C0-AUK-667

THE CAMBRIDGE BIBLE
FOR SCHOOLS AND COLLEGES

THE GOSPEL ACCORDING TO
ST MATTHEW

CAMBRIDGE UNIVERSITY PRESS WAREHOUSE,
C. F. CLAY, MANAGER.
London: FETTER LANE, E.C.
Edinburgh: 100, PRINCES STREET.

Leipzig: F. A. BROCKHAUS.
Berlin: A. ASHER AND CO.
New York: G. P. PUTNAM'S SONS.
Bombay and Calcutta: MACMILLAN & CO. LTD

THE GOSPEL ACCORDING TO

ST MATTHEW

Edited by

THE REV. A. CARR, M.A.
Formerly Fellow of Oriel College, Oxford;
Late Assistant Master at Wellington College

CAMBRIDGE:
at the University Press
1908

"Novum Testamentum in vetere latet,
Vetus Testamentum in novo patet."
Ambrose.

First Edition 1878.
Reprinted 1878 (*three times*), 1879, 1880 (*twice*), 1881 (*twice*), 1882, 1883 (*twice*), 1884 (*twice*), 1885, 1886, 1887 (*twice*), 1888, 1889, 1890, 1891, 1893, 1894, 1896, 1898, 1902, 1905, 1908.

PREFACE

BY THE GENERAL EDITOR.

THE General Editor of *The Cambridge Bible for Schools* thinks it right to say that he does not hold himself responsible either for the interpretation of particular passages which the Editors of the several Books have adopted, or for any opinion on points of doctrine that they may have expressed. In the New Testament more especially questions arise of the deepest theological import, on which the ablest and most conscientious interpreters have differed and always will differ. His aim has been in all such cases to leave each Contributor to the unfettered exercise of his own judgment, only taking care that mere controversy should as far as possible be avoided. He has contented himself chiefly with a careful revision of the notes, with pointing out omissions, with suggesting occasionally a reconsideration of some question, or a fuller treatment of difficult passages, and the like.

Beyond this he has not attempted to interfere, feeling it better that each Commentary should have its own individual character, and being convinced that freshness and variety of treatment are more than a compensation for any lack of uniformity in the Series.

CONTENTS.

*** The Text adopted in this Edition is that of Dr Scrivener's *Cambridge Paragraph Bible.* A few variations from the ordinary Text, chiefly in the spelling of certain words, and in the use of italics, will be noticed. For the principles adopted by Dr Scrivener as regards the printing of the Text see his Introduction to the *Paragraph Bible*, published by the Cambridge University Press.

INTRODUCTION.

CHAPTER I.

LIFE OF ST MATTHEW.

LEVI the son of Alphæus[1] was a tax-gatherer at Capernaum. His special duty would be to collect tolls from the fisheries on the Lake, and perhaps from the merchants travelling southward from Damascus. One day Jesus coming up from the Lake side passed near the custom-house where Levi was seated in Oriental fashion, and He saith unto him, Follow me, and he arose and followed Him (ch. ix. 9). That Jesus ever addressed Levi before, we are not told; but it is reasonable to suppose that he was expecting the summons, that he was already a disciple of Jesus, and prepared as soon as Christ gave the word to leave all for His sake. At any rate, Levi must have heard of the Great Rabbi and of His preaching, and have already resolved to adopt the view of the kingdom of God which Jesus taught.

When Levi became a follower of Jesus he changed his name from Levi to Matthew[2], which means "the Gift of God," and is the same as the Greek name Theodore. This practice was not unusual, and may be illustrated by the instances of Saul and of Simon, who also adopted new names in the new life.

The same day Matthew made a feast—perhaps a farewell feast to his old associates—to which he invited Jesus and His

[1] Alphæus being also the name of the father of James the Apostle it has been conjectured that James and Matthew were brethren. This is of course possible, but can hardly be called probable.

[2] This is indeed an inference, but one which is accepted by the best commentators to harmonise the "Levi" of the second and third Gospels with the "Matthew" of the first Gospel.

disciples. We may conceive what a joyous banquet that was for Matthew, when for the first time as an eye-witness he marked the words and acts of Jesus, and stored within his memory the scene and the conversation which he was inspired to write according to his clerkly ability for the instruction of the Church in all after ages.

After this Matthew is not once named in the Gospel history, except in the list of the Twelve; in the other Gospels he appears seventh on the list, in his own Gospel eighth—the last in the second division. In his own Gospel again—a further mark of humility—he designates himself as "Matthew the publican." His nearest companion seems to have been Thomas (whose surname Didymus has led to the belief that he was Matthew's twin-brother), and in the same group or division were Philip and Bartholomew. Such are the scanty details which the Gospels record of St Matthew. These few notices however suggest some inferences as to the religious position, character and teaching of the Evangelist.

Since Capernaum was in the tetrarchy of Herod Antipas, it may be inferred that Levi was an officer in the service of that prince, and not in the service of the Roman government, as is sometimes tacitly assumed. This is not unimportant in estimating the call and conversion of St Matthew.

A Hebrew who entirely acquiesced in the Roman supremacy could hardly have done so at this period without abandoning the national hopes. Jesus alone knew the secret of reconciling the highest aspirations of the Jewish race with submission to Cæsar. But to acknowledge the Herodian dynasty was a different thing from bowing to Rome. Herod was at least not a foreigner and a Gentile in the same sense as the Roman. Idumea had coalesced with Israel. It is therefore conceivable that a Jew who was waiting for the Messiah's reign may in very despair have learned to look for the fulfilment of his hopes in the Herodian family. If it was impossible to connect Messianic thoughts with an Antipas, or even with the more reputable Philip, still might not a prince hereafter spring from that house to restore the kingdom to Israel? Might not God in His providence fuse by some means the house and lineage of Herod with the house and lineage of David? It was not impossible, and probably the tyrannical Antipas owed the stability of his throne in some measure to a party among the Jews who cherished these ideas.

No one can read St Matthew's Gospel without perceiving that he was no Hellenist, but a Hebrew of the Hebrews, deeply learned in the history and prophecies of his race, and eagerly looking forward to their realisation; but he had been content to find, or at least to expect that realisation in the family of Herod. These views were suited to his nature in two ways. For we may infer first, that he was influenced by what is almost an inherent passion in his race—the love of gain; (had it not been so he would never have chosen a career which at its best was despised and odious); secondly, that he loved a life of contemplation and quiet, and was well pleased to separate himself from the fiery enthusiasm and headstrong schemes of the Galileans who surrounded him. Such may have been the hopes to which Levi clung. But when the plan and teaching of Jesus were unfolded to his mind stored with national memories, he instantly recognised the truth and beauty and completeness of that ideal, and gave himself up heart and soul to the cause of the Son of David. For that cause and for the kingdom of God he resigned all his hopes of advancement in Herod's kingdom, his lucrative calling, and the friends he had made.

It may be that Matthew's wealth was not in an absolute sense great, but it was great for the little Galilean town. It was great to him. And if like St Paul he had left a record of his personal religious feelings, he might have related how he counted up all the several items of gain, and found the sum total loss compared with the excellency of the knowledge of Christ Jesus[1].

If we may judge from the silence of the Gospels, the position which Matthew held among his fellow-disciples was a humble one. He was not among the chosen three. No incident connects itself with his name, as with the names of Andrew and Simon, of Philip, of Thomas, or of Bartholomew, of Judas [the brother] of James, of the sons of Zebedee. No one word of his to Christ is recorded. Even when he was called he rose and followed in silence.

[1] Phil. iii. 7, 8.

We may picture Matthew to ourselves as a silent, unobtrusive, contemplative man, "swift to hear and slow to speak," unobservant of the minutiæ of outward action but with a mind teeming with the associations of his nation and deeply conscious of the momentous drama which was being enacted before him, of which he felt himself called upon to be the chronicler and interpreter to his own people.

No special mention is made of St Matthew in the Acts of the Apostles, or in the Epistles, but some light is thrown upon his after life by fragmentary notices of early Christian writers.

We gather that he remained in Palestine longer than the rest of the Apostles, and that he made his fellow-countrymen familiar with the words and works of Jesus. More will be said below as to the nature and special scope of his teaching ; but an interesting point of Christian history, and one that bears upon St Matthew's character, recorded by Eusebius, may be mentioned here. St Matthew, says the historian, being about to depart for distant lands to preach to others also, left as a memorial to his Palestinian converts the story of the New Covenant committed to writing in their own tongue, the Aramaic or Hebrew dialect which they used. This parting gift of the Evangelist was the origin of the written Gospels.

Later authorities have named Æthiopia, Parthia, Egypt and Macedonia, as fields of his missionary work. Clement of Alexandria states that Matthew devoted himself to a strictly ascetic life, abstaining from the use of animal food.

By the most ancient testimony the death of this apostle is attributed to natural causes. The traditions of the Greek Church and the pictures of the Greek artists represent him dying peacefully. But the Western Church has placed Matthew on the list of martyrs, and in the works of Italian painters he is portrayed perishing by the executioner's sword. It is characteristic of this silent, unmarked life, in which the personality of the Evangelist is lost in the voice of the message which he was inspired to utter, that Matthew's name has been less prominent in the Churches and nations of Christendom than others of his co-apostles, or even than many saints, whose services to the Church of Christ have been infinitely less. None of the great

Churches of Christendom have been called by his name, no guild or fraternity, no college in our great Universities, no state or nation, has chosen him for a patron. Scarcely one famous picture has taught the lesson of his call. The personal memory, like the personal life of St Matthew, withdraws itself from the observation of men.

CHAPTER II.

AUTHORSHIP, ORIGIN AND CHARACTERISTICS OF THE GOSPEL.

1. The authorship of the first gospel has been ascribed by an unbroken tradition to the Apostle Matthew.

2. The date is uncertain. Irenæus however states that St Matthew wrote his gospel when SS. Peter and Paul were founding the Church in Rome: and the fact that it was published first of the written Gospels rests upon early and uncontradicted testimony. The date of publication then should probably be fixed not many years after the Ascension.

3. St Matthew's Gospel was primarily intended for the use of the Jewish converts in Palestine. It is this fact that gives its special character to this Gospel. No other of the evangelists has so completely developed the idea that in Christ the nation lived again, that towards Christ all prophecy moved, that in Him all national aspirations were centred and satisfied. No other inspired writer has pictured so vividly the critical interest of the Messianic days as the meeting point of the world's past and future.

According to St Matthew Jesus is from first to last Christ the King, the King of whom all the prophets spake in the past, but He is also the one figure round whom the historical interest of the future was destined to gather. Hence the twofold aspect of this Gospel, on the one hand it is the most national and the most retrospective of the Gospels; on the other it is the most universal and the most prophetic; in one sense St Matthew is more gentile than St Luke, in another he is truly a Hebrew of the Hebrews.

The very depth of St Matthew's patriotism impels him to glory in the universality of the Messianic reign. The Kingdom of God *must* over-pass the limits of the Chosen race. Hence it is no matter of surprise that the Hebrew historian should alone commemorate the coming of the Magi and the refuge in Egypt, and that he and not St Luke should tell the story of the Canaanitish woman.

The following points confirm the received account of the origin of this Gospel and indicate its special reference to the Jews.

(1) The numerous quotations from prophecy.

(2) The appeals to history as fulfilled in Christ.

(3) The rare explanation of Jewish words and customs.

(4) The strong and special denunciation of the Jews and of their rulers.

(5) The special reference to the Law in the Sermon on the Mount.

(6) The Genealogy traced from Abraham and David.

(7) The Mission of the Seventy omitted.

(8) The absence of Latin words, with very few exceptions.

(9) The prominence given to the Jewish thought of a Kingdom of Heaven; (*a*) in the general scope of the Gospel; (*b*) in the parables; (*c*) in the account of the Passion.

4. The question of style cannot be fully or satisfactorily discussed without a direct appeal to the original, but it may be observed that St Matthew's manner is less vivid and picturesque than St Mark's, more even and unvaried than St Luke's, whose diction is greatly influenced by the various sources whence he derived the details which he incorporates into his Gospel. Consequently although no passages in St Matthew's Gospel recall the classical ring like the introduction to St Luke's Gospel; on the other hand the Hebrew idiom never so manifestly shews itself in the first Gospel as in the opening chapters of the third.

St Matthew was an eyewitness of the events which he chronicles, yet it is often remarked that his descriptions are less graphic and full of detail than those of St Mark, who wrote what he had heard from the lips of others. This need not be a matter of surprise. It is indeed a phenomenon that meets us every day. It is not the contemporary and the eyewitness, but the historian of a succeeding age who takes the keenest interest in minute detail and records with faithful accuracy the less prominent circumstances of a great event. It is the Herodotus or the Macaulay—the historian, the 'questioner'—who gathers from every source materials for a minute and brilliant picture, rather than the actual spectator who is often too deeply absorbed by the one point of supreme interest in a scene to notice the looks and acts of other bystanders, or so impressed by the speaker's glowing thoughts, as to deem them alone worthy of record.

But though St Mark enables us to realize more exactly the external accessories of the various incidents, St Matthew has treasured up for the Church more fully than the other synoptists the words and discourses of Jesus; such especially as present Him in the character of the Great Prophet, who, like the prophets of old time, denounces national sins and predicts the future of the nation and the Church. Instances of this characteristic are the full report of the Sermon on the Mount (ch. v. vi. vii.), the charge to the Apostles ch. x; the great series of prophetic parables in ch. xiii. peculiar to this gospel; the denunciation of the Scribes and Pharisees in ch. xxiii., the parables of the Passion ch. xxv., the predictions of the fall of Jerusalem, and of the second Advent chs. xxiv. and xxv.

5. The ablest critics are agreed that St Matthew does not observe the chronological order of events. By the arrangement followed by this Evangelist, as may be seen by the accompanying analysis of the Gospel, special incidents and sayings are so grouped together as to illustrate the different aspects of our Lord's life and teaching.

6. The most interesting literary question in connection with this Gospel concerns the language in which it was written. Is the Hellenistic Greek version which we possess, (1) the original Gospel, or (2) a translation from a Hebrew or Aramaic original; further, if a translation by whom was the translation made, by (*a*) St Matthew himself, or (*b*) by some other?

Apart from the antecedent probability of a Hebrew Gospel—a version of the New Covenant to correspond with the Hebrew of the Old Covenant, and to meet the requirements of those

Jews who gloried in their knowledge of the Hebrew tongue, and their adhesion to Hebrew customs, who would listen more gladly to the Gospel if it were preached to them in the language of their fathers—direct testimony to the existence of an Aramaic original of St Matthew's Gospel is borne by a succession of the earliest Christian writers.

(1) Papias in the beginning of the second century writes:—"Matthew arranged the 'oracles' (or sayings of Christ) in the Hebrew language."

(2) Irenæus says "Matthew among the Hebrews brought out a writing of the Gospel in their own tongue."

(3) Pantænus, according to Eusebius (*H. E.* v. 10), is said to have gone to preach to the Indians and to have found among them a copy of the Hebrew Gospel according to St Matthew which had been left by the Apostle Bartholomew.

(4) In later times evidence for the belief in a Hebrew original is drawn from the writings of Origen, Eusebius, Jerome, and many others.

Against this testimony in favour of a Hebrew original, arguments tending to an opposite conclusion are grounded on (1) the disappearance of the Hebrew Gospel: (2) the authority which the existing version has always had in the Church: (3) the similarity of expression to certain portions of the other Gospels: (4) the apparent originality of style.

(1) That no copy of the Hebrew Gospel is extant need not excite surprise. With the destruction of Jerusalem the Hebrew speaking Christians would be for the most part scattered far and wide over the limits of the Roman Empire. Necessity would impel them to become familiar with the Greek tongue. Their Jewish compatriots in foreign countries would be acquainted with no other. Everywhere the credit of the Greek version of St Matthew's Gospel would be fully established; to that version the original Hebrew edition would soon give place. It seems probable too that copies of this Gospel were purposely altered and mutilated to serve the ends of heretical sects, and thus the genuine Hebrew text would become more and more difficult to obtain, and finally would be discredited and lost to the Church. The preface of St Luke's Gospel suggests the

thought that many more or less complete "Gospels" once extant have disappeared. Moreover, most critics are agreed that the existing Epistles of St Paul do not comprise the whole number which he wrote to the Churches.

The points raised in the second (2) and third (3) arguments are considered below.

(4) The question of originality cannot be decisively settled by an appeal to the style of the Greek Gospel. There are, however, certainly some characteristics in St Matthew's Gospel that seem to indicate a translation. The style is uniform, almost monotonous. Hebraisms are regularly and evenly distributed, not as in St Luke, prominent in some parts and altogether absent in others. The actual Hebrew words are few. This is what we should expect in a translation, but not in an original Gospel addressed principally to Jewish converts. St Matthew's Gospel deals with quotations from the Old Testament in a twofold manner. When the narrative is closely parallel with the other Synoptic Gospels, the quotations are also parallel following generally the text of the LXX., but presenting the same variations from that text which appear in the other Synoptic Gospels. But in those portions of this Gospel which are independent of the others, the quotations approach more nearly to the Hebrew text. This phenomenon must be taken into account in drawing any conclusion as to the existence of the Aramaic original.

The following theory is advanced as a natural way of explaining the facts. It can hardly be doubted that St Matthew in the first instance composed a Gospel for the use of the Palestinian Jews. But on the disruption of the Jewish polity Aramaic would cease to be intelligible to many, and the demand would come for a Greek version of the Gospel according to St Matthew. How would this demand be met? Either Matthew himself, or else some faithful scribe, would use the Hebrew Gospel as the basis of a Greek version. Many of the familiar parables and sayings of Jesus, which were orally afloat in all the Churches, he would (for the sake of old association) incorporate with little alteration, but he would preserve throughout the plan of the original, and, in passages where the special teaching of this

Gospel came in, the version would be a close rendering of the Aramaic. This theory explains the verbal coincidence of some parts of St Matthew's Gospel with the parallel Synoptic passages, and accounts for the facts in regard to the quotations stated above.

Such a version, especially if made by St Matthew himself, would indeed be rather an original work than a translation, and would speedily in either case acquire the authority of the original Aramaic. Accordingly we find that even those writers who speak of the Hebrew Gospel themselves quote from the Greek version as authoritative.

NOTE I.

(A) *Miracles.* (B) *Parables.* (C) *Discourses.* (D) *Incidents peculiar to this Gospel.*

(A) *Miracles.*

(1) Cure of two blind men .... ix. 27—31.
(2) The stater in the fish's mouth .... xvii. 24—27.

(B) *Parables.*

(1) The tares .... xiii. 24—30.
(2) The hid treasure .... xiii. 44.
(3) The pearl of great price .... xiii. 45, 46.
(4) The draw net .... xiii. 47—50.
(5) The unmerciful servant .... xviii. 23—35.
(6) The labourers in the vineyard .... xx. 1—16.
(7) The two sons .... xxi. 28—32.
(8) Marriage of the king's son .... xxii. 1—14.
(9) The ten virgins .... xxv. 1—13.
(10) The talents .... xxv. 14—30.

(C) *Discourses.*

(1) A large part of the sermon on the Mount.
(2) Invitation to the heavy laden .... xi. 28—30.
(3) Idle words .... xii. 36, 37.
(4) The blessing pronounced on Peter .... xvi. 17—19.
(5) The greater part of ch. xviii. on humility and forgiveness.
(6) The rejection of the Jews .... xxi. 43.
(7) The denunciation of the Scribes and Pharisees as a connected discourse ...... xxiii.
(8) The description of the judgment .... xxv. 31—46.
(9) The last commission and promise .... xxviii. 18—20.

(D) *Incidents.*

(1) The whole of ch. ii.

(α) The coming of the Magi, guided by the star in the east.

(β) The massacre of the innocents.

(γ) The flight into Egypt.

(δ) The return to Nazareth.

(2) The coming of the Pharisees and Sadducees to John's baptism ....iii. 7.

(3) Peter's attempt to walk upon the water......xiv. 28—31.

(4) Payment of the Temple Tax ....xvii. 24—27.

(5) In connection with the Passion:

(α) The covenant of Judas for thirty pieces of silver; his repentance, and his end xxvi. 14—16; xxvii. 3—10.

(β) The dream of Pilate's wife ....xxvii. 19.

(γ) The appearance of saints in Jerusalem......xxvii. 52.

(6) In connection with the Resurrection:

(α) The watch placed at the sepulchre......xxvii. 62—66.

(β) The soldiers bribed to spread a false report ....xxviii. 11—15.

(γ) The earthquake ....xxviii. 2.

CHAPTER III.

ANALYSIS OF THE GOSPEL.

PART I.

The Birth and Childhood of the King:—i.—ii. 23.

(1) The lineage of Jesus Christ ....i. 1—17.
(2) His birth ....i. 18—25.
(3) The visit of the Magi ....ii. 1—12.
(4) The flight into Egypt and the return......ii. 13—23.

According to St Matthew's plan Jesus Christ is represented as (*a*) the King; (*β*) descended from David; (*γ*) who fulfils the words of prophecy; (*δ*) whose Kingdom is recognised by the Gentiles; (*ε*) who is the representative of His nation, and fulfils their history.

PART II.

The Beginning of the Kingdom :—iii.—iv. 11.

(1) The forerunner of the Kingdom............iii. 1—12.
(2) The baptism of Jesus ....iii. 13—17.
(3) The Temptation ....iv. 1—11.

This part corresponds to the opening verses of St Mark's Gospel; it contains the announcement and victory of the King, and His entrance upon His reign; the true kingdom of God is opposed to the false conception of the Kingdom.

PART III.

The Works and Signs of the Kingdom of God :—iv. 12—xvi. 12.

Section (i). At Capernaum..........................iv.—viii. 17.
(α) Preaching of repentance (*Metanoia*) ......iv. 17.
(β) Call of four disciples ....iv. 18—22.
(γ) Various diseases are cured ....iv. 23—25.
(δ) The sermon on the mount ....v., vi., vii.
(ε) Cleansing of a leper ....viii. 1—4.
(ζ) Cure of the centurion's servant ....viii. 5—13.
(η) Cure of Peter's wife's mother ....viii. 14—17.

The preparation for the Kingdom is amendment of life, a changed heart. It is a Kingdom of love shewn by deeds of mercy. The Law of the Kingdom is the highest fulfilment of the old Law.

Section (ii). Jesus crosses the Lake ....viii. 18—34.
(α) Fitness for discipleship ....viii. 18—22.
(β) The winds and the sea obey Him ....viii. 23—27.
(γ) The Gergesene demoniacs ....viii. 28—34.

Jesus shews that self-denial is essential to His subjects; He exhibits His power over nature, and over the spiritual world.

Section (iii). Return to Capernaum ....ix.—xiii. 52.
(α) Cure of a paralytic ....ix. 1—8.
(β) Call of Levi ....ix. 9.
(γ) Feast in Levi's house. Jesus the friend of sinners ....ix. 10—13.
(δ) Fasting ....ix. 14—17.
(ε) The daughter of Jairus.—The woman with an issue ....ix. 18—26.
(ζ) Two blind men cured ....ix. 27—31.
(η) The dumb demoniac..........................ix. 32—34.

(θ) The good works of Christ ....ix. 35.
(ι) The labourers are few ....ix. 36—38.
(κ) The choice and mission of the Twelve ...x.
(λ) John the Baptist—his message to Jesus—his position as a prophet ....xi. 1—19.
(μ) The unrepentant cities—The yoke of Christ.. ....xi. 20—30.
(ν) The observance of the Sabbath ....xii. 1—13.
(ξ) Plot of the Pharisees—Retirement of Jesus ....xii. 14—21.
(ο) Cure of the blind and dumb man—Blasphemy of the Pharisees ....xii. 22—37.
(π) Rebuke to those who ask for a sign ......xii. 38—45.
(ρ) The kinsfolk of Jesus ....xii. 46—50.
(σ) Teaching by parables ....xiii. 1—52.

In these Chapters the teaching of the Kingdom is further developed in its relation (1) to John, as the greatest of the Prophets before the Kingdom; (2) to the religious system of the Pharisees. The Church of Christ is founded by the call of His disciples. Its future is foreshewn in the charge to the Twelve, and in the Parables of ch. xiii.

Section (iv). At Nazareth.
His own receive Him not ....xiii. 53—58.

Section (v). In different parts of Galilee ....xiv.—xvi. 12.
(α) Herod, who has slain John, asks concerning Christ ....xiv. 1—12.
(β) Jesus retires ....xiv. 13, 14.
(γ) The feeding of Five Thousand............xiv. 15—21.
(δ) The passage to Gennesaret—Jesus walks on the sea ....xiv. 22—36.
(ε) The tradition of the elders—Hypocrisy...xv. 1—20.
(ς) The Canaanite woman.........................xv. 21—28.
(η) Cure of many sick ....xv. 29—31.
(θ) The feeding of Four Thousand ....xv. 32—38.
(ι) A sign refused ....xvi. 4.
(κ) The leaven of the Pharisees ....xvi. 5—12.

Here the Kingdom of God is brought into contrast with (1) the kingdom of Herod—a point of special interest to Matthew; and (2) with legal righteousness. Jesus indicates the extension of His Church to the Gentiles. He manifests His creative power.

PART IV.

The Predictions of the Passion:—xvi. 13—xx. 34.

Section (i). Near Cæsarea Philippi ....xvi. 13—28.
(α) Peter's acknowledgment of the Son of God—The first prediction ....xvi. 13—20.
(β) Peter rebuked—The true subjects of the King ....xvi. 21—28.

The Confession of St Peter is the central point of interest in the education of the disciples. The importance of the crisis is shewn by the expression '*from that time*' (xvi. 21). Possessing this truth the disciples may learn the other truth—the sufferings of the Son of Man. Each prediction presents the same contrast—a lesson of glory, and a lesson of humiliation.

Section (ii). The second prediction of the Passion ....xvii. 1—xviii. 35.
(α) The Transfiguration..........................xvii. 1—13.
(β) Cure of the lunatic boy ....xvii. 14—21.
(γ) The prediction ....xvii. 22, 23.
(δ) The Temple Tax ....xvii. 24—27.
(ε) Contention for greatness ... .xviii. 1—6.
(ζ) Offences and forgiveness ....xviii. 7—35.

A glimpse of the glorified Kingdom of God contrasted with the misery of earth. All that follows the prediction shews the inability of the disciples to understand as yet the truth about the Kingdom.

Section (iii). The third prediction of the Passion...xix.—xx. 34.
(α) Journey through Peræa ....xix. 1, 2.
(β) Question of divorce ....xix. 3—12.
(γ) Children brought to Christ..................xix. 13—15.
(δ) The rich young ruler................ ....xix. 16—22.
(ε) Riches—Rewards of Christ's followers ...xix. 23—30.
(ζ) Parable of the labourers in the vineyard...xx. 1—16.
(η) The prediction ....xx. 17—19.
(θ) The petition of Salome for her sons ......xx. 20—28.
(ι) Two blind men are cured ....xx. 29—34.

Compare the exactness of detail in this third Prediction with the less definite first and second Predictions.

The social life of the subjects of the King—marriage and the use of riches—must be moulded to the laws of the Kingdom. There are great rewards in store for Christ's faithful followers.

PART V.

The Triumph of the King:—xxi.—xxv.

Sunday and Monday Nisan 9 and 10.

(α) The King enters the Holy City in triumph .... xxi. 1—11.
(β) The cleansing of the Temple .... xxi. 12—14.
(γ) The children's praise .... xxi. 15, 16.
(δ) Bethany—The cursing of the fig-tree .... xxi. 17—22.
(ε) The victories of the King .... xxi. 23—xxiii.
  (1) Over the Sanhedrin—The parables of the Two Sons, the Vineyard, and the Marriage Feast .... xxi. 23—xxii. 14.
  (2) Over the Pharisees—The tribute money .... xxii. 15—22.
  (3) Over the Sadducees—The Resurrection .... xxii. 23—33.
  (4) Over a certain lawyer—The greatest commandment .... xxii. 34—40.
  (5) By a counter-question—David's Son xxii. 41—46.
  (6) Rebuke of the Pharisees .... xxiii.
(ς) Discourse concerning the fall of Jerusalem and the end of the world—Type and antitype .... xxiv.
(η) Parables of the Advent .... xxv. 1—30.
(θ) The judgment of the nations .... xxv. 31—46.

Here Jesus is set forth (1) as the King who triumphs; (2) as victorious over all adversaries; (3) as the Prophet who must perish in Jerusalem.

PART VI.

The Passion.

Wednesday, Nisan 12—Friday, Nisan 14, xxvi. xxvii.

(α) A fourth prediction of the Passion .... xxvi. 1, 2.
(β) A meeting of the Sanhedrin .... xxvi. 3—5.
(γ) The feast in Simon's house—Judas agrees to betray Jesus .... xxvi. 6—16.
(δ) The Last Supper .... xxvi. 17—30.
(ε) All shall be offended .... xxvi. 31—35.
(ς) The agony in the garden of Gethsemane... xxvi. 36—46.
(η) The arrest of Jesus .... xxvi. 47—56.
(θ) The trial before Caiaphas .... xxvi. 57—68.
(ι) The denial of Peter .... xxvi. 69—72.
(κ) The formal trial before the Sanhedrin ... xxvii. 1.

(λ) The remorse of Judas—The Roman trial...xxvii. 2—26.
(μ) The mockery by Roman soldiers.........xxvii. 27—30.
(ν) The crucifixion and death of Jesus.........xxvii. 31—56.
(ξ) The entombment ....xxvii. 57—66.

The Triumph of the King is followed by the Humiliation, true to the Predictions of Jesus. "He humbled Himself even unto the death upon the Cross."

PART VII.

The Resurrection :—xxviii.

(α) The empty sepulchre ....xxviii. 1—8.
(β) The appearance of the Lord to the women ....xxviii. 9, 10.
(γ) The soldiers bribed to silence ....xxviii. 11—15.
(δ) Jesus in Galilee ....xxviii. 16, 17.
(ε) The last commission..........................xxviii. 18—20.

The Gospel of the Kingdom ends fittingly with the victory over death; with the declaration by the Lord Jesus of His universal power, and His commission to the disciples to teach all nations.

CHAPTER IV.

EXTERNAL HISTORY DURING THE LIFE AND MINISTRY OF JESUS CHRIST.

1. *Summary.*

B.C. 3. (see note ch. ii. 1) Octavianus Augustus had been sole ruler of the Roman Empire from B.C. 30.
Twice during that period the temple of Janus had been closed in sign of peace.

B.C. 1. Death of Herod. Rising of the Jews against the Procurator Sabinus. Repression of the revolt by Varus: 2000 Jews crucified.

A.D. 6. Resistance to the Census of Quirinus by Judas the Gaulonite and his Galilæan followers.

A.D. 7. Banishment of Archelaus.

1—12. Campaigns against the Germans, Pannonians, Dalmatians, conducted by Tiberius and Germanicus.
The disastrous defeat of Varus in Germany.
Final success and triumph of the Roman Generals.

14. Death of Augustus and succession of Tiberius.

15—17. Germanicus continues the war against the Germans, and triumphs.

18. Death of Ovid and of Livy.

19. Death of Germanicus.
Jews banished from Italy.

20—31. Hateful tyranny of Tiberius. Ascendancy of Sejanus.
Fall of Sejanus A.D. 30.

26. Pontius Pilate appointed as the sixth Procurator of Judæa.

2. *The Imperial Rule.*

It will be seen from this summary, that while Jesus was passing a quiet childhood in the Galilæan valley, few startling events disturbed the peace of the world. But it was an epoch of the greatest historical interest. It was a crisis in the kingdoms of the world as well as in the Kingdom of God. Rome had completed her conquests—no formidable rival was left to threaten her power in any direction. But the moment when the Roman people secured the empire of the world, they resigned their own liberties into the hands of a single master.

Cæsar Octavianus, afterwards named Augustus, the successor of the great Julius Cæsar, was the first to consolidate this enormous individual power; it was he who bequeathed to the world the proudest titles of despotic rule—Emperor—Kaiser—Czar. With him the true nature of the monarchy was veiled over by the retention of Republican forms, and by a nominal re-election at intervals. The justice and clemency of his rule kept out of sight the worst abuses of unlimited power. And partly owing to the fact that the most brilliant age of Roman literature coincided with the reign of Augustus, his name is associated rather with literary culture and refinement, than with despotic sway.

When Jesus grew up to manhood, the grace and culture and

the semblance of liberty which had gilded the despotism of Augustus vanished under the dark influence of the morose and cruel Tiberius. If ever men suffered from hopeless tyranny and wrong, it was in this reign. It is a miserable history of lives surrounded by suspicion and fear, and of the best and purest citizens yielding to despair or removed by secret assassination.

It can perhaps be scarcely a matter of surprise, that a Jewish patriot, alive to the horrors of this despotism and recalling the prophetic images of a triumphant Messiah, should sometimes have dreamed that the Kingdom of God would be manifested by the overthrow of this monstrous evil, and in turn establish itself as an external power stronger and more resistless than Rome. It is this thought that gives point to the third temptation presented to our Lord. (ch. iv. 8, 9).

3. *The Provincial System.*

A glance at the Provincial system of Rome with especial reference to Palestine will shew how truly, in an external sense, Christ came in the fulness of time.

Under the Empire the condition of the provinces was happier than formerly. The rapacity of individual governors was checked by the imperial supervision. Moreover, great consideration was in many cases shewn to a conquered people. National customs were allowed to continue; even native princes were in several instances confirmed in their rule on condition of becoming tributary to Rome.

In accordance with this principle, the Herodian dynasty was tolerated in Palestine. Observe how the changes in that dynasty affected the life of Christ. When Jesus was born, Herod was reigning in Jerusalem; hence the events that led to the flight into Egypt. On the return of Jesus with Mary and Joseph, the kingdom was divided; hence the possibility of taking refuge from the cruelty of an Archelaus under the more tolerant Antipas in the home at Nazareth. The banishment of Archelaus a few years afterwards brought about the establishment in Judæa of the Roman government, which with its accustomed liberality left the national system represented by the Sanhedrin, not wholly unimpaired, indeed, but still influential.

Important consequences followed this precise political position. The Jewish nation was still responsible. It was Israel and not Rome that rejected the Messiah—Israel that condemned to death the Lord of Life. But it was Rome that executed the will of the Jewish people. Jesus suffered, by the law of Rome, death on the Roman cross, with all its significance, its agreement with prophecy, and its divine fitness. The point to be observed is that under no other political conditions could this event have taken place in that precise manner, which was wholly in accordance with the Scriptures that foretell the Messiah.

4. *A time of Peace.*

The lull of peace that pervaded the Roman world, was another element in the external preparation for the advent of Christ. In the generation which preceded and in that which followed the life of Christ on earth, Palestine, and indeed the whole empire, was disquieted by the greatest political confusion. In the generation before the Christian Era, Antony and Augustus were contending for the mastery of the world, and a disputed succession disturbed the peace of Palestine. The succeeding generation was filled with the horrors of the Jewish war, of which Galilee was the focus, and which culminated in the fall of Jerusalem. It is clear that the conditions of Christ's ministry could not have been fulfilled in either of these conjunctures.

5. *The various nationalities in Palestine.*

A further point of interest at the particular period when Jesus lived on earth, is the variety of nationalities which the special circumstances of the time brought together in Palestine.

A political epoch that found a Roman governor in the south (where the native ecclesiastical rule still prevailed), Idumean kings in the north and east, wild mountain and desert tribes pressing on the frontiers in one direction, peaceful Phœnicians in another, involved a mixture and gathering of populations which made Palestine an epitome of the whole world. The variety of life and thought, which must have resulted from these different social elements, is one of those external circumstances which have rendered the Gospel so fit to instruct every age and every condition of men.

6. *The religious condition of the Empire.*

The wider and more interesting question of the religious state of the world at this epoch, cannot be fully discussed here. In Greece and in Rome, the most civilised portions of the earth, Religion allowed, or at least was ineffectual to prevent, a state of morality which St Paul describes with terrible plainness in the first chapter of his Epistle to the Romans. Gross immorality entered even into the ritual of worship; Religion raised no voice against the butchery of gladiatorial shows, or against infanticide, or slavery, or suicide, or even against the horrors of human sacrifice.

Little real belief in the gods and goddesses remained; and though ancient superstitions still lingered among the vulgar, and interested motives on the part of priests and communities kept alive the cult of special deities, and supported shrines and temples in various parts of the world, and though, credulity gaining ground as true religious feeling passed away, the mysterious rites of Egypt and the East, the worship of Isis and of Mithras flourished at Rome in spite of repressive edicts—all this was external and unreal, a thin cover for deep-seated and widespread scepticism.

Philosophy did but little to fill the void. Stoicism, the favourite creed with the practical Roman, though apparently nearest to Christianity in some respects, was deeply opposed to the Christian spirit by its pride, its self-sufficiency, its exclusiveness, its exaltation of human nature, its lack of love, its approval of suicide. Epicurism had degenerated from a high ideal to a mere pursuit of sensual pleasure.

It was in the midst of a world thus corrupt to the core, that the beautiful and novel conception rose of a religion, which recognizing no limits of race or language, should without distinction draw all men to itself by its appeal to the sin-stricken conscience, and by the satisfaction it brought to the deepest needs of humanity.

NOTE II.

A GENEALOGICAL TABLE OF THE HERODIAN FAMILY, INCLUDING THOSE MEMBERS OF IT WHO ARE MENTIONED IN THE GOSPEL ACCORDING TO ST MATTHEW.

HEROD THE KING (ch. ii. 1, 16, 19) married ten wives, among whom were:

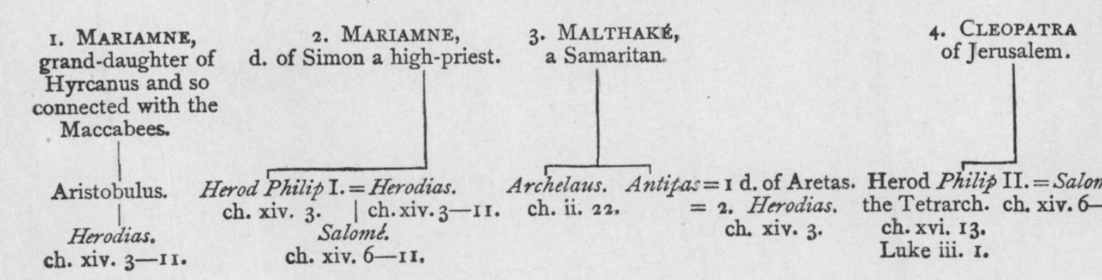

Note III.

The New Testament: ἡ καινὴ διαθήκη (ch. xxvi. 28), more correctly *the New Covenant*, a rendering which preserves the sense of a continuity between the past history of Israel and the future history of the Church as revealed by the Gospel. In the Saviour's words, God renewed the ancient Covenant which He made with the patriarchs. The universal adoption of the other possible rendering of διαθήκη, *Testament*, has obscured this connection, which St Matthew places in the greatest prominence throughout his Gospel.

Gospel (*Good News*)*:* a most felicitous translation into a Saxon compound of the Greek εὐαγγέλιον, which means: (1) reward for good news, (2) good news. The Continental languages have naturalised the Greek word: *évangile* (French), *evangelium* (German), *evangelo* (Italian). A similar instance of felicitous word-formation is "passover"; see note, ch. xxvi. 2.

According to: the Gospel is more correctly spoken of as *according to* than as *of* St Matthew. It is the Gospel of Jesus Christ, but it is variously presented according to the plan and aims of the different writers inspired to meet the requirements of particular readers, and to satisfy special needs.

Synoptic: a term applied to the first three Gospels, because they take a synopsis or conspectus of the same group and succession of events. The fourth Gospel deals mainly with the works of Christ in Judæa as distinct from His circuits in Galilee and His life at Capernaum. The great discourses of that Gospel are also supplementary to the records of the Synoptists.

Note IV.

On the MSS. of the New Testament.

No Classical work has so many valuable ancient MSS. on which to establish its text as the New Testament. The earliest of these MSS. are beautifully written on fine *vellum*, (prepared skin of calves or kids) in *uncial* or large capital letters. The later MSS. are called *cursive*, from being written in a *cursive* (curro) or running hand.

The subjoined brief account of the five oldest uncial MSS. of the N. T. will be of interest.

א. *Codex Sinaiticus.* This is probably the oldest MS. of the N. T. now extant, and is assigned to the *fourth* century. It was discovered by Tischendorf in the Convent of St Catharine on Mount Sinai, in 1859. "It contains both Old and New Testaments—the latter perfect without the loss of a single leaf. In addition it contains the entire Epistle of Barnabas and a portion of the 'Shepherd' of Hermas" (Tischendorf). This Codex is now at St Petersburg.

A. *Codex Alexandrinus.* This MS. belongs to the *fifth* century. It contains, with very few exceptions, the whole of the LXX. version of the O. T.; in the N. T. the missing portions are Matt. i. 1—xxv. 6, John vi. 50—viii. 52, 2 Cor. iv. 13—xii. 6. It is now in the British Museum, having been presented to Charles I. by Cyrillus Lucaris, Patriarch of Constantinople, who had previously brought it from Alexandria in Egypt.

B. *Codex Vaticanus* also contains the LXX. Version of the O. T. with the exception of a large portion of Genesis and Psalms cv—cxxxvii; in the N. T. the latter part of the Epistle to the Hebrews is lacking (from ch. ix. 14—end), also the Pastoral Epistles and the Apocalypse. It is probably either contemporary with א, or a little later. This MS. is now, as the name implies, in the Vatican Library.

C. *Codex Ephraemi rescriptus:* a *palimpsest;* i.e. on the vellum which contained the worn-out ancient letters (the value of the MS. not being recognised) were written the works of the Syrian Saint Ephraem. In the seventeenth century the older writing was observed beneath the more modern words, and a great portion of this valuable *fifth*-century codex has been recovered and published. It contains portions of the LXX. Version of the O. T., and fragments of every book of the N. T. with the exception of 2 John and 2 Thessalonians, which are entirely lost. This Codex is in the National Library of Paris.

D. *Codex Bezæ:* a MS. of the sixth or seventh century, containing the Gospels and Acts, between which the Catholic Epistles once stood. Of these, 3 John. *vv.* 11—15 is the only extant portion. The interpolations and various readings of this MS. are of a remarkable character. There are several lacunæ. It is now in the Cambridge University Library, to which it was presented by Beza in 1581. (See Wetstein's *Proleg. in N. T.* pp. 28—101. Scrivener, *Introduction to the Criticism of the N. T.* pp. 83—118. Tischendorf, *Introduction to the Tauchnitz Edition of the N. T.* Smith's *Dictionary of the Bible;* Art. New Testament, pp. 513, 514.)

THE HOLY LAND.

Palestine (*Philistia*) or the Holy Land was about 140 miles in length. The distance from Dan to Beersheba was less than that between London and Manchester; the distance from Capernaum to Jerusalem was nearly the same as that from Rugby to London. The average breadth was 40 miles.

The political divisions are indicated as they existed during our Lord's ministry. At the date of His birth all the districts included in this map were comprised in the Kingdom of Herod the Great. After Herod's death, Archelaus ruled over Samaria and Judæa. When Archelaus was banished these divisions were placed under the rule of a Roman Procurator.

Mount Hermon, called also Sirion (the Glitterer), and Shenir (Deut. iii. 9), and Sion (Deut. iv. 48), ch. xvii. 1.

Cæsarea Philippi, ch. xvi. 13.

Syro-Phœnicia or *Canaan*, ch. xv. 22 and Mark vii. 26.

Nazareth, ch. ii. 23.

Mount Tabor, the traditional scene of the Transfiguration; at this time its summit was probably occupied by a fortress. Ch. xvii. 1.

Gerasa, not mentioned in this gospel; see ch. viii. 28, and cp. Mark v. 1, where one reading is Gerasenes, inhabitants of a *different* Gerasa or Gergesa.

Ephraim, the supposed site of the Ephraim mentioned John xi. 54, to which Jesus retired shortly before his last Passover.

Ramah, ch. ii. 18.

Arimathæa, ch. xxvii. 57.

Jericho, ch. xx. 29.

Bethphage, ch. xxi. 1.

Bethany, ch. xxi. 17, xxvi. 6.

Bethlehem, ch. ii. 1.

Machærus, the scene of John Baptist's imprisonment and death, ch. iv. 12 and xiv. 10.

PLACES in
THE HOLY LAND
Referred to in
St Matthew's Gospel
Sidon
Tyre
SYRO PHŒNICIA
or CANAAN
(THE LOWLANDS)
DAMASCUS
SYRIA
Mt Hermon
Dan
Cæsarea Philippi
ITURÆA
TETRARCHY
GAULANITIS
OF
HEROD PHILIP
TRACHONITIS
GALILEE
TETRARCHY
Chorazin
Capernaum
Bethsaida
(Julias)
Sea of Galilee
Magdala
Nazareth
Mt Tabor
Nain
Gadara
DECAPOLIS
Ford
Cæsarea
Stratonis
THE GREAT SEA
(MEDITERRANEAN)
SAMARIA
Gerasa
HEROD
ANTIPAS
PERÆA
Beyond Jordan
River Jordan
ROMAN PROVINCE UNDER THE PROCURATOR PONTIUS PILATE
Rantieh
Roman Road
Ephraim
Arimathea?
Jericho
Ford
Ramah
JERUSALEM
Bethany
Bethlehem
to Egypt
JUDÆA
Juttah
Wilderness of Judæa
The Salt Sea
(Dead Sea)
Machærus
Prison of St John
Kerioth
Beer-sheba
IDUMÆA
Scale of English Miles
10 5 0 10 20 30
JERUSALEM
Mt of Olives
Bethphage
Bethany
Siloam
Brook Kidron
High Level Aqueduct
M. Moriah (Temple)
Z. Zion (Upper City)
B. Bezetha (New City)
A. Acra (Lower City)
C. Golgotha ?
G. Gethsemane
P. Pool of Siloam
F. Potter's Field
35
36
33
32
31
Copyright.
H. Courtier F.R.G.S.

ST MATTHEW.

1—17. *The Lineage of the King. The Genealogy.*

THE book of the generation of Jesus Christ, the son of 1
David, the son of Abraham. Abraham begat Isaac; 2
and Isaac begat Jacob; and Jacob begat Judas and his
brethren; and Judas begat Phares and Zara of Thamar; 3
and Phares begat Esrom; and Esrom begat Aram; and 4

CH. I. 1—17. THE LINEAGE OF THE KING. THE GENEALOGY. Luke iii. 23—38.

1. *The book of the generation*] i.e. the pedigree extracted from the public archives which were carefully preserved and placed under the special care of the Sanhedrin. The expression recalls, perhaps designedly, Gen. v. 1: The book of the Generations of Adam.

(1) The genealogy is an answer to the question which would be asked by every Jew of any one who claimed to be the Messiah, "Is he of the house of David?" for by no name was the Messiah more frequently spoken of by Jews and by foreigners (see ch. xv. 22), and designated in the Talmud, than by that of the Son of David.

(2) Both this genealogy and that in St Luke's Gospel trace Joseph's descent. But see below, *v.* 16.

(3) St Matthew proves that Jesus is the Son of David and of Abraham; St Luke, true to the scope of his Gospel, traces the pedigree from the common Father of Jew and Gentile.

(4) St Matthew traces the *royal succession*, St Luke, the family *lineage*. This accounts for many variations in names.

(5) This genealogy *descends* from father to son, and is therefore probably the most exact transcript of the original document. St Luke's *ascends* from son to father.

3. *Thamar*] St Matthew also differs from St Luke in naming women in the genealogy. Of the four mentioned two—Rahab and Ruth—are foreigners, and three—Thamar, Rahab and Bathsheba—were stained with sin. The purpose of the Evangelist in recording their names may be to shew that He who came to save "that which was lost," the Friend of sinners, does not scorn such descent.

Aram begat Aminadab; and Aminadab begat Naasson; and
5 Naasson begat Salmon; and Salmon begat Booz of Rachab;
6 and Booz begat Obed of Ruth; and Obed begat Jesse; and
Jesse begat David the king; and David the king begat
7 Solomon of *her that had been* the *wife* of Urias; and Solomon
begat Roboam; and Roboam begat Abia; and Abia begat
8 Asa; and Asa begat Josaphat; and Josaphat begat Joram;
9 and Joram begat Ozias; and Ozias begat Joatham; and
10 Joatham begat Achaz; and Achaz begat Ezekias; and
Ezekias begat Manasses; and Manasses begat Amon; and
11 Amon begat Josias; and Josias begat Jechonias and his
brethren, about the time they were carried away to Babylon:
12 and after they were brought to Babylon, Jechonias begat Sala-
13 thiel; and Salathiel begat Zorobabel; and Zorobabel begat
Abiud; and Abiud begat Eliakim; and Eliakim begat Azor;
14 and Azor begat Sadoc; and Sadoc begat Achim; and Achim

5. *Salmon...Jesse*] According to the received chronology the space of time between Salmon and Jesse was not less than 400 years. In that space there are only four generations recorded in the text. Either then the received chronology is wrong or the genealogy not complete. In all probability the former is at fault, and the shortening of the period named would bring "Jewish history into harmony with Egyptian and with the internal evidence of the Israelitish history itself." See art. Genealogy in *Bib. Dict.* for this and other points.

6. *David the king*] A special hint of Christ the King, of whom David was the type.

It is at this point that St Luke's genealogy branches off. According to *natural* descent Joseph was a descendant of *Nathan*, not of *Solomon*. The genealogies meet again in the names of Zorobabel and Salathiel. See below, *v.* 12.

8. *Joram begat Ozias* (Uzziah)] The names of Ahaziah, Joash and Amaziah are here omitted; see note, *v.* 17.

11. *Josias begat Jechonias* (Jehoiakim)] but in the next *v.* Jechonias =Jehoiachin. Read, as in the margin, "Josias begat Jakim (Jehoiakim), and Jakim begat Jechonias (Jehoiachin).

Jechonias and his brethren] Jehoiachin had no brethren, but Jehoiakim had three: a further proof that Jechonias in this verse=Jehoiakim.

12. *Jechonias begat Salathiel*] Jehoiachin had no children of his own, "write ye this man childless" (Jer. xxii. 30). Salathiel was the son of Neri (Luke), but heir to Jehoiachin.

13. *Zorobabel begat Abiud*] Here a step is omitted, Abiud—the Hodaiah of 1 Chron. iii. 24—being the grandson of Zerubbabel. Rhesa, who is named as Zerubbabel's son (Luke iii. 27), is a title: the text in Luke should run, "which was the son of Rhesa Zorobabel." The Juda of Luke is the same as Abiud.

begat Eliud; and Eliud begat Eleazar; and Eleazar begat 15
Matthan; and Matthan begat Jacob; and Jacob begat 16
Joseph the husband of Mary, of whom was born Jesus, who
is called Christ. So all the generations from Abraham to 17
David *are* fourteen generations; and from David until the
carrying away into Babylon *are* fourteen generations; and
from the carrying away into Babylon unto Christ *are* fourteen
generations.

18—25. *The Birth of Jesus Christ.*

Now the birth of Jesus Christ was on this wise: When as 18
his mother Mary was espoused to Joseph, before they came

16. *Jacob begat Joseph*] "Joseph which was the son of Heli" (Luke), see last note; probably Joseph was the son of Heli and the heir to Jacob. It is conjectured with much probability that Jacob was Mary's father. In that case, although both genealogies show Joseph's descent, they are in fact equally genealogies of Mary's family.

Matthan or Matthat

(According to Matthew) Jacob — Heli (according to Luke)

Mary (?) — Joseph

17. This division into three sets, each containing fourteen steps of descent, is an instance of a practice familiar to readers of Jewish antiquities. Lightfoot says, "They do so very much delight in such kind of concents, that they oftentimes screw up the strings beyond the due measure and stretch them till they crack." Such a system necessitates the omission of steps in the descent: see notes *vv.* 8 and 13.

18—25. The Birth of Jesus Christ. Luke i. 26—56 and ii. 4—7.

St Mark and St John give no account of the birth of Jesus, St Luke narrates several particulars not recorded by Matthew, (1) the annunciation, (2) Mary's salutation of Elizabeth in a city of Juda (or Juttah), and (3) the journey from Galilee to Bethlehem.

18. *Jesus*] see *v.* 21.

Christ (anointed)] The *title* of Jesus as Prophet, Priest and King; for among the Jews, Prophets, Priests and Kings were anointed on entering upon their office. *Christos*, very rare as a classical Greek word, is a translation of the Hebr. *Mashiach*, a term applied to the Saviour in one passage only of the O. T. (Dan. ix. 25, 26). In the N. T. the Hebrew form is used twice (John i. 41 and iv. 25), where it is explained "which is called Christ." Note that one title—Messiah or Christ—has been adopted almost to the exclusion of others quite as common in the O. T., "The Branch," "He that cometh" (Habba), "The Prophet." This is partly due to the great influence of Daniel's prophecy, partly to the appropriateness of the title to the Son of David.

19 together, she was found with child of the Holy Ghost. Then
Joseph her husband, being a just *man*, and not willing to
make her a publick example, was minded to put her away
20 privily. But while he thought on these *things*, behold, *the*
angel of the Lord appeared unto him in a dream, saying,
Joseph, *thou* son of David, fear not to take unto *thee* Mary
thy wife: for that which is conceived in her is of the Holy
21 Ghost. And she shall bring forth a son, and thou shalt call
his name JESUS: for he shall save his people from their
22 sins. Now all this was done, that it might be fulfilled which
23 was spoken of the Lord by the prophet, saying, Behold, a
virgin shall be with child, and shall bring forth a

Mary] The Hebr. form is Miriam; the Greek Maria.

espoused (betrothed)] Among the Jews the betrothal took place a year before marriage, and during the interval the betrothed maiden remained with her own family. But from the day of betrothal the pair were regarded as man and wife.

19. *being a just man*] i.e. one who observed the law, and, therefore, feeling bound to divorce Mary. But two courses were open to him. He could either summon her before the law-courts to be judicially condemned and punished, or he could put her away by a bill of divorcement before witnesses, but without assigning cause. This is meant by "*putting her away privily*," the more merciful course which Joseph resolved to adopt.

21. *Jesus* = Saviour] *Jesus* represents the Greek form, while *Joshua* represents the Hebrew form of the same name. The same Hebrew root occurs in the salutation *Hosanna:* see note, ch. xxi. 9. Joshua who led the Israelites into the Promised Land, and Joshua or Jeshua, who was high priest at the time of the return from the Babylonish Captivity, are types of Jesus Christ in respect both of work and name.

save his people from their sins] An announcement of a Spiritual Kingdom. Contrary to the thought of many Jews the salvation which Jesus brought was not to be a saving from the Roman or Herodian rule, but a life protected from sin.

22. *was done*] Rather, **has come to pass**. The Evangelist speaks as a contemporary.

that it might be fulfilled] By this formula the Evangelist recognises in the event described a fulfilment of a type or prophecy. It matters little whether we regard "that" (ἵνα) as (1) *final*, "in order that," or (2) by a late use *consecutive*, "so that," in other words (1) as marking the conscious intention of the prophet or of God speaking through the prophet, or (2) a reflection of the Evangelist viewing the historical fact in connection with the prophecy—and finding in the prophecy an analogy, if not a definite prediction. For in regard to divine action the intention and result are identical, that is, we cannot conceive of any result being unintentional with God.

son, and they shall call his name Emmanuel, which
being interpreted is, God with us. Then Joseph being raised 24
from sleep did as the angel of the Lord had bidden him,
and took unto *him* his wife: and knew her not till she had 25
brought forth her firstborn son: and *he* called his name
JESUS.

1—12. *The Visit of the Magi.*

Now when Jesus was born in Bethlehem of Judea in 2

23. *a virgin shall be with child*] Properly, according to the Greek text and to the original Hebrew, "The virgin shall be with child, and shall bring forth a son, and they (Hebr. she) shall call his name God with us;" see Is. vii. 14. The historical crisis was this, Ahaz is alarmed by the threatened invasion of Pekah and Rezin—the confederate kings of Samaria and Damascus. Isaiah reassures Ahaz, who hypocritically refuses to ask for a sign. Yet a sign is given. She, who is now unmarried, shall bear a son, probably a scion of the royal house of David; he shall be called Emmanuel, and before he arrives at years of discretion the deliverance shall come, though a heavier distress is at hand.

The prophecy is distinctly Messianic, but the sign in Isaiah is not concerned with the *manner* of the child's birth, but with the name and the deliverance which should happen in his infancy. Therefore, the weight of the reference is to the name "Emmanuel" and to the true Son of David, whose birth was the sign of His people's deliverance.

25. *knew her not till*] This expression cannot be considered as in any way decisive of the question, whether the Virgin Mary had or had not children besides our blessed Lord.

her firstborn son] The oldest MSS. omit the word "first-born:" translate "a son."

CH. II. 1—12. THE VISIT OF THE MAGI. Recorded by St Matthew only.

1. *Jesus was born*] The year 3 before the Christian Era has been fixed almost beyond a doubt as the date of the Nativity. The present year—1877—is therefore correctly A.D. 1880. The data on which the computation is founded are (1) the first rule of Quirinus (Luke ii. 2), (2) the accession of Tiberius A.D. 14, (3) the Paschal full moon at the time of the crucifixion probably A.D. 33, (4) the reign of Herod, which began in B.C. 36 and ended in B.C. 1. The last-named date has been accurately determined in a paper read before the Society of Biblical Archæology by Mr J. W. Bosanquet,—which see for a learned discussion of the whole question.

in Bethlehem] St Matthew omits the circumstances which brought Mary to Bethlehem.

Bethlehem] ('The House of Bread,' cp. John vi. 51), the city of David, situate on a limestone ridge a few miles S. of Jerusalem. The old name

the days of Herod the king, behold, there came wise men
2 from the east to Jerusalem, saying, Where is he that is born
King of the Jews? for we have seen his star in the east, and

of Bethlehem was Ephrath or Ephratah; it is now called Beit-lahm. It is worthy of remark that no visit of Jesus or of His disciples to Bethlehem, His birthplace and the cradle of His race, is recorded.

Herod] Called afterwards, but not in his lifetime, Herod the Great; he was an Idumæan (Edomite) who, chiefly through the friendship of M. Antony, became king of Judæa. For date of reign see above. The title of *King* distinguishes him from the other Herods named in the gospels. Antipas, who tried in vain to obtain the title, is called King by courtesy, Mark vi. 14.

Herod was not an absolute monarch, but subject to the Roman empire, much in the same way as some of the Indian princes are subject to the British government, or as Servia was till recently subject to the Porte.

behold] The use of this word in the original is a mark of the Hebrew style influencing the Greek.

wise men] Lit. Magi, originally the name of a Median tribe, who, according to Herodotus, possessed the power of interpreting dreams. Their religion consisted in the worship of the heavenly bodies and of the elements. At this date the name implied a religious caste—the followers of Zoroaster, who were the astrologers of the East. Their tenets had spread widely; and as the East is a vague term, it is difficult to determine from what country these Magi came. A theory, stated below, connects them with Egypt, or at least with an Egyptian system of chronology. The common belief that the Magi were three in number is a mere tradition, which has been perpetuated by great painters. It was probably an inference from *v.* 11. An equally groundless tradition has designated the Magi as kings, and has assigned names to them. Every reader of the Classics knows how common a failing it is with ancient annotators to state deductions from the text as proved facts.

2. *King of the Jews*] A title unknown to the earlier history of Israel and applied to no one except the Messiah. It reappears in the inscription over the Cross (ch. xxvii. 37).

his star in the east] The simplest explanation of this is that a Star or Meteor appeared in the sky to guide the Magi on their way first to Jerusalem, then to Bethlehem. It is, however, quite possible that the Magi were divinely led to connect some calculated phenomenon with the birth of the "King of the Jews." Among many conjectures may be mentioned one recently propounded by Prof. Lauth of Munich. It appears to be proved that the dog-star Sirius rose heliacally, i.e. appeared at sunrise, on the first of the Egyptian month Mesori, for four years in succession, viz. 5, 4, 3, 2 before our era. The rising of this star of special brilliance on the first of this special month (Mesori = birth of the prince) would have a marked significance. By the Magi it might well be connected with the prophecy of "the star of Jacob," and become the cause of their journey to Jerusalem.

are come to worship him. When Herod the king had heard 3
these things, he was troubled, and all Jerusalem with him.
And when he had gathered all the chief priests and scribes 4
of the people together, he demanded of them where Christ
should be born. And they said unto him, In Bethlehem of 5
Judea: for thus it is written by the prophet, And thou 6
Bethlehem, *in* the land of Juda, art not the least
among the princes of Juda: for out of thee shall
come a Governor, that shall rule my people Israel.

This theory explains Herod's edict, *v.* 16, for the destruction of all male children "from two years old and under," for, as according to the date assigned to the Nativity of Christ, the arrival of the Magi at Jerusalem would coincide with the year 3 before the Christian era, the star had appeared for two years.

The theory, supported by Alford, which identifies this "star" with a conjunction of Jupiter and Saturn, forces the meaning of the word "star," is inconsistent with the latest chronological results, and is shown to be scientifically impossible by Prof. Pritchard in *Dict. of the Bible, sub voc.* "Star of the Magi."

The connection of the birth of the Messiah with the appearance of a Star is illustrated by the name Barchochab ("Son of a Star"), assumed by a false Messiah who appeared in the year 120 A.D. It has also been noticed that in the *Cartouche* or Egyptian royal symbol of Vespasian, the word "God" is for the first time expressed by a Star. (Dr Lauth, *Trans. Bib. Arch. Soc.* IV. 2.)

3. *all Jerusalem with him*] Fearing some fresh outbreak of cruelty.

4. *gathered all the chief priests and scribes of the people together*] i.e. summoned a meeting of the Sanhedrin, a body often indicated in this way. Others contend that this was an irregular meeting of all the chief priests and learned men.

The chief priests were those who had served the office of high priest, and also the heads of the courses into which the priests were divided. Scribes were those who transcribed or copied the law and who expounded it. They are called lawyers in St Luke's gospel.

where Christ should be born] Lit. **where the Christ or Messiah is born**. Where do your sacred writings represent him to be born? For a similar use of the indicative cp. John vii. 52.

5. *by the prophet*] Lit. **by means of, through**—the prophet is regarded as the instrument. In *v.* 17 and iii. 3, some MSS. have the preposition signifying personal agency (ὑπό), instead of the instrumental preposition (διά); but the usual formula is as in *v.* 15, "by the Lord through the prophet."

Bethlehem of Judea] To distinguish this Bethlehem from the Bethlehem in the tribe of Zebulun (Josh. xix. 15).

6. *And thou Bethlehem, &c.*] Micah v. 2. The quotation nearly corresponds with the Hebrew text, the literal translation of which is: **But thou Bethlehem Ephratah, though thou be little to be among the**

7 Then Herod, when he had privily called the wise men,
inquired of them diligently what time the star appeared.
8 And he sent them to Bethlehem, and said, Go and search
diligently for the young child; and when ye have found
him, bring me word again, that I may come and worship
9 him also. When they had heard the king, they departed;
and lo, the star, which they saw in the east, went before
them, till it came and stood over where the young child
10 was. When they saw the star, they rejoiced *with* exceeding
11 great joy. And when they were come into the house, they
saw the young child with Mary his mother, and fell down,
and worshipped him: and when they had opened their
treasures, they presented unto him gifts; gold, and frank-

thousands of Judah, yet out of thee shall come forth unto me he that is to be ruler in Israel.

The LXX. is singularly different both in words and construction—a proof of the Hebrew original of this gospel; for the Greek translation of the prophecy is evidently independent of the LXX.

A reflection of this prophecy became prevalent in the East. Accordingly the Roman historians designate the Emperor Vespasian as the Eastern Prince who was destined to rule the world: "Percrebuerat Oriente toto vetus et constans opinio esse in fatis ut eo tempore Judæa profecti rerum potirentur. Id de Imperatore Romano quantum postea eventu paruit prædictum Judæi ad se trahentes rebellarunt." Suet. *Vesp.* IV. Similarly Tac. *Hist.* V. 13. Comp. Joseph. *B. J.* VI. 5. 4. See above, *v.* 2.

7. *inquired of them diligently*] Rather, **having accurately ascertained**; the word is used of scientific exactness. The reason of this inquiry appears in *v.* 16.

what time the star appeared] Literally, **the time of the star which was appearing**, i.e. when it first appeared and how long it would continue.

8. *he sent them to Bethlehem*] Up to this point the Magi are not said to have been guided by the Star; they go to Bethlehem in accordance with Herod's directions, which were based on the report of the Sanhedrin; as they went the star again appeared in the East.

11. *the house*] St Matthew gives no hint that "the house" was an inn, or that the babe was lying in a manger. Perhaps here as in other places we are misled by the ideas suggested by great pictures; and in truth the visit of the Magi should be placed at least some days after the events recorded in Luke ii. 1—38.

their treasures] Properly caskets or chests in which treasures were placed. Such offerings to kings were quite in accordance with Eastern usage. Seneca says "No one may salute a Parthian king without bringing a gift;" cp. Ps. lxviii. 29, lxxii. 10.

incense, and myrrh. And being warned of God in a dream 12
that *they* should not return to Herod, they departed into
their own country another way.

13—15. *The Flight into Egypt.*

And when they were departed, behold, *the* angel of the 13
Lord appeareth to Joseph in a dream, saying, Arise, and
take the young child and his mother, and flee into Egypt,
and be thou there until I bring thee word: for Herod will
seek the young child to destroy him. When he arose, he 14
took the young child and his mother by night, and departed
into Egypt: and was there until the death of Herod: that 15
it might be fulfilled which was spoken of the Lord by the
prophet, saying, Out of Egypt have I called my son.

frankincense and myrrh were products of Arabia, and, according to Herodotus, of that country only. They were both used for medicinal purposes and for embalming; cp. John xix. 39.

13—15. THE FLIGHT INTO EGYPT.

13. *the young child*] Named first, as the most precious charge and the most exposed to danger.

Egypt] at all times the readiest place of refuge for the Israelites, whether from famine or from political oppression. It had sheltered many thousands of Jews from the tyranny of the Syrian kings. Consequently large settlements of Jews were to be found in various cities of Egypt and Africa. In Alexandria the Jews numbered a fifth of the population. Wherever therefore the infant Saviour's home was in Egypt, it would be in the midst of His brethren according to the flesh.

At this time Egypt was a Roman province. This incident of Christ's stay in Egypt would be regarded as a precious memory by the African church—the church of Cyprian, Origen and Augustine.

15. *until the death of Herod*] According to the chronology adopted above this would be for a space of less than two years.

that it might be fulfilled] See note on ch. i. 22.

Out of Egypt have I called my son] Better, **I called my son.** The history of Israel is regarded as typical of the Messiah's life. He alone gives significance to that history. He is the true seed of Abraham. In Him the blessing promised to Abraham finds its highest fulfilment. (See Lightfoot on Gal. iii. 16.) Even particular incidents in the Gospel narrative have their counterpart in the O.T. history. Accordingly St Matthew, who naturally reverts to this thought more constantly than the other Evangelists, from the very nature of his gospel, recognises in this incident an analogy to the call of Israel from Egypt.

The quotation is again from the original Hebrew of Hosea xi. 2, and again the LXX. differs considerably. Cp. Ex. iv. 22, 23: "Israel is

16—18. *The Slaying of the Children at Bethlehem.*

16 Then Herod, when he saw that he was mocked of the
wise men, was exceeding wroth, and sent forth, and slew all
the children that were in Bethlehem, and in all the coasts
thereof, from two years old and under, according to the
time which he had diligently inquired of the wise men.
17 Then was fulfilled that which was spoken by Jeremie the
18 prophet, saying, In Rama was there a voice heard,
lamentation, and weeping, and great mourning,
Rachel weeping for her children, and would not be
comforted, because they are not.

my son, even my firstborn: and I say unto thee, Let my son go, that he may serve me."

16—18. THE SLAYING OF THE CHILDREN AT BETHLEHEM.

16. *and sent forth, and slew*] i.e. he sent assassins to slay.

all the children] Lit. **all the male children.**

coasts] i.e. borders or neighbourhood.

from two years old and under] If we adopt the hypothesis regarding the star mentioned above, a satisfactory explanation is given for Herod's directions, which otherwise it is difficult to explain. Even if the above theory is not the true one, the two years mentioned in the text are clearly connected with the astronomical appearances described by the Magi, in answer to Herod's "diligent inquiries."

Profane history passes over this atrocity in silence. But Josephus may well have found his pages unequal to contain a complete record of all the cruel deeds of a tyrant like Herod. Macaulay relates that the massacre of Glencoe is not even alluded to in the pages of Evelyn, a most diligent recorder of passing political events. Besides, the crime was executed with secrecy, the number of children slain was probably very inconsiderable, for Bethlehem was but a small town; and though it was possibly crowded at the time (Luke ii. 7), the number of very young children would not have been considerably augmented by those strangers.

The whole scene must have been very different from that which is presented to us on the canvas of the great mediæval artists.

17. *Then was fulfilled*] This turn of expression may be regarded as identical with the more usual "that it might be fulfilled."

by] See note *v.* 5.

18. Jer. xxxi. 15, in LXX. xxxviii. 15. In a singularly touching passage, Rachel, the mother of the tribe of Benjamin (whose tomb was close to Bethlehem: Gen. xxxv. 19), is conceived of as weeping for her captive sons at Ramah—some of whom were possibly doomed to die; cp. Jer. xl. 1.

The Evangelist pictures Rachel's grief re-awakened by the slaughter of the infants at Bethlehem.

19—21. *The Return from Egypt.*

But when Herod was dead, behold, an angel of the Lord 19
appeareth in a dream to Joseph in Egypt, saying, Arise, 20
and take the young child and his mother, and go into the
land of Israel: for they are dead which sought the young
child's life. And he arose, and took the young child and 21
his mother, and came into the land of Israel.

22, 23. *The Dwelling at Nazareth.*

But when he heard that Archelaus did reign in Judea in 22
the room of his father Herod, he was afraid to go thither:
notwithstanding, being warned of God in a dream, he
turned aside into the parts of Galilee: and he came and 23
dwelt in a city called Nazareth: that it might be fulfilled
which was spoken by the prophets, He shall be called a
Nazarene.

The Ramah alluded to by Jeremiah, generally identified with the modern Er-Rama, was about 5 miles N. of Jerusalem, and in the tribe of Benjamin. There is no proof of another Ramah near Bethlehem. The analogy therefore must not be pressed.

19—21. The Return from Egypt.

20. *they*] Plural by a euphemism, the reference being to Herod alone.

22. *Archelaus*] A son of Herod the Great. His mother was Malthaké, a Samaritan. After a cruel and disturbed reign (under the title of Ethnarch) of about eight years he was banished to Vienna in Gaul—the modern Vienne. His dominions, including Samaria, Judæa, and Idumæa, then passed into the direct government of Rome. See note, ch. xiv. 1, and Introduction, p. 25.

22, 23. The Dwelling at Nazareth.

22. *notwithstanding*] Rather "but" or "so."

he turned aside] Rather, **retired** or **withdrew.** The English 'anchorite' is derived from the Greek word in the original. The same word is translated in *vv.* 12 and 13, "departed."

Galilee] Now under the government of Herod Antipas, full brother of Archelaus. For the extent of his dominions see *Map.*

23. *a city called Nazareth*] St Matthew gives no intimation of any previous residence of Mary and Joseph at Nazareth.

Nazareth] Said to signify "the Protectress" (Hebr. *natsar*), a small town of central Galilee, on the edge of the plain of Esdraelon, beautifully situated on the side of a steep hill within a sheltered valley.

He shall be called a Nazarene] The meaning of this passage was probably as clear to the contemporaries of St Matthew, as the other

1—12. *John Baptist preaches in the Wilderness of Judæa.*

3 In those days came John the Baptist, preaching in the
2 wilderness of Judea, and saying, Repent ye: for the kingdom

references to prophecy *vv.* 15, 17; for us it is involved in doubt. First, it may be said Nazarene cannot = Nazarite: the word differs in form, and in no sense could Christ be called a Nazarite. Secondly, the quotation is probably not from a lost prophecy. One meaning of the word *Nazoræus* is an inhabitant of Nazareth, but the word either (1) recalls the Hebrew word *netser* a Branch, a title by which the Messiah is designated Isai. xi. 1, or (2) connects itself in thought with the Hebr. *natsar*, to save or protect (see above), and so has reference to the name and work of Jesus, or (3) is a synonym for "contemptible" or "lowly," from the despised position of Nazareth. Of these (3) is perhaps the least probable explanation. The play upon words which (1) and (2) involve is quite characteristic of Hebrew phraseology. The sound of the original would be either (1) He whom the prophet called the "Netser" dwells at "Netser"—(for this form of Nazareth see Smith's *Bib. Dict.*), or (2) He who is called "Notsri" (my protector) dwells at "Natsaret" (the protectress).

In any case the passage gains fresh interest from the fact that the early Christians were called Nazarenes in scorn. Cp. Acts xxiv. 5. For them it would be a point of triumph that their enemies thus unconsciously connected them with a prophetic title of their Master.

CH. III. **1—12.** JOHN BAPTIST PREACHES IN THE WILDERNESS OF JUDÆA. Mark i. 2—8; Luke iii. 1—18; John i. 15—34.

St Luke does not name the Pharisees and Sadducees, he gives the particular exhortations to the various classes of people who came to hear John. In the fourth Gospel the Baptist's disclaimer of the Messiahship (cp. also ch. iii. 25—36) and his teaching respecting the person of Christ are reported more fully.

1. *In those days*] See Luke iii. 1, where the time is defined.

came] Rather, **cometh**. The same word and the same tense as in *v.* 13.

John the Baptist] So named by the other Synoptists and by Josephus: in the fourth gospel he is called simply John, a note of the authenticity of St John's gospel. Josephus mentions the great influence of John and speaks of the crowds that flocked to hear him preach and to be baptized of him. He says John taught men "Justice in regard to one another and piety towards God."

preaching] Lit. **heralding**, a word appropriate to the thought of the proclamation of a King.

the wilderness of Judea] i. e. the uncultivated Eastern frontier of Judah. The term also includes the cliffs and Western shore of the Dead Sea. In this wild and nearly treeless district there were formerly a few cities, and there are still some luxuriant spots. See Tristram's *Topog. of H. L.* Ch. IV.

of heaven is at hand. For this is he that was spoken of by 3
the prophet Esaias, saying, The voice of one crying in
the wilderness, Prepare ye the way of the Lord,
make his paths straight. And the same John had his 4
raiment of camel's hair, and a leathern girdle about his
loins; and his meat was locusts and wild honey. Then 5
went out to him Jerusalem, and all Judea, and all the region round about Jordan, and were baptized of him in 6

2. *Repent ye*] The original implies more than "feel sorrow or regret for sin," it is rather "change the life, the heart, the *motive* for action." It was a call to self-examination and reality of life.

the kingdom of heaven] St Matthew alone uses this expression, but he also employs the equivalent phrase, the Kingdom of God, in common with the other N. T. writers. In itself the expression was not new. It connected itself in Jewish thought with the theocracy—the direct rule of God—of which the Earthly Kingdom was a shadow. It implied the reign of the Messiah (cp. Dan. vii. 14). It became the watchword of the zealots "no King but God." Jesus took up the word and gave it a new deep and varied spiritual significance, which is rather illustrated than defined.

The principal meanings of the Kingdom of Heaven in N. T. are (1) The presence of Christ on earth. (2) His Second Advent. (3) His influence in the heart. (4) Christianity, (*a*) as a Church, (*b*) as a faith. (5) The life eternal.

3. *by*] See note on ch. ii. 5.

by the prophet Esaias] The reference in Is. xl. 3 is to the promised return from Babylon. A herald shall proclaim the joyous news on mountains and in the desert through which the return should be. This incident in the national history is transferred to the more glorious deliverance from bondage and to the coming of the true King.

The voice] The message is more than the messenger, the prophet's personality is lost in the prophetic voice.

make his paths straight] The image would be familiar to Eastern thought, a Semiramis or a Xerxes orders the mountains to be levelled or cut through, and causeways to be raised in the valleys.

4. *the same John*] Translate, "John himself."

raiment of camel's hair] A kind of tunic or shirt coarsely woven of camel's hair, "one of the most admirable materials for clothing, it keeps out the heat, cold and rain." *Recovery of Jerusalem*, p. 445.

his meat was locusts and wild honey] Thomson, *Land and Book*, pp. 419, 420, states that though tolerated, as an article of food, only by the very poorest people, locusts are still eaten by the Bedawin. Burckhardt mentions having seen locust shops at Medina and Tayf. After being dried in the sun the locusts are eaten with butter and honey. Sometimes they are sprinkled with salt and either boiled or roasted. Thomson adds that wild honey is still gathered from trees in the wilderness and from rocks in the Wadies.

7 Jordan, confessing their sins. But when he saw many of the
Pharisees and Sadducees come to his baptism, he said unto
them, O generation of vipers, who hath warned you to flee
8 from the wrath to come? Bring forth therefore fruits meet
9 for repentance: and think not to say within yourselves, We

6. *baptized*] John introduced no new custom, for ceremonial ablution or baptism was practised in all ancient religions. Among the Jews proselytes were baptized on admission to the Mosaic covenant. John's baptism was the outward sign of the purification and "life-giving change," and contained the promise of forgiveness of sins. Christ too adopted the ancient custom and enriched it with a new significance, and a still mightier efficacy.

7. *Pharisees*] The name signifies "Separatists;" the party dates from the revival of the National life, and observances of the Mosaic Law under the Maccabees. Their ruling principle was a literal obedience to the written law and to an unwritten tradition. Originally they were leaders of a genuine reform. But in the hands of less spiritual successors their system had become little else than a formal observance of carefully prescribed rules. "The real virtues of one age become the spurious ones of the next." Prof. Mozley, *Sermon on Pharisees*. The "hypocrisy" of the Pharisees, which stifled conscience and made them "*incapable of repentance*," is the special sin of the day rebuked more than any other by the Saviour.

Politically they were the popular party, supporters of an isolating policy, who would make no terms with Rome or any other foreign power. The *Zealots* may be regarded as the extreme section of the Pharisees.

The *Sadducees* were the aristocratic and priestly party, they acquiesced in foreign rule, and foreign civilization. They refused to give the same weight as the Pharisees to unwritten tradition, but adhered strictly to the written law of Moses. Their religious creed excluded belief in a future life, or in angels and spirits (Acts xxiii. 8). The name is probably derived from Zadok the priest in David's time. Others with less probability connect it with Zadok, a disciple of Antigonus of Socho, who lived in the second century B.C. The derivation from *tsaddik* (righteous) is untenable.

O generation of vipers] Translate "offspring or 'brood' of vipers."

the wrath to come] In a technical sense "wrath" is (1) the divine attitude towards sin, and as a result (2) the divine judgment upon sin (Rom. ii. 5). "Fleeing from the wrath to come" implies agreeing with God's view of sin and therefore "Repentance" or change of heart.

8. *meet for repentance*] "Answerable to amendment of life." (*Margin.*)

9. *think not to say*] i.e. "Do not persuade yourselves to say," "be not so proud as to say." For a similar use of the word see Phil. iii. 4, "If any other man thinketh that he hath whereof he might trust in the flesh."

have Abraham to *our* father: for I say unto you, that God
is able of these stones to raise up children unto Abraham.
And now also the axe is laid unto the root of the trees: 10
therefore every tree which bringeth not forth good fruit is
hewn down, and cast into the fire. I indeed baptize you 11
with water unto repentance: but he that cometh after me is
mightier than I, whose shoes I am not worthy to bear: he
shall baptize you with the Holy Ghost, and *with* fire: whose 12
fan *is* in his hand, and he will throughly purge his floor,

We have Abraham to our father] Or, '*as* our father.' The Jewish doctors taught that no one who was circumcised should enter Gehenna.

of these stones to raise up children] Stones are regarded as the most insensate, the furthest removed from life of created things. May there not be a play on the words *banim* (children) *abanim* (stones)?

10. *which bringeth not forth*] Lit. **if it bring not forth.**

fruit] The Oriental values trees only as productive of fruit, all others are cut down as cumberers of the ground. He lays his axe literally at the root. *Land and Book*, p. 341.

the fire] Rather, **fire**, there is no definite article in the original.

11. *unto repentance*] i.e. to be a symbol of the changed life.

whose shoes I am not worthy to bear] The work of the meanest slaves. John, great prophet as he was, with influence sufficient to make even Herod tremble for his throne, is unworthy to be the meanest slave of the Stronger One—the Son of God.

with the Holy Ghost] Lit. **in the Holy Ghost.** This preposition is used in Greek and especially in Hellenistic Greek to signify the instrument, but it also expresses the surrounding influence or element in which an act takes place. With water = in water; with the Holy Ghost = surrounded by, influenced by the Holy Ghost.

The matured Christian conception of the Holy Ghost would not be present to the mind of John. Some of his disciples at Ephesus said to Paul "we have not so much as heard whether there be any Holy Ghost." Acts xix. 2.

fire] This metaphor implies: (1) Purification, (2) Fiery zeal or enthusiasm, (3) Enlightenment; all which are gifts of the Holy Spirit. In the ancient hymn by Robert II. of France the third point is brought out:

"Et emitte cælitus
Lucis tuæ radium
*   *   *   *   *
Veni lumen cordium."

12. *fan*] An instrument by which the corn after being threshed is thrown up against the wind to clear it of chaff.

floor] Here put for the contents of the threshing-floor, the mingled grain and chaff.

St Matthew represents the picturesque side of John's preaching,

and gather his wheat into the garner; but will burn up the chaff with unquenchable fire.

13—17. *Jesus comes to be baptized of John.*

13 Then cometh Jesus from Galilee to Jordan unto John, to
14 be baptized of him. But John forbad him, saying, I have
15 need to be baptized of thee, and comest thou to me? And
Jesus answering said unto him, Suffer *it to be so* now: for
thus it becometh us to fulfil all righteousness. Then he
16 suffered him. And Jesus, when he was baptized, went up
straightway out of the water: and lo, the heavens were

these verses are full of imagery. How many similes are compressed into his teaching! The vipers, the stones, the trees, the slave, the threshing-floor, are all used to illustrate his discourse. St Luke throws into prominence the great teacher's keen discrimination of character. St John has recorded a fragment of the Baptist's deeper teaching as to the nature and mission of the Son of God.

13—17. JESUS COMES TO BE BAPTIZED OF JOHN. Mark i. 9—11; Luke iii. 21, 22; John i. 32—34.

St Luke adds two particulars: that the Holy Spirit descended on Jesus (1) "in a bodily shape," and (2) "while He was praying."

In the fourth gospel, where John Baptist's own words are quoted, the act of baptism is not named; a touch of the Baptist's characteristic humility.

13. *Then cometh Jesus...to be baptized of him*] Jesus who is the pattern of the New life submits to the baptism which is a symbol of the New life (*metanoia*). He who has power to forgive sins seems to seek through baptism forgiveness of sins. But in truth by submitting to baptism Jesus shows the true efficacy of the rite. He who is most truly man declares what man may become through baptism—clothed and endued with the Holy Spirit, and touched by the fire of zeal and purity.

There is no hint in the gospel narrative of that beautiful companionship and intercourse in childhood between Jesus and the Baptist with which Art has familiarized us. See John i. 31, a passage which tends to an opposite conclusion.

to Jordan] Probably at "Ænon near to Salim" (John iii. 23), a day's journey from Nazareth, "close to the passage of the Jordan near Succoth and far away from that near Jericho." *Sinai and Palestine*, p. 311.

14. *forbad him*] Rather, **was preventing**, or, **endeavoured to prevent.**

15. *righteousness*] Here = the requirements of the law.

16. *the heavens*] A literal translation of the Hebrew word, which is a plural form.

+ 24th day

opened unto him, and he saw the Spirit of God descending like a dove, and lighting upon him: and lo a voice from 17
heaven, saying, This is my beloved Son, in whom I am well
pleased.

1—11. *The Temptation of Jesus.*

Then was Jesus led up of the Spirit into the wilderness to 4

he [*Jesus*] *saw*] We should infer from the text that the vision was to Jesus alone, but the Baptist also was a witness as we learn from John i. 32. "And John bare record, I saw the Spirit descending from heaven like a dove, and it abode upon him." This was to John the sign by which the Messiah should be recognised.

17. *a voice from heaven*] Thrice during our Lord's ministry it is recorded that a voice from heaven came to Him. The two other occasions were at the Transfiguration and in the week of the Passion (John xii. 28).

heaven] lit. as above **heavens**.

beloved] The original word is used specially and only of the Saviour in the Gospels, Mark xii. 6 and Luke xx. 13 cannot be called exceptions. In late Greek it is nearly interchangeable with "only-begotten."

CH. IV. **1—11.** THE TEMPTATION OF JESUS. Mark i. 12, 13; Luke iv. 1—13.

St Mark's account is short; the various temptations are not specified; he adds the striking expression "he was with the wild beasts." St Luke places the temptation of the Kingdoms of the World before that of the Pinnacle of the Temple.

Generally it may be remarked the account can have come from no other than Jesus Himself. The words of the Evangelist describe an actual scene—not a dream. The devil *really* came to Jesus, but in what form he came is not stated. These were not isolated temptations in the life of Jesus. Cp. Luke xxii. 28, "Ye are they which have continued with me in my *temptations*." But they are typical temptations, comprehending all the forms of temptation by which human nature can be assailed. For, as it has often been said, the three temptations cover the same ground as "the lust of the flesh, the lust of the eyes, and the pride of life" (1 John ii. 16) in which St John sums up the evil of the world.

Viewing the temptation in a personal reference to Jesus Christ we discern Him tempted (1) As the Son of Man—the representative of humanity—in whom human nature in its perfection triumphs over sin. An important element in the Atonement. (2) As the second Adam regaining for man what the first Adam lost for man. (3) As the Son of Abraham following the fortunes of his race, tempted in the wilderness as the Hebrews were tempted. A thought present implicitly in our Lord's answers. (4) As the true Messiah or Christos rejecting the unreal greatness which was the aim of false Messiahs.

2 be tempted of the devil. And when he had fasted forty
3 days and forty nights, he was afterward a hungred. And
when the tempter came to him, he said, If thou be the Son
4 of God, command that these stones be made bread. But he
answered and said, It is written, Man shall not live by
bread alone, but by every word that proceedeth
5 out of the mouth of God. Then the devil taketh him
up into the holy city, and setteth him on a pinnacle of the

The lesson of each and all of the temptations is trust in God and submission to God's will—the result of *metanoia* (repentance).

1. *led up of the Spirit*] The agency of the Spirit of God is named in each of the Synoptists. St Mark uses the strong expression "the Spirit driveth him forth." St Luke uses the preposition ἐν (in) denoting the influence in which Jesus passed into the wilderness.

the wilderness] See note on ch. iii. 1, but the locality of the temptation is not known.

The desert unpeopled by men was thought to be the abode of demons. So Jesus meets the evil spirit in his own domains, the Stronger One coming upon the strong man who keepeth his palace (Luke xi. 21, 22). The retirement preparatory to the great work may be compared with that of Elijah and of Paul. It is perhaps an invariable experience in deeply religious lives to be taken into the desert of their own hearts and there to meet and resist the temptations that assailed Christ.

of the devil] Gk. διάβολος. Hebr. Satan = one who opposes, an adversary. The Greek word conveys the additional ideas of (1) deceiving, (2) calumniating, (3) accusing.

2. *he was afterward a hungred*] The words imply that the temptation was not throughout the forty days, but at the end of the forty days.

3. *that these stones be made bread*] The temptation is addressed to the appetite, Use thy divine power to satisfy the lusts of the flesh.

4. Jesus answers by a quotation from Deut. viii. 3. The chapter sets forth the teaching of the wilderness. The forty years were to the Jews what the forty days are to Jesus. The Lord God proved Israel "to know what was in thine heart, whether thou wouldest keep his commandments or no. And he humbled thee, and suffered thee to hunger, and fed thee with manna...that he might make thee know that man doth not live by bread only, but by every [word, omitted in Hebr.] that proceedeth out of the mouth of the Lord doth man live."

Christ's test of sonship is obedience and entire trust in God who alone is the giver of every good gift. The devil's test of sonship is supply of bodily wants, external prosperity, &c.

5. *taketh him up*] The situation of Jerusalem is remarkably high. It was probably the loftiest capital in the ancient world.

the holy city] Jerusalem is so designated by St Matthew alone.

a pinnacle] strictly the pinnacle—pinnacle, lit. 'a little wing,' an architectural term for a wing-like projection. The particular pinnacle

temple, and saith unto him, If thou be the Son of God, cast 6
thyself down: for it is written, He shall give his angels
charge concerning thee: and in *their* hands they
shall bear thee up, lest at any time thou dash thy
foot against a stone. Jesus said unto him, It is written 7
again, Thou shalt not tempt the Lord thy God. Again, 8
the devil taketh him *up* into an exceeding high mountain, and
sheweth him all the kingdoms of the world, and the glory of
them; and saith unto him, All these *things* will I give thee, 9
if thou wilt fall down and worship me. Then saith Jesus 10
unto him, Get thee hence, Satan: for it is written, Thou
shalt worship the Lord thy God, and him only

was probably on the roof of one of the Temple Porches overlooking the deep valley of the Kedron or of Hinnom. Josephus speaking of the "Royal Porch" says "if anyone looked down from the top of the battlements he would be giddy, while his sight could not reach to such an immense depth." *Antiq.* xv. 11. 5.

6. *it is written*] Ps. xci. 11, 12. The words "to keep thee in all thy ways" are omitted in the text. The omission distorts the meaning of the original, which is that God will keep the righteous on their journeys, and is no inducement to tempt God by rash venture or needless risk. The Psalmist himself probably quotes Prov. iii. 23. "Thus [i.e. by obedience: see preceding verses] shalt thou walk in thy way safely, and thy foot shall not stumble."

7. *Thou shalt not tempt the Lord thy God*] Deut. vi. 16. The verse ends "as ye tempted him in Massah." The reference to Massah (Numb. xx. 7—12) shews the true meaning of the Saviour's answer. Moses and Aaron displayed distrust in God when they tried to draw to themselves the glory of the miracle instead of "sanctifying the Lord." Jesus will not glorify Himself in the eyes of the Jews by a conspicuous miracle. His work as the Son of Man is to glorify the Father's name through obedience. Cp. John xii. 28.

8. *an exceeding high mountain*] It is idle to ask what this mountain was, or in what sense Jesus saw the kingdoms of the world. It is enough that the thought and the temptation of earthly despotism and glory were present to the mind of Jesus.

9. *All these things will I give thee*] Satan, the "prince of this world," (John vii. 31) claims the disposal of earthly thrones. This is more clearly brought out by St Luke (ch. iv. 6), "All this power will I give thee and the glory of them, for that is delivered unto me, and to whomsoever I will I give it." The arrogance, selfishness, and cruelty of contemporary rulers would give force to such an assumption. A Tiberius or a Herod Antipas might indeed be thought to have worshipped Satan.

10. *Get thee hence, Satan*] It is instructive to find these words addressed to Peter (ch. xvi. 23) when he put himself as it were in the place of the tempter. See note *ad loc.*

11 shalt thou serve. Then the devil leaveth him, and behold, angels came and ministered unto him.

12—16. *Jesus returns to Galilee.*

12 Now when Jesus had heard that John was cast into prison,
13 he departed into Galilee; and leaving Nazareth, he came
and dwelt in Capernaum, which is upon the sea coast, in the

him only shalt thou serve] Deut. vi. 10—13. Idolatry, multiplicity of aims, and forgetfulness of God are the dangers of prosperity and ambition. See context of passage in Deut.

12—16. JESUS RETURNS INTO GALILEE.

Mark i. 14; Luke iv. 14, who assigns no reason; John iv. 1—3. St John gives a further reason "when the Lord knew how the Pharisees had heard that Jesus made and baptized more disciples than John, he left Judæa, &c."

12. *when Jesus had heard*] probably also *because* he had heard. It was a needful precaution against the cruel treachery of Herod Antipas. At Capernaum He would be close to the dominions of Herod Philip.

John was cast into prison] at Machærus. The cause of John's imprisonment is stated at length ch. xiv. 3, 4 (where see note) and Luke iii. 19, 20.

On hearing of the *death* of John the Baptist Jesus retired into the wilderness. See ch. xiv. 13.

departed into Galilee] by the shortest route through Samaria. John iv. 4. During this journey must be placed the conversation with the woman of Samaria. This was after a ministry in Judæa, which had lasted eight months (Ellicott, *Lectures on the life of our Lord*, p. 130), some incidents of which are related by St John, ii. and iii.

Galilee]=a circle or circuit originally confined to a "circle" of 20 cities given by Solomon to Hiram 1 Kings ix. 11. Cp. Josh. xx. 7. From this small beginning the name spread to a larger district, just as the name of Asia spread from a district near the Mæander, first to the Roman Province, then to a quarter of the Globe. The Jews were in a minority in those parts. The population mainly consisted of Phœnicians, Arabs, and Greeks.

13. *leaving Nazareth*] partly because of the unbelief of the Nazarenes, partly (we may infer) in order to be in a frontier town from which He might easily pass from the jurisdiction of Antipas.

Capernaum] or Capharnaum, a town on the N.W. shore of the Sea of Galilee. The exact site is keenly disputed. It was, perhaps, at Khan Minyeh (see map), not quite on the Sea, but on the plain of Gennesaret, at a short distance from the sea. It was the scene of a considerable traffic, and had a large Gentile element in its population.

Others identify Capernaum with the modern Tell Hûm, at the N. end of the Lake in the plain of the Jordan. The name Tell Hûm nearly

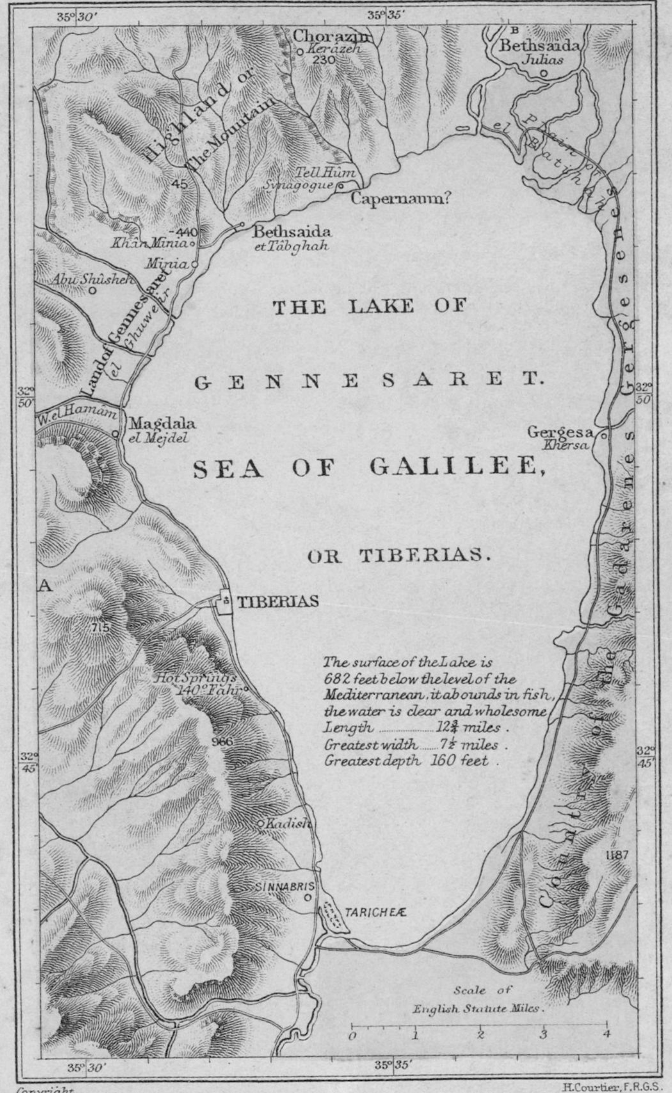

H. Courtier, F.R.G.S.

THE SEA OF GALILEE,

called the Lake of Gennesareth (Luke v. 1), the Sea of Tiberias (John vi. 1 and xxi. 1).

Bethsaida Julias, rebuilt by Herod Philip, the tetrareh, and called Julias after Julia, daughter of Augustus. See note, ch. xiv. 19.

Kerazeh, identified by Capt. Wilson with *Chorazin*. Ch. xi. 21.

Highland or *The Mountain*, the probable scene of the Sermon on the Mount and of the appearance of Jesus Christ, ch. xxviii. 16.

Tell Hûm, the site of *Capernaum*, according to Thomson (*Land and Book*), Capt. Wilson, Dean Stanley *latterly*, and others.

Et Tabigah, by some thought to be the *Bethsaida* ("House of Fish"), mentioned as being the home of Peter, Andrew and Philip (John i. 44); see chs. viii. 14 and xi. 21. Near Et Tabigah is a large fountain, probably "the fountain of Capharnaum" mentioned by Josephus, *B. J.* III. 10. 8, from which water was conveyed by an aqueduct to the plain of Gennesareth. Traces of this aqueduct and of an octagonal reservoir are distinctly visible. See *Recovery of Jerusalem*, p. 349.

Khan Minyeh, the site of Capernaum according to Dean Stanley in *S. and P.* (in Preface to *Rec. of Jerusalem* the Dean inclines to the Tell Hûm site), Dr Robinson, Mr Macgregor (Rob Roy), and others.

El Ghuweir or *The Land of Gennesareth*, a fertile plain 2½ miles in length, about 1 mile in breadth; ch. xiv. 34.

Mejdel, the Magdala of ch. xv. 39.

Tiberias. Not mentioned in this Gospel. But possibly Herod Antipas was holding his Court here when John Baptist was put to death at Machærus; ch. xiv. 6 foll. It was built by Herod Antipas and named Tiberias in honour of the Emperor. See note, ch. xiv. 13—21, and cp. John vi. 1, 23.

K'hersa, identified with *Gergesa*. *Gerasa* (not the well-known Gerasa N. of the Jabbok; see Smith, *Bib. Dic.* sub voc.) is probably another form of the same name. See ch. viii. 23.

Gadara, the capital of "the country of the Gadarenes," to which district Gergesa belonged.

A and *B*, disputed sites for the miracle of feeding 5000; ch. xiv. 13—21.

14 borders of Zabulon and Nephthalim: that it might be ful-
15 filled which was spoken by Esaias the prophet, saying, The
land of Zabulon, and the land of Nephthalim, *by* the
way of the sea, beyond Jordan, Galilee of the Gen-
16 tiles; the people which sat in darkness saw great
light; and to them which sat in the region and
shadow of death light is sprung up.

17—22. *The Call of Peter and Andrew and the sons of Zebedee.*

17 From that time Jesus began to preach, and to say, Repent:
18 for the kingdom of heaven is at hand. And Jesus, walking by the sea of Galilee, saw two brethren, Simon called

corresponds with Kefr na Hum, thought by some to have been the ancient form of Capernaum. The most interesting point in the identification is that among the ruins at Tell Hûm are remains of a Synagogue, in which some of the Saviour's "mighty works" may have been wrought. See map.

Whatever the truth may be in this question it is certain that in passing from Nazareth to Capernaum Jesus left a retired mountain home for a busy and populous neighbourhood, "the manufacturing district of Palestine."

14. *Esaias*] Read the whole of the prophecy (ch. viii. 11—ix. 6) which is unfortunately broken in the E. V. by the division into chapters.

15. *Galilee of the Gentiles*] See above, *v.* 12.

16. *the people which sat in darkness*] The invasion of Tiglath-pileser, whom Ahaz called in to assist him against Rezin and Pekah, fell with great severity on the Northern tribes (2 Kings xv. 29). Yet even they are promised a great deliverance ["there shall not hereafter be darkness in the land that was distressed," Is. ix. 1], in the first instance, by the destruction of Sennacherib, from temporal distress (cp. Is. chs. x. and xi. with ch. ix. 1—6); secondly, by the advent of the Messiah, from spiritual darkness.

17—22. The Call of Peter and Andrew and of the sons of Zebedee. See Mark i. 16—20.

In Luke Simon is mentioned without any introduction, ch. iv. 38. The narrative of Luke v. 3—11 must be referred to a different occasion, though *v.* 11 corresponds with *v.* 22 of this chapter. St Luke adds that the sons of Zebedee were partners with Simon. John, i. 35—42, refers to a previous summons. We learn there that Andrew was a disciple of John the Baptist, and that Bethsaida was the city of Andrew and Peter.

17. For *Metanoia* (Repentance) and the *Basileia* (Kingdom), which are the key-notes of our Saviour's preaching, see note, ch. iii. 2.

Peter, and Andrew his brother, casting a net into the sea:
for they were fishers. And he saith unto them, Follow me, 19
and I will make you fishers of men. And they straightway 20
left *their* nets, and followed him. And going on from thence, 21
he saw other two brethren, James the *son* of Zebedee, and
John his brother, in a ship with Zebedee their father, mend-
ing their nets; and he called them. And they immediately 22
left the ship and their father, and followed him.

23—25. *Jesus preaches the Gospel and cures Diseases in Galilee.*

And Jesus went about all Galilee, teaching in their syna- 23
gogues and preaching the gospel of the kingdom, and

18. *a net*] a casting-net; the Greek word is used only here and Mark i. 16. Cp. Verg. *Georg.* I. 141, Alius latum *funda* jam verberat amnem.

fishers] The fisheries on the Sea of Galilee, once so productive, are now deserted. It seems that the Bedawin have an invincible dislike and dread of the sea. Consequently there is scarcely a boat to be seen, and the Lake yields no harvest. See *Land and Book*, 401.

19. *fishers of men*] A condensed parable explicitly drawn out, ch. xiii. 47—50.

22. *and their father*] St Mark (i. 20) adds "with the hired servants." We may infer that Zebedee and his sons and their partners were raised above the lowest social rank.

23—25. Jesus preaches the Gospel and cures Diseases in Galilee.

Special instances of cure are recorded in Mark i. 13 and foll.; Luke iv. 31 and foll.

23. *their synagogues*] The synagogue, built on a hill or on the highest place in the city, distinguished sometimes by a tall pole corresponding to a modern steeple, was as familiar and conspicuous in a Jewish town as the Church is in an English village. Sometimes, however, the synagogue was placed on the bank of a river. Sometimes it was constructed without a roof and open to the sky.

1. Divine service was held in the synagogue on the Sabbath and also on the second and fifth day of each week.

2. The service consisted in reading the Law and the Prophets by those who were called upon by the "Angel of the Church," and in prayers offered up by the minister for the people; the people responding "Amen" as with us.

3. But the Synagogues were not churches alone. Like Turkish mosques they were also Courts of Law in which the sentence was not only pronounced but executed, "they shall scourge you in their synagogues." Further, the Synagogues were Public Schools, "the boys that were

healing all *manner of* sickness and all *manner of* disease
24 among the people. And his fame went throughout all
Syria: and they brought unto him all sick people that were
taken with divers diseases and torments, and those which
were possessed with devils, and those which were lunatick,

scholars were wont to be instructed before their masters in the synagogue" (Talmud). Lastly, the Synagogues were the Divinity Schools or Theological Colleges among the Jews.

4. The affairs of the Synagogue were administered by ten men, of whom three, called "Rulers of the Synagogue," acted as judges, admitted proselytes and performed other important functions. A fourth was termed the "Angel of the Church" or bishop of the congregation; three others were deacons or almoners. An eighth acted as "interpreter," rendering the Hebrew into the Vernacular; the ninth was the master of the Divinity School, the tenth his interpreter; see ch. x. 27.

It is interesting to trace in the arrangements of the Synagogue part of the organization of the Christian Church. This note is chiefly due to Lightfoot ad loc.

preaching the gospel of the kingdom] i. e. "heralding the good tidings," for the thought see ch. iv. 3 note, and cp. Is. xl.

The word translated gospel does not occur in St Luke or St John, it is a favourite word with St Paul, but is elsewhere used twice only in the N. T., viz. 1 Peter iv. 17 and Rev. xiv. 6.

It is desirable to observe the original and spiritual form of the expression, "to preach the gospel," for the words are sometimes used in a narrow and polemical sense.

24. *throughout all Syria*] The fame passes to the north and east, rather than to the south. Galilee is connected by trade and affinity with Damascus rather than with Jerusalem.

torments] The original Greek word signifies a "touch-stone," then "torture," the touch-stone of justice; then a disease that racks and agonizes the limbs like the torture which many a poor Galilean had experienced in the courts of law.

possessed with devils] The possession of the human soul by spiritual powers or beings is distinguished from ordinary diseases here, and also by St Luke, who, as a physician, is exact in his description of the various forms of disease. The distinguishing feature of such demoniacal possession may be described as the phenomenon of double consciousness. The occult spiritual power becomes, as it were, a second self, ruling and checking the better self. The Greek word in the text, lit. **subject to a dæmon or dæmonion**, has no precise English equivalent. The word "devil" should be confined to the translation of διάβολος, see note, ch. iv. 1. It is most unhappily used as a rendering of δαιμόνια in 1 Cor. x. 20, 21. In classical Greek the word is used of the divine voice which warned Socrates, and of the divine power or force which Demosthenes sometimes fancied to be hurrying on the Hellenic race in a fatal course.

and those that had the palsy; and he healed them. And 25
there followed him great multitudes *of people* from Galilee,
and *from* Decapolis, and *from* Jerusalem, and *from* Judea,
and *from* beyond Jordan.

V.—VII. *Sermon on the Mount.*

And seeing the multitudes, he went up into a mountain: 5

those which were lunatick] Lit. **affected by the moon**; the changes of the moon being thought to influence mad persons. The passage is important as distinguishing dæmoniacal possession from lunacy.

The only special instance of curing a lunatic is recorded in ch. xvii. 14—21 and in the parallel passages. The origin of mental disease may often be traced to licentious living. Observe the frequent instances of unclean spirits met with in these districts.

The Christian Church has followed her divine Founder's example in this tendance of bodily ailment. The founding of hospitals and the care of the sick are distinguishing features of Christianity and among the most blessed fruits of it. A deeper respect for life and a deeper sense of purity have followed as necessary consequences.

It is contended by some that the "several house" of 2 Chron. xxvi. 21 was a hospital. Possibly this was so, but the spirit of Judaism in this respect was not the spirit of Christianity. It may readily be acknowledged, however, that the Jews of the present day are the foremost in works of charity and tender regard for the sick.

25. *Decapolis*] Lit. **a group of ten cities**. The cities included in this group are variously named by different authors, they lay to the E. and S. of the Sea of Galilee; by some Damascus is mentioned as belonging to the group.

Ch. V.—VII. Sermon on the Mount.

It is instructive to find the Sermon on the Mount following close upon the works of mercy which would open men's hearts to receive the Saviour's words. It is a discourse about the changed life or *Metanoia*, showing its conditions; and about the Kingdom or *Basileia*, showing its nature, legislation, and privileges.

The description of the Kingdom here given may be compared with the thoughts suggested by Satan in the Temptation. Jesus makes no promise to conquer the world, or to dazzle men by a display of power, or to satisfy bodily wants, making poverty cease.

In regard to *heathenism* the sermon is a contrast, in regard to the *Jewish Law* it is a sublime fulfilment. Again, instead of curses there are blessings, instead of penalties, reward.

Two questions are raised in regard to the Sermon on the Mount (1) Is it a connected discourse, and not merely a collection of our Lord's sayings? (2) Is it to be identified with the Sermon on the Plain, Luke vi. 17—49?

It is probable that the answer should be in the affirmative to each

2 and when he was set, his disciples came unto him: and he opened his mouth, and taught them, saying,

question. 1. (*a*) This is the most natural inference from the Evangelist's words and from the manner in which the discourse is introduced. (*b*) An analysis points to a close connection of thought and to a systematic arrangement of the different sections of the Sermon. (*c*) The objection that some of the sayings are found in a different connection in St Luke's Gospel cannot have great weight. For it is more than probable that our Lord repeated on many occasions various portions of His teaching. 2. (*a*) The beginning and end are identical as well as much of the intervening matter. (*b*) The portions omitted—a comparison between the old and the new legislation—are such as would be less adapted for St Luke's readers than for St Matthew's. (*c*) The "mount" and the "plain" are not necessarily distinct localities. The plain is more accurately translated "a level place," a platform on the high land. (*d*) The place in the order of events differs in St Luke, but it is probable that here as well as elsewhere St Matthew does not observe the order of time.

Here the question of time is important as bearing on a further question, whether Matthew was himself among the audience. Was the Sermon delivered after the call of the twelve (Luke) or before (Matthew)?

The following analysis may be of use in showing the connection.

A. The Subjects of the Kingdom, v. 3—16.

(1) Their character and privileges, v. 3—12.

(2) Their responsibility, v. 13—16.

B. The Kingdom of Heaven in relation (1) to the Law, v. 17—48; and (2) to Pharisaic rules, vi. 1—34.

(1) It is the highest fulfilment of the law in regard to (*a*) The Decalogue, v. 21—37. (*b*) The law of Retaliation, 38—42. (*c*) Love or Charity, 43—48.

(2) It exceeds the righteousness of the Pharisees in regard to (*a*) Almsgiving, vi. 1—4; (*b*) Prayer, vi. 5—15; (*c*) Fasting, vi. 16—18; (*d*) Earthly possessions and daily cares, vi. 19—34.

C. Characteristics of the Kingdom, vii. 1—27. (*a*) Judgment on others, vii. 1—6. (*b*) The Father's love for the Children of the Kingdom, 7—12. (*c*) The narrow entrance therein, 13, 14. (*d*) The danger of false guides to the narrow entrance, and the test of the true, 15—23. (*e*) A description of the true subjects of the Kingdom, as distinguished from the false, 24—27.

1. *a mountain*] Accurately, **the** mountain, the high land bordering on the Lake, behind Tell Hûm or Et Tabigah, which the inhabitants of those places would naturally call "the mountain" (see map). It was the Sinai of the New Law. Cp. Ps. lxxii. 3.

Blessed *are* the poor in spirit: for theirs is the kingdom 3
of heaven.
Blessed *are* they that mourn: for they shall be com- 4
forted.
Blessed *are* the meek: for they shall inherit the 5
earth.
Blessed *are* they which do hunger and thirst after right- 6
eousness: for they shall be filled.
Blessed *are* the merciful: for they shall obtain mercy. 7

he was set] The usual position of a Jewish teacher. In the Talmud "to sit" is nearly synonymous with "to teach."

his disciples came unto him] This may be regarded as the beginning of the Christian Church.

A. The Subjects of the Kingdom, v. 3—16.

(1) Their character and privileges, v. 3—12.

3. *Blessed are the poor in spirit*] The beatitudes—so called from the opening word "beati" (blessed), in the Vulgate. Mark the Christian growth step by step. First, spiritual poverty, the only character which is receptive of repentance, therefore alone admissible into the Kingdom. Secondly, sadness for sin. Thirdly, meekness, implying submission to the will of God, a characteristic of Jesus Himself, who says "I am meek and lowly in heart." Fourthly, the soul-hunger for righteousness. Then three virtues of the Christian life, each of which wins, without seeking it, a reward in an ascending scale—mercy, purity, peacemaking. (It is a little remarkable that the English language supplies no abstract term to express this last, the highest grace of the Christian life.) The last two beatitudes vv. 10, 11 may be regarded as encouragements to the disciples, and as tests of their true discipleship.

poor in spirit] Opposed to the spiritually proud, the just who need no repentance. St Luke omits "in spirit," showing that the literal poor are primarily meant, St Matthew shows that they are not exclusively meant.

4. *mourn*] Those who mourn for sin are primarily intended; but the secondary meaning, "those who are in suffering and distress," is not excluded. The first meaning is illustrated by 2 Cor. vii. 10, "For godly sorrow worketh repentance to salvation not to be repented of, but the sorrow of the world worketh death."

5. *the meek*] Ps. xxxvii. 11. "But the meek shall inherit the earth." See note *v.* 3. Meekness is mentioned with very faint praise by the greatest of heathen moralists, Aristotle. He calls it "a mean inclining to a defect." It is indeed essentially a Christian virtue.

6. This longing for righteousness is God's gift to the meek.

7. *they shall obtain mercy*] This principle in the divine Government that men shall be dealt with as they deal with their fellow-men is taught in the parable of the Unmerciful Servant, ch. xviii., and underlies the fifth petition in the Lord's Prayer, ch. vi. 12.

8 Blessed *are* the pure in heart: for they shall see God.
9 Blessed *are* the peacemakers: for they shall be called the children of God.
10 Blessed *are* they which are persecuted for righteousness' sake: for theirs is the kingdom of heaven.
11 Blessed are ye, when *men* shall revile you, and persecute *you*, and shall say all manner of evil against you falsely, for my sake.
12 Rejoice, and be exceeding glad: for great *is* your reward in heaven: for so persecuted they the prophets which were before you.
13 Ye are the salt of the earth: but if the salt have lost his
savour, wherewith shall it be salted? it is thenceforth good

8. *pure in heart*] Purity is a distinguishing virtue of Christianity. It finds no place even in the teaching of Socrates, or in the system of Aristotle. Pure *in heart* "non sufficit puritas ceremonialis." Bengel.

shall see God] The Christian education is a gradual unveiling of God, all have glimpses of Him, to the pure He appears quite plainly. Cp. 1 John iii. 2, 3. In a further sense the unveiled sight of God is reserved for the Eternal life.

9. *peacemakers*] not only in the sense of those who heal dissension. Peace is used in a deeper sense, "the peace of God," Phil. iv. 7; "the peace of Christ," Col. iii. 15.

children of God] These are most akin to the divine nature, perfect as their Father which is in heaven is perfect, *v.* 48, cp. 1 John iii. 1, "Behold what manner of love the Father hath bestowed upon us that we should be called the Sons of God."

10, 11. *for righteousness' sake... ..for my sake*] Observe these limitations. The *cause* in which a man suffers is everything. Many Galilæan zealots who had been persecuted, reviled, traduced, when they rose against Herod or the Roman power had no share in this blessedness.

12. *so persecuted they the prophets...*] Persecution is a test and token of true discipleship, that which naturally brings distress and despair to men will bring delight in the kingdom of God. The passion and death of Christ gave a fresh force to these words, see 1 Peter iv. 13, 14.

(2) Their responsibility, v. 13—16.

13. *Ye are the salt of the earth*] Here the disciples and primarily the Apostles are addressed. Those who fulfil the condition of discipleship have a responsibility laid upon them.

have lost his savour] i.e. become tasteless. Salt is essential to all organized life, it is also the great preservative from corruption. If these virtues pass from it, it is worse than useless. It cannot even be thrown on the fields, it must be cast into the street to be trodden under foot. (See a very interesting illustration of this in *Land and Book*,

for nothing, but to be cast out, and to be trodden under
foot of men. Ye are the light of the world. A city that is 14
set on a hill cannot be hid. Neither do *men* light a candle, 15
and put it under a bushel, but on a candlestick; and it
giveth light unto all that are in the house. Let your light so 16
shine before men, that they may see your good works, and
glorify your Father which is in heaven.

Think not that I am come to destroy the law, or the pro- 17
phets: I am not come to destroy, but to fulfil. For verily I 18

pp. 381, 382.) So to the apostles who hold the highest and most necessary places in the kingdom of God, there is no middle course, either they must be the salt of the earth, be its very life, or fall utterly. If not Peter, then Judas.

14. *the light of the world*] See John viii. 12, where Jesus says of Himself "I am the light of the world." Cp. Phil. ii. 15, "Ye shine as lights (rather 'luminaries') in the world."

a city that is set on a hill...] Stanley remarks (*S. and P.* 337) that in Northern Palestine "the plain and mountain-sides are dotted with villages...situated for the most part (not like those of Judæa, on hill-tops, or Samaria, in deep valleys, but) as in Philistia, on the slopes of the ranges which intersect or bound the plain." The image in the text therefore recalls Judæa rather than Galilee, Bethlehem rather than Nazareth. Some however have conjectured that the lofty Safed was in sight, and was pointed to by our Lord. *Land and Book*, 273.

15. *a bushel*] Rather, **the** bushel, i.e. the common measure found in every Jewish house. Strictly speaking, the *modius*, translated "bushel," denoted a smaller measure equal to about two gallons.

candle...candlestick...] Or rather, **lamp...lampstand.** The lamp in a Jewish house was not set on a table, but on a tall pedestal or stand, sometimes made with a sliding shaft.

all that are in the house] i.e. the Jews. St Luke, true to the character of his gospel, says "that they which enter in," i.e. the Gentiles, "may see the light."

16. *Let your light so shine...*] The word translated "shine" is rendered "giveth light" in the preceding verse. It would be better to use the same English word in both cases. *So*="in like manner." *That* is final, not consecutive='in order that.'

B. The Kingdom of Heaven is a fulfilment of the law, v. 17—48.
Stated generally, v. 17—20.

17. *I am come...*] Lit. **I came.**

18. *verily...*] The Hebr. *Amen* is retained in the Greek text. This particle is used (*a*) to confirm the truth of what has been said. (*b*) To affirm the truth of what is about to be said. The second (*b*) is a Syriac use, and therefore more usual in the N.T. than in the O.T. where the use is nearly limited to (*a*).

say unto you, Till heaven and earth pass, one jot or one
tittle shall in no wise pass from the law, till all be fulfilled.
19 Whosoever therefore shall break one of these least commandments, and shall teach men so, he shall be called the
least in the kingdom of heaven: but whosoever shall do and
teach *them*, the same shall be called great in the kingdom of
20 heaven. For I say unto you, That except your righteousness
shall exceed *the righteousness* of the scribes and Pharisees, ye
shall in no case enter into the kingdom of heaven.
21 Ye have heard that it was said by them of old time, Thou
shalt not kill; and whosoever shall kill shall be in danger
22 of the judgment: but I say unto you, That whosoever is
angry with his brother without a cause shall be in danger of
the judgment: and whosoever shall say to his brother, Raca,

one jot...] "*yod*" (י) the smallest of the Hebr. characters, generally a silent letter, rather the adjunct of a letter than an independent letter. Still a critical interpretation might turn on the presence or absence of *yod* in a word. The controversy as to the meaning of Shiloh, Gen. xlix. 10, is an instance of this. The letter *yod* makes the difference between Sarai and Sarah. It is the first letter in Jehovah and in the Hebrew form of Jesus or Joshua.

tittle] The English word means a "point," from Anglo-Saxon *thyd-an* to prick, connected with "thistle." The Greek word means lit. **a horn.** Here the extremity of a letter, a little point, in which one letter differs from another.

fulfilled] The Greek word is different from that which has the same rendering in *v.* 17.

19. Again addressed to the Apostles as teachers. The union of doing and teaching is essential. It was the grave sin of the Pharisees that they taught without doing. See ch. xxiii. 2, 3. This explains the *for* of next verse.

20. *scribes*] See note, ch. vii. 29.

(*a*) Instances from the Decalogue, v. 21—37. (*α*) Murder, v. 21—26.

21. *Ye have heard*] Rather, **ye heard** either in the service of the synagogue or in the teaching of the scribes.

by them of old time] Better, **to** them of old time.

in danger of] Lit. **bound by them, liable, exposed to.**

22. *I say*] A most emphatic formula, which implies the authority of a lawgiver.

without a cause] The Greek word is omitted in the oldest MSS., and has probably been inserted by a copyist desirous of softening the expression.

the judgment] = the local court: see next note.

shall be in danger of the council: but whosoever shall say,
Thou fool, shall be in danger of hell fire. Therefore if thou 23
bring thy gift to the altar, and there rememberest that thy
brother hath ought against thee; leave there thy gift before 24
the altar, and go thy way; first be reconciled to thy brother,

Raca] A word of contempt, said to be from a root meaning to "spit." The distinction between *Raca* and *Thou fool* is lost, and naturally, for they belong to that class of words, the meaning of which depends entirely on the usage of the day. An expression innocent and unmeaning in one age becomes the watchword of a revolution in another. There is, however, clearly a climax. (1) Feeling of anger without words. (2) Anger venting itself in words. (3) Insulting anger. The gradation of punishment corresponds; liable (1) to the local court; (2) to the Sanhedrin; (3) to Gehenna.

council] i.e. the **Sanhedrin.** See note ch. xxvi. 3.

hell fire] Lit. **Gehenna of fire,** i.e. "burning Gehenna." *Gehenna* is the Greek form of the Hebrew Ge-Hinnom or "Valley of Hinnom," sometimes called "Valley of the son of Hinnom," also "Tophet" (Jer. vii. 31). It was a deep narrow glen S. W. of Jerusalem, once the scene of the cruel worship of Moloch; but Josiah, in the course of his reformation, "defiled Tophet, that no man might make his son or his daughter to pass through the fire to Moloch" (2 Kings xxiii. 10). Cp. Milton, *Paradise Lost* I.:

"First Moloch, horrid king, besmeared with blood
Of human sacrifice and parents' tears;
Though, for the noise of drums and timbrels loud,
Their children's cries unheard that passed through fire
To his grim idol."

After that time pollutions of every kind, among them the bodies of criminals who had been executed, were thrown into the valley. From this defilement and from its former desecration Gehenna was used to express the abode of the wicked after death. The words "of fire" are added, either because of the ancient rites of Moloch, or, if a Rabbinical tradition is to be credited, because fires were always burning in the valley, or, further, as a symbol of everlasting punishment.

23. *if thou bring thy gift to the altar*] i.e. **thy offering,** such as a lamb or a pair of doves.

rememberest that thy brother hath ought against thee] that thy brother hath cause of complaint against thee, just or unjust, if the quarrel is still not made up.

24. *before the altar*] Stay the sacrifice, though begun, for God will not accept it unless the heart be free from anger, and the conscience from offence. It is an application of the great principle summed up in "I will have mercy and not sacrifice." Cp. also Ps. xxvi. 6, "I will wash my hands in innocency, O Lord, and so will I go to thine altar."

25 and then come and offer thy gift. Agree with thine adversary
quickly, whiles thou art in the way with him; lest at any
time the adversary deliver thee to the judge, and the judge
deliver thee to the officer, and thou be cast into prison.
26 Verily I say unto thee, Thou shalt by no means come out
27 thence, till thou hast paid the uttermost farthing. Ye have
heard that it was said by them of old time, Thou shalt not
28 commit adultery: but I say unto you, That whosoever
looketh on a woman to lust after her hath committed adultery
29 with her already in his heart. And if thy right eye offend
thee, pluck it out, and cast *it* from thee: for it is profitable
for thee that one of thy members should perish, and not *that*
30 thy whole body should be cast into hell. And if thy right
hand offend thee, cut it off, and cast *it* from thee: for it is
profitable for thee that one of thy members should perish,
31 and not *that* thy whole body should be cast into hell. It
hath been said, Whosoever shall put away his wife, let him
32 give her a writing of divorcement: but I say unto

25. *Agree*] Lit. **be friendly with.** The participle in the orig. conveys the idea of continuance. The thought of the preceding verse is extended and generalised. By the "adversary" are meant those against whom we harbour that resentment which keeps us from the kingdom of God. "While there is time in this life put away the resentment. Show thyself to be a son of God by being a peacemaker." *v.* 9.

The imagery is taken from the law-courts. It would be well for a man to compound with his creditor before the case should be brought before the judge.

(β) Adultery, 27—32.

28. *to lust after her* i.e. "with a view to lust after her."

in his heart] Contrast with the pure *in heart*, *v.* 8.

29. *thy right eye*] suggested by the preceding verse. The eye and the hand are not only in themselves good and serviceable, but *necessary*. Still they may become the occasion of sin to us. So pursuits and pleasures innocent in themselves may bring temptation, and involve us in sin. These must be resigned, however great the effort implied in "cast it from thee."

offend thee] "cause thee to fall."

31. *a writing of divorcement*] See note on ch. i. 19. The greatest abuses had arisen in regard to divorce, which was permitted on very trivial grounds. One Rabbinical saying was "If any man hate his wife, let him put her away." Copies of these bills of divorce are still preserved. The formula may be seen in Lightfoot, *Hor. Hebr.* ad loc. The same facility of divorce prevails in Mohammedan countries.

you, That whosoever shall put away his wife, saving for the
cause of fornication, causeth her to commit adultery: and
whosoever shall marry her that is divorced committeth
adultery.

Again, ye have heard that it hath been said by them of old 33
time, Thou shalt not forswear thyself, but shalt perform unto the Lord thine oaths: but I say unto you, Swear 34
not at all; neither by heaven; for it is God's throne: nor by 35
the earth; for it is his footstool: neither by Jerusalem; for it
is the city of the great King. Neither shalt thou swear by 36
thy head, because thou canst not make one hair white
or black. But let your communication be, Yea, yea; Nay, 37
nay: for whatsoever is more than these cometh of evil.

32. *causeth her to commit adultery*] By adopting a slightly different reading in the original with Lachmann, Tischendorf, and Tregelles, the idea of wilful sin on the woman's part is removed.

that is divorced] Lit. **when she hath been divorced.**

(γ) Oaths, 33—37.

33. *Thou shalt not forswear thyself*] The special reference may be to the third commandment. Cp. also Levit. xix. 12, "Ye shall not swear by my name falsely, neither shalt thou profane the name of thy God." In the kingdom of God no external act or profession as distinct from the thought of the heart can find a place. But such words as those of the Apostle, "The God and Father of our Lord Jesus Christ, which is blessed for evermore, knoweth that I lie not" (2 Cor. xi. 31), will prevent Christians observing the letter rather than the spirit of our Blessed Saviour's words.

34. *Swear not at all*] The prohibition must be understood of rash and careless oaths in conversation, not of solemn asseveration in Courts of Justice.

for it is God's throne] Such was the prevalent hypocrisy that the Jews of the day thought that they escaped the sin of perjury if in their oaths they avoided using the name of God. One of the Rabbinical sayings was "As heaven and earth shall pass away, so passeth away the oath taken by them." Our Lord shows that a false oath taken by heaven, by earth, or by Jerusalem is none the less a profanation of God's name.

Hypocrisy reproduces itself. Louis XI. "admitted to one or two peculiar forms of oath the force of a binding obligation which he denied to all others, strictly preserving the secret, which mode of swearing he really accounted obligatory, as one of the most valuable of state mysteries." Introd. to *Quentin Durward*.

36. *by thy head*] A common form of oath in the ancient world: cp. "Per caput hoc juro per quod pater ante solebat." Verg. *Æn.* IX. 300.

38 Ye have heard that it hath been said, An eye for an
39 eye, and a tooth for a tooth: but I say unto you, That
ye resist not evil: but whosoever shall smite thee on thy
40 right cheek, turn to him the other also. And if any man
will sue thee at the law, and take *away* thy coat, let him
41 have *thy* cloke also. And whosoever shall compel thee to
42 go a mile, go with him twain. Give to him that asketh thee,
and from him that would borrow of thee turn not thou
away.
43 Ye have heard that it hath been said, Thou shalt love
44 thy neighbour, and hate thine enemy. But I say unto

(*b*) The law of retaliation, 38—42.

38. *An eye for an eye*] See Exod. xxi. 24. The Scribes draw a false inference from the letter of the law. As a legal remedy the *lex talionis* was probably the best possible in a rude state of society. The principle was admitted in all ancient nations. But the retribution was exacted by a judicial sentence for the good of the community, not to gratify personal vengeance. The deduction that it was morally right for individuals to indulge revenge could not be justified.

39. *resist not evil*] i.e. **do not seek to retaliate evil.**

turn to him the other also] To be understood with the limitation imposed on the words by our Lord's personal example, John xviii. 22, 23.

The gradation of the examples given is from the greater to the less provocation.

40. *coat*] Lit. **tunic**, the under garment. It had sleeves, and reached below the knees, somewhat like a modern shirt. *cloke*, the upper garment. A large square woollen robe, resembling the modern Arab *abba* or *abayeh*. The poorest people wore a tunic only. Among the richer people many wore two tunics besides the upper garment. Wealth is often shown in the East not only by the quality but also by the amount of clothing worn. For the general sense cp. 1 Cor. vi. 7, "There is utterly a fault...suffer yourselves to be defrauded."

41. *compel thee to go a mile*] The Greek text has a Persian word here signifying "to press into service as a courier" for the royal post, then, generally, "to force to be a guide," "to requisition," men or cattle. This was one of the exactions which the Jews suffered under the Romans. Alford quotes Joseph. *Ant.* XIII. 2, 3, where Demetrius promises not to press into service the beasts of burden belonging to the Jews. For an instance of this forced service see ch. xxvii. 32.

42. *from him that would borrow of thee*] Luke has "lend, hoping for nothing again." Forced loans have been a mode of oppression in every age, for which, perhaps, no people have suffered more than the Jews.

(*c*) Love or Charity, 43—48.

43. *Thou shalt love thy neighbour*] Levit. xix. 18, "Thou shalt

you, Love your enemies, bless them that curse you, do
good to them that hate you, and pray for them which
despitefully use you, and persecute you; that ye may be 45
the children of your Father which is in heaven: for he
maketh his sun to rise on the evil and *on* the good, and
sendeth rain on the just and *on* the unjust. For if ye love 46
them which love you, what reward have ye? do not even

love thy neighbour as thyself." The second clause does not occur in Levit., but was a Rabbinical inference. *Enemies*, all who are outside the chosen race, the etymological force of the Greek word. Heathen writers bear testimony to this unsocial characteristic of the Jews. Juvenal says it was their rule—

> "Non monstrare vias eadem nisi sacra colenti,
> Quaesitum ad fontem solos deducere verpos."—*Sat.* XIV. 104.

44. Several editors, with high MS. authority, omit the words "bless them that curse you, do good to them that hate you," and "despitefully use you and." The omission, however, breaks the gradation and balance of the paragraph. The contrast between love and hate is exhibited in four degrees, the antithesis widens, the deeper the hate the higher the love. (1) Feel love towards those who are enemies by position merely. (2) Say loving words in return for enmity that shews itself in curses. (3) Towards those who hate you do not only *feel* love, but *prove* love by charitable deeds. (4) To enemies whose hate is active, even to persecution, offer the highest act of love in prayer.

despitefully use you] A forcible word, meaning "to vex out of spite with the sole object of inflicting harm." In 1 Peter iii. 16 it is rendered "to accuse falsely." The word occurs also in Luke vi. 28.

45. *that ye may be the children of your Father*] See note on *v.* 9. To act thus would be to act like God, Who blesses those who curse Him and are His enemies, by the gifts of sun and rain. This is divine. Mere return of love for love is a human, even a heathen virtue.

46. *publicans*] **taxgatherers**; not collectors of a regular tax fixed by government as with us, but men who farmed or contracted for the *publicum* (state revenue), hence called Publicani. At Rome the equestrian order enjoyed almost exclusively the lucrative privilege of farming the state revenues.

The publicans of the N. T. however are a lower class of taxgatherers, to whom the contractors sublet the collection of taxes. These men repaid themselves by cruel and oppressive exactions. Only the least patriotic and most degraded of the population undertook these functions which naturally rendered them odious to their fellow-citizens.

It is this system pursued in the Turkish Empire that produces much frightful misery and illegal oppression.

47 the publicans the same? And if ye salute your brethren
only, what do ye more *than others?* do not even the publi-
48 cans so? Be ye therefore perfect, even as your Father
which is in heaven is perfect.

1—4. *Almsgiving.*

6 Take heed that *ye* do not your alms before men, to be
seen of them: otherwise ye have no reward of your Father
2 which is in heaven. Therefore when thou doest *thine* alms,
do not sound a trumpet before thee, as the hypocrites do in
the synagogues and in the streets, that they may have glory
of men. Verily I say unto you, They have their reward.

47. *salute your brethren only*] See *v.* 43. The Hebrew salutation was *Shalom* (peace).

The higher MS. authority gives "Gentiles" or "heathen," instead of "publicans."

48. *Be ye*] Lit. **Ye shall be** *perfect.* Either (1) in reference to a future state, "if ye have this true love or charity ye shall be perfect hereafter;" or (2) the future has an imperative force, and *perfect* is limited by the preceding words = perfect in respect of love, i. e. "love your enemies as well as your neighbours," because your Father being perfect in respect of love does this.

CH. VI. 1–4. ALMSGIVING.

(2) The Kingdom of Heaven exceeds the righteousness of the Pharisees in regard to (*a*) Almsgiving, 1—4.

1. *alms*] The best MSS. have "righteousness;" the two words were nearly synonymous with the Jews, partly because the poor had a right to share in the produce of the land; partly because almsgiving is the most natural and obvious external work of righteousness. In the same way *agapé* (love), the leading Christian virtue, has lost its original breadth of meaning and has sunk to the modern and restricted sense of "charity."

2. *do not sound a trumpet before thee*] The chests for alms in the Court of the Women, where the temple-treasury was placed, were called "trumpets" from their shape. Possibly the words of the text contain an allusion to these alms-chests. See Edersheim's *Temple in the time of our Lord*, ch. II. p. 26. But perhaps the expression means simply, "avoid ostentation in almsgiving."

hypocrites] Lit. **actors**; those who play a part in life, whose actions are not the true reflection of their thoughts, whose religion is external and unreal. Such men begin by deceiving others, but end in self-deception. It is against these that our Lord's severest reproofs are delivered.

in the synagogues] To this day alms are given in the Jewish synagogues.

They have] Strictly, **have in full.** Their reward is *now* and *on earth.*

But when thou doest alms, let not thy left hand know what 3
thy right hand doeth: that thine alms may be in secret: 4
and thy Father which seeth in secret himself shall reward
thee openly.

And when thou prayest, thou shalt not be as the hypo- 5
crites *are:* for they love to pray standing in the synagogues
and in the corners of the streets, that they may be seen of
men. Verily I say unto you, They have their reward. But 6
thou, when thou prayest, enter into thy closet, and when
thou hast shut thy door, pray to thy Father which is in
secret; and thy Father which seeth in secret shall reward
thee openly. But when ye pray, use not vain repetitions, as 7
the heathen *do:* for they think that they shall be heard for
their much speaking. Be not ye therefore like unto them: 8
for your Father knoweth what *things* ye have need of, before
ye ask him.

3. *when thou doest alms*] Observe that the singular number is used throughout these instructions on the subject of almsgiving and prayer, and in these only. These duties are essentially personal and individual. The teaching of the Talmud commends secrecy in almsgiving in such sayings as "he that doeth alms in secret is greater than Moses." But the spirit of hypocrisy prevailed; the Pharisees taught and did not.

4. *himself*] God, not man, will reward.

(*b*) Prayer, 5—15.

5. *pray standing*] The posture of standing was as closely associated with prayer as that of sitting was with teaching.

6. *closet*] A private oratory or place of prayer. These were usually in the upper part of the house. The Greek word in the original is translated (1) "Secret Chambers," ch. xxiv. 26; (2) "Storehouse," Luke xii. 24.

pray to thy Father which is in secret] Christ was the first to enjoin clearly secret and silent prayer. Certainly to pray aloud and in public appears to have been the Jewish practice; it is still the practice with the heathen and Mahomedans. The Roman looked with suspicion on private prayer: "quod scire hominem nolunt deo narrant" (Seneca). Cp. Hor. *Ep.* I. 16. 59—62, where see Macleane's note. Cp. also Soph. *Electra*, 638, where Clytemnestra apologises for offering up a secret prayer.

7. *use not vain repetitions*] It is not the length of time spent in prayer or the fervent or reasonable repetition of forms of prayer that is forbidden, but the mechanical repetition of set words, and the belief that the efficacy of prayer consists in such repetition. The word itself lit. means **to stammer**, then to "repeat uselessly."

as the heathen] The Jews also had a saying, "Every one that multiplies prayer is heard."

8. *for your Father knoweth...before ye ask him*] Our Father knows

9—13. *The Lord's Prayer.*

9 After this manner therefore pray ye:
Our Father which art in heaven, Hallowed be thy name.
10 Thy kingdom come. Thy will be done in earth, as *it is* in
11 heaven. Give us this day our daily bread. And forgive us
12
13 our debts, as we forgive our debtors. And lead us not into

our wants, still we are bound to express them. Why? because this is a proof of our faith and dependence upon God, which are the conditions of success in prayer.

9—13. The Lord's Prayer.

St Luke xi. 2—4, where the prayer is found in a different connection, and is given by our Lord in answer to a request from the disciples to teach them to pray, "even as John taught his disciples." The text of St Luke as it stands in E. V. has probably been supplemented by additions from St Matthew.

9. *Our Father*] It is of the essence of Christian prayer that God should be addressed as a Father to whose love we appeal, not as a God whose anger we appease. The analogy removes nearly all the real difficulties on the subject of prayer. A wise earthly father does not grant *all* requests, but all which are for the good of his children and which are in his power to grant. Again, the child asks without fear, yet no refusal shakes his trust in his father's love or power.

Hallowed] "held sacred," "revered." Each of these petitions implies an obligation to carry out on our own part what we pray God to accomplish.

10. *Thy kingdom come*] See note ch. iii. 2. Lightfoot quotes an axiom from the Jewish Schools, "that prayer wherein there is not mention of the Kingdom of God is not a prayer."

11. *this day*] In Luke, "day by day."

our daily bread] The Greek word translated "daily" occurs only in the Lord's Prayer here and Luke xi. 3, it is not found in any classical author. The rendering of the E. V. "daily" as nearly as possible represents the probable force of the word, which is strictly (bread) "for the coming day," i.e. for the day now beginning. Others render "bread for the future," taking bread in a spiritual sense; others, following a different etymology, translate "bread of subsistence." *Bread*, primarily the bread on which we subsist (see Prof. Lightfoot in appendix to his work *On a Fresh Revision of the N. T.*); subsistence as distinct from luxury; but the spiritual meaning cannot be excluded, Christ the Bread of Life is the Christian's daily food.

12. *debts*] Sins are debts, shortcomings in the service due to God.

forgive] The aorist should be read in the Greek text. The force would then be that an act of forgiveness on man's part is past before he prays to receive forgiveness. Cp. ch. v. 23, 24, also the parable of the unforgiving servant, ch. xviii. 23 seqq.

temptation, but deliver us from evil: For thine is the kingdom, and the power, and the glory, for ever. Amen.
For if ye forgive men their trespasses, your heavenly 14
Father will also forgive you: but if ye forgive not men 15
their trespasses, neither will your Father forgive your trespasses.
Moreover when ye fast, be not as the hypocrites, of a sad 16
countenance: for they disfigure their faces, that they may
appear unto men to fast. Verily I say unto you, They have
their reward. But thou, when thou fastest, anoint thine 17
head, and wash thy face; that thou appear not unto men 18
to fast, but unto thy Father which is in secret: and thy
Father, which seeth in secret, shall reward thee openly.
Lay not up for yourselves treasures upon earth, where 19
moth and rust doth corrupt, and where thieves break through

13. *lead us not into temptation*] The statement of James, i. 2, "Count it all joy when ye fall into divers temptations," is not really contradictory. The Christian character is strengthened and purified by temptation, but no one can think of temptation without dread.

deliver] Lit. **draw to thyself**, "rescue," as from an enemy. Cp. 1 Thess. i. 10, "Jesus which delivered us from the wrath to come."

from evil] Or, **from the Evil One**, Satan. The Greek bears either rendering, but the neuter is preferable and gives a deeper sense. We pray to be delivered not only from external evil, but from the evil within us.

For thine is the kingdom, &c.] This doxology is not supported by high MS. authority, it was doubtless an insertion from the liturgy. The Roman use omits the doxology. In the retention of it the English Church follows the Greek and Gallican uses.

(*c*) Fasting, 16—18.

16. Fasting, in itself a natural result of grief, as anyone who has witnessed deep sorrow knows, easily degenerates into a form without reality.

disfigure] Either (1) make unseen, "veil," or (2) cause to disappear, so "destroy," "mar," by leaving the face unwashen. The same word is translated "corrupt," *v.* 19.

The apparent play upon the Greek words for "disfigure" and "appear" has been adduced in support of their view by those who consider Greek to have been the original language of the gospel.

(*d*) Earthly possessions and daily cares, 19—34.

19. *treasures upon earth*] Love of amassing wealth has been characteristic of the Jews in all ages.

moth and rust] Oriental wealth consisted to a great extent in stores

20 and steal: but lay up for yourselves treasures in heaven,
where neither moth nor rust doth corrupt, and where thieves
21 do not break through nor steal: for where your treasure is,
22 there will your heart be also. The light of the body is the
eye: if therefore thine eye be single, thy whole body shall
23 be full of light. But if thine eye be evil, thy whole body
shall be full of darkness. If therefore the light that is in
thee be darkness, how great *is* that darkness?
24 No *man* can serve two masters: for either he will hate
the one, and love the other; or else he will hold to the one,
and despise the other. Ye cannot serve God and mammon.

of linen, embroidered garments, &c., which were handed down and left as heir-looms.

moth] The English word = "the devourer."

rust] Money was frequently buried in the ground in those unsettled times, and so would be more liable to rust. Banks in the modern sense were unknown. *Rust*, lit., an **eating away**, it is not confined to corrosion of metals.

break through and steal] An expression applicable to the mud walls of Oriental huts.

21. *where your treasure is*] The words gain point if we think of the hoards buried in the *earth*.

22. *The light*] Rather, **lamp**, or **candle** as it is translated ch. v. 15. The eye is not itself the light, but contains the light; it is the "lamp" or candle of the body, the light-conveying principle. If the eye or lamp is single, it admits the influx of the pure light only; if an eye be evil, i.e. affected with disease, the body can receive no light at all. The whole passage is on the subject of the *singleness* of service to God. There can be but one treasure, one source of light, one master. The eye is the spiritual faculty, through which the light of God's truth is recognised and admitted into the soul.

The connection in which the words occur in Luke xi. 34 is instructive. The inference there is that the spiritual perception of the Pharisees is dimmed, so that they cannot recognise Christ.

23. *the light that is in thee*] Here the Greek word is correctly rendered "light." If the light admitted to the body be distorted and obscured by the diseased medium, how great will be the darkness!

24. Another illustration of the singleness of the Christian character, "the simplicity that is in Christ" (2 Cor. xi. 3), drawn from the relation of master and slave.

serve two masters] Strictly, **be a slave to two masters.** The absolute subjection of the slave must be considered. The interests of the "two masters" are presupposed to be diverse.

mammon] A Syriac word meaning "wealth." There is no proof that it was the name of a god. It stands here for all that mostly estranges men from God: cp. "covetousness, which is idolatry," Col. iii. 5.

Therefore I say unto you, Take no thought for your life, 25
what ye shall eat, or what ye shall drink; nor yet for your
body, what ye shall put on. Is not the life more than meat,
and the body than raiment? Behold the fowls of the air: 26
for they sow not, neither do they reap, nor gather into
barns; yet your heavenly Father feedeth them. Are ye not
much better than they? Which of you by taking thought 27
can add one cubit unto his stature? And why take ye 28
thought for raiment? Consider the lilies of the field, how

25—34. The parallel passage (Luke xii. 22—31) follows immediately the parable of the "Rich Fool."

25. *Therefore*] i.e. because this double service is impossible there must be no distraction of thought.

Take no thought] "Do not be anxious," which was the meaning of "take no thought," when the E. V. was made. The same word occurs Phil. iv. 6, "Be careful for nothing." Cp. 1 Peter v. 7, "Casting all your care [or anxiety] upon him." See Prof. Lightfoot, *On a Fresh Revision of the New Testament, &c.*, p. 171.

The argument in the verse is: such anxiety is unnecessary; God gave the life and the body; will He not give the smaller gifts of food and clothing?

26. *fowls*] Old English for birds; cp.

"Smale fowles maken melodie
That slepen all the night with open yhe." Chaucer.

There is no argument here against forethought or labour. In one sense "trusting to providence" is idleness and a sin. God has appointed labour as the means whereby man provides for his wants. Even birds shew forethought, and search for the food which God has provided for them.

27. *can add one cubit unto his stature*] As the word translated "stature" also = duration of life, the meaning may be "add a cubit to his life." Comp. Ps. xxxix. 6 (P. B.), "Thou hast made my days as it were a span long." This rendering falls in better with the connection. With all his anxiety man cannot add to his length of days, or clothe himself like the flowers.

28. *for raiment*] The birds are an example of God's care in providing food, the flowers of His care in providing apparel.

the lilies of the field] identified by Dr Thomson (*Land and Book*, p. 256), with a species of lily found in the neighbourhood of Hûlêh. He speaks of having met with "this incomparable flower, in all its loveliness...around the northern base of Tabor, and on the hills of Nazareth, where our Lord spent His youth." Canon Tristram (*Nat. Hist. of the Bible*) claims this honour for the beautiful and varied *anemone coronaria*. "If in the wondrous richness of bloom which characterises the Land of Israel in spring any one plant can claim pre-eminence, it is the anemone, the most natural flower for our Lord to

29 they grow; they toil not, neither do they spin: and yet I
say unto you, That even Solomon in all his glory was not
30 arrayed like one of these. Wherefore, if God so clothe the
grass of the field, which to day is, and to morrow is cast
into the oven, *shall he* not much more *clothe* you, O ye of
31 little faith? Therefore take no thought, saying, What shall
we eat? or, What shall we drink? or, Wherewithal shall we
32 be clothed? (For after all these *things* do the Gentiles
seek): for your heavenly Father knoweth that ye have need
33 of all these *things*. But seek ye first the kingdom of God,
and his righteousness; and all these *things* shall be added
34 unto you. Take therefore no thought for the morrow: for
the morrow shall take thought for the *things* of itself. Sufficient unto the day *is* the evil thereof.

7 Judge not, that ye be not judged. For with what judgment
2

pluck and seize upon as an illustration, whether walking in the fields or sitting on the hill-side."

29. *was not arrayed*] Rather, **arrayed not himself.** The middle voice has a special force. Though he arrayed himself, the lilies, who trusted to God for their array, are more beautiful than he.

30. *which to day is*] Rather, **though it is to-day.**

cast into the oven] The Jewish oven was a vessel narrower at the top than at the bottom, made of baked clay. Sometimes the fuel was placed within, and the cakes laid against the sides. Sometimes the oven was heated by a fire kindled beneath or around it. Eastern travellers state that wood being rare in most parts of the East, grass, twigs, and straw are commonly used for fuel.

31. *take no thought*] See *v.* 25.

32. *the Gentiles seek*] Seek with eagerness. A compound verb. The simple verb is used below in the next verse. For the aims of the heathen world read Juvenal *Sat.* x., or Johnson's imitation of it "The Vanity of Human Wishes."

34. *the morrow shall take thought for the things of itself*] The morrow shall have its own anxieties; sufficient for the day is its own distracting evil or distress. This seems to be the force of the Greek word for "evil." See Schleusner sub voc.

CH. VII. C. Characteristics of the Kingdom, 1—27.

After contrasting the New Law with the Mosaic Law and with Pharisaic rules and conduct, Jesus proceeds to lay down rules for the guidance of His disciples in the Christian life.

(*a*) Judgment on others, 1—6.

The passage occurs in St Luke's report of the Sermon on the Mount (ch. vi. 37, 38), with a different context, and a further illustration of "full measure."

ye judge, ye shall be judged: and with what measure ye
mete, it shall be measured to you again. And why behold- 3
est thou the mote that is in thy brother's eye, but considerest
not the beam that is in thine own eye? Or how wilt thou 4
say to thy brother, Let me pull out the mote out of thine
eye; and behold, a beam *is* in thine own eye? *Thou* hypo- 5
crite, first cast out the beam out of thine own eye; and then
shalt thou see clearly to cast out the mote out of thy brother's
eye.

Give not *that which is* holy unto the dogs, neither cast ye 6

1. *Judge not*, &c.] This is the form which the "lex talionis," or law of reciprocity, takes in the kingdom of heaven.

The censorious spirit is condemned, it is opposed to the ἐπιείκεια, "forbearance," "fairness in judgment," that allows for faults, a characteristic ascribed to Jesus Christ Himself, 2 Cor. x. 1; cp. also Rom. xiv. 3 foll.

that ye be not judged] by Christ on the Last Day.

2. *judgment*] The same Greek word is used Rom. ii. 2, 3 of the divine sentence or decision: see that passage and context which are closely parallel to these verses: cp. also Mark xii. 40, where the same word is translated "damnation."

3. *the mote*] The English word is either connected with *mite* (the coin) from a Latin root (minutum), or mite (the insect) from an Anglo-Saxon root meaning "to cut," "sever," or from one meaning "to eat." The Greek word = a "dry particle" of dust, wool, &c.

beholdest...considerest] It is the contrast between judging from the outside, and examination of the heart. The Greek verbs in this, and the Greek prepositions in the following verses, convey this contrast.

4. *a beam is in thine own eye*] Which (1) ought to prevent condemnation of another for a less grave offence; and which (2) would obscure the spiritual discernment, and so render thee an incapable judge. The Pharisaic sin of hypocrisy (see next verse) was deeper and more fatal to the spiritual life than the sins which the Pharisee condemned.

out of] Greek ἀπό (a reading which rests on the highest MS. authority) = "from the outside surface," which alone the Pharisee discerns—

5. *out of*] Greek ἐκ = "from within," of the deep-seated root of sin which the Pharisee may discern only when he has cast out the beam from his own eye.

(*b*) The Father's love for the children of the Kingdom shewn by answering prayer, 7—11.

6. The connection between this verse and the preceding section is not quite obvious. It seems to be this. Although evil and censorious judgment is to be avoided, discrimination is needful. The Christian must be judicious, not judicial.

that which is holy] i.e. "spiritual truths." Some have seen in the

your pearls before swine, lest they trample them under their
feet, and turn *again* and rent you.
7 Ask, and it shall be given you; seek, and ye shall find;
8 knock, and it shall be opened unto you: for every one that
asketh receiveth; and he that seeketh findeth: and to him
9 that knocketh it shall be opened. Or what man is there of
you, whom if his son ask bread, will he give him a stone?
10 11 Or if he ask a fish, will he give him a serpent? If ye then,
being evil, know *how* to give good gifts unto your children,
how much more shall your Father which is in heaven give
12 good *things* to them that ask him? Therefore all *things*
whatsoever ye would that men should do to you, do ye even
so to them: for this is the law and the prophets.

expression a reference to the holy flesh of the offering (Hag. ii. 12). But this allusion is very doubtful; see Meyer on this passage.

dogs...swine] Unclean animals; see the proverb quoted 2 Pet. ii. 22; cp. Phil. iii. 2, "Beware of dogs, beware of evil workers;" also Hor. *Ep.* I. 2. 25, "vel canis immundus vel amica luto sus." See note on ch. xv. 26.

pearls] The only gems mentioned in the Gospels, twice named by Jesus: here, where they signify the deepest spiritual thoughts of God and heaven, and ch. xiii. 46, where "the pearl of great price" is the kingdom of heaven itself. The general sense is "use discrimination, discern between holy and unholy, between those who are receptive of these high truths and those who are not." The profane will despise the gift and put the giver to shame. Want of common sense does great harm to religion.

7. *Ask, and it shall be given*] The connection is again difficult. The verse may be the answer to the disciples' unspoken questions: (1) "How shall *we* discriminate?" or (2) "Who are fit to receive these divine truths?" The words of Christ teach, (1) that discernment will be given, among other "good things," in answer to prayer; (2) that prayer in itself implies fitness, because it implies desire for such truths.

8. The triple formula covers every kind of want. The prayer shall be granted, the treasure found, the gate of heaven opened. St Luke xiii. 24, 25. Observe the climax: ask—seek—knock; the fervour of the prayer must grow more and more intense.

9. *bread...a stone...fish...a serpent*] The things contrasted have a certain superficial resemblance, but in each case one thing is good, the other unclean or even dangerous.

11. *good things*] For this St Luke (xi. 13) has "the Holy Spirit," shewing that spiritual rather than temporal "good things" are intended.

12. *Therefore*] The practical result of what has been said both in regard to judgment and to prayer is mutual charity. The thought of the divine judgment teaches forbearance; the thought of the divine goodness teaches kindness.

Enter ye in at the strait gate: for wide *is* the gate, and 13
broad *is* the way, that leadeth to destruction, and many
there be which go in thereat: because strait *is* the gate, and 14
narrow *is* the way, which leadeth unto life, and few there be
that find it.

Beware of false prophets, which come to you in sheep's 15
clothing, but inwardly they are ravening wolves. Ye shall 16
know them by their fruits. Do *men* gather grapes of thorns,
or figs of thistles? *Even* so every good tree bringeth forth 17
good fruit; but a corrupt tree bringeth forth evil fruit. A 18
good tree cannot bring forth evil fruit, neither *can* a corrupt
tree bring forth good fruit. Every tree that bringeth not 19
forth good fruit is hewn down, and cast into the fire. Where- 20
fore by their fruits ye shall know them.

Not every one that saith unto me, Lord, Lord, shall enter 21
into the kingdom of heaven; but he that doeth the will of
my Father which is in heaven. Many will say to me in 22
that day, Lord, Lord, have we not prophesied in thy name?

(*c*) The narrow entrance to the Kingdom, 13, 14.

These verses are linked to the preceding by the thought of prayer, for it is by prayer chiefly that the narrow entrance must be gained.

13. *The broad and the narrow way*, Luke xiii. 24, 25. The illustration seems to be drawn from a mansion having a large portal at which many enter, and a narrow entrance known to few.

strait = narrow.

14. *because*] To be taken after "enter ye" as in preceding verse, or it gives a reason why many go in at the wide gate.

narrow] Literally, **pressed, confined.**

(*d*) The false guides to the narrow entrance, and the test of the true, 15—23.

15. *false prophets*] who will not help you to find the narrow way.

in sheep's clothing] Not in a literal sense, but figuratively, "wearing the appearance of guilelessness and truth."

16. *thorns*] The Greek word means, probably, a kind of acacia, or perhaps "thistles." There is a Greek proverb οὐ γὰρ ἄκανθαι, "no thistles," i.e. "nothing useless."

thistles] Rather, **caltrop**, a prickly water-plant.

19. *Every tree that bringeth not forth good fruit*, &c.] To this day in the East trees are valued only so far as they produce fruit.

22. *in that day*] The day of judgment. This is a forecast far into the distant future, when it would be worth while to assume Christianity, when hypocrisy would take the form of pretending to be a follower of

and in thy name have cast out devils? and in thy name
23 done many wonderful works? And then will I profess unto
them, I never knew you: depart from me, ye that work
iniquity.
24 Therefore whosoever heareth these sayings of mine, and
doeth them, I will liken him unto a wise man, which built
25 his house upon a rock: and the rain descended, and the
floods came, and the winds blew, and beat upon that house;
26 and it fell not: for it was founded upon a rock. And every
one that heareth these sayings of mine, and doeth them not,
shall be likened unto a foolish man, which built his house
27 upon the sand: and the rain descended, and the floods

the now despised Jesus. (See Canon Mozley's sermon *On the reversal of human judgment.*)

For the pathetic repetition, Lord, Lord, cp. ch. xxiii. 37; Luke xxii. 31.

prophesied] i.e. preached. The greatest of preachers dreads such a sentence. 1 Cor. ix. 27, "Lest that by any means, when I have preached to others, I myself should be a castaway."

devils] See note, ch. iv. 24.

23. *I never knew you*] "Never recognised you as my disciples. While my name was on your lips, your hearts were far from me." Clement of Rome (*Ep.* II. 4), referring to this passage, says: "let us then not only call Him 'Lord,' for that will not save us;" he then quotes the words of *v.* 21.

iniquity] Literally, **lawlessness.**

(*e*) A description of the true subjects of the Kingdom as opposed to the false. The wise and foolish builders, 24—27.

Luke vi. 47—49, where the phraseology differs a good deal from St Matthew. St Matthew, who living near the lake had often witnessed such sudden floods as are described, uses more vigorous language and draws the picture more vividly. St Luke marks the connection with the insincere "Lord, Lord," more distinctly, but omits the reference to the last day and to the future of the Church.

24. *whosoever heareth*] Cp. *v.* 26, **every one that heareth.** Both classes of men hear the word. So far they are alike. In like manner the two houses have externally the same appearance. The great day of trial shews the difference. The imagery is from a mountain country where the torrent-beds, sometimes more than half a mile in width in the plain below the mountain, are dry in summer, and present a level waste of sand and stones. We may picture the foolish man building on this sandy bottom, while the wise or prudent man builds on a rock planted on the shore, or rising out of the river bed, too high to be affected by the rush of waters. In the autumn the torrents stream down filling the sandy channel and carrying all before them. For the spiritual sense of the parable see 1 Cor. iii. 10 foll.

came, and the winds blew, and beat upon that house; and
it fell: and great was the fall of it. And it came to pass, 28
when Jesus had ended these sayings, the people were astonished at his doctrine: for he taught them as *one* having 29
authority, and not as the scribes.

1—4. *A Leper is cleansed.*

When he was come down from the mountain, great multi- 8
tudes followed him. And behold, there came a leper and 2

27. *the rain descended*, &c.] In the original both the tense and the position of the verbs give great vivacity to the description.

29. *having authority*] He was Himself a lawgiver. His teaching was not a mere expansion of the old law. Much less did he confine himself to the words of any particular Rabbi.

the scribes] *Sopherim* = either (1) "those who count;" because the Scribes counted each word and letter of the Scriptures; or (2) "those occupied with books." The Scribes, as an organized body, originated with Ezra, who was in a special sense the "*Sopher*" or Scribe. This order of *Sopherim*, strictly so called, terminated B.C. 300. Their successors in our Lord's time were usually termed *Tanaim*, "those who repeat, i.e. teach the Law." They are called "lawyers" (ch. xxii. 35; Luke v. 17; Acts v. 34), also "the wise," "Elders," and "Rabbis."

A scribe's education began as early as in his fifth year. At thirteen he became a "son of the precept," *Bar-mitsvah*. If deemed fit, he became a disciple. At thirty he was admitted as a teacher, having tablets and a key given him. See note, ch. xvi. 19. His functions were various; he transcribed the law (here the greatest accuracy was demanded); he expounded the law, always with reference to authority—he acted as judge in family litigation, and was employed in drawing up various legal documents, such as marriage contracts, writings of divorce, etc. (See Kitto's *Cycl. Bib. Lit.* and Smith's *Bib. Dict.* art. Scribes.)

The alliance between Scribes and Pharisees was very close, each taught that the law could be interpreted, fenced round and aided by tradition, in opposition to the Sadducees, who adhered to the strict letter of the written law.

CH. VIII. 1—4. A LEPER IS CLEANSED.

St Mark i. 40—44; St Luke v. 12, where the cure is placed in "a certain city."

2. *a leper*] St Luke has "full of leprosy," a term implying the gravity of the disease,—not that it covered the whole body, in which case the leper was pronounced clean, Levit. xiii. 12, 13, 16, 17. See *Our Lord's Miracles of Healing*, ch. IV. (Belcher). Leprosy is to be regarded as especially symbolic of sin: the beginning of the disease is almost unnoticed, it is contagious (this point is disputed, but see in confirmation of the note Belcher, *Our Lord's Miracles of Healing*, ch. IV., also

worshipped him, saying, Lord, if thou wilt, thou canst make
3 me clean. And Jesus put forth *his* hand, and touched him,
saying, I will; be thou clean. And immediately his leprosy
4 was cleansed. And Jesus saith unto him, See thou tell no
man; but go thy way, shew thyself to the priest, and offer
the gift that Moses commanded for a testimony unto them.

5—13. *Cure of a Centurion's Servant.*

5 And when Jesus was entered into Capernaum, there came
6 unto him a centurion, beseeching him, and saying, Lord,
my servant lieth at home sick of the palsy, grievously tor-

Meyer ad loc. who takes the same view), in its worst form it is incurable except by the touch of Christ; it separated a man and classed him with the dead.

worshipped him] The imperfect in the original marks that persistency in prayer, which Jesus had just promised should win acceptance; while the leper's words imply a faith which is another condition of acceptance.

4. *the gift that Moses commanded*] "two birds alive and clean, and cedar wood, and scarlet and hyssop." And on the eighth day "two he lambs without blemish, and one ewe lamb of the first year without blemish, and three tenth deals of fine flour for a meat offering, mingled with oil, and one log of oil." Levit. xiv. 4, 10.

for a testimony unto them] Either (1) to the priests, or (2) to the people who were following Jesus; in either case to shew that Jesus came to fulfil the law. Christ enjoins the cleansed leper to tell no one, thus instructing us that He would not have people converted by His miracles. Christ addresses Himself to men's hearts not to their eyes or ears. He will not fling Himself from the height of the temple to persuade men.

5—13. Cure of a Centurion's Servant.

St Luke vii. 1—10, where the incident is placed immediately after the Sermon on the Mount. The centurion sends a deputation of Jewish elders to Jesus, who speak of the worthiness of the centurion and of his love to the nation, "he built us a synagogue." St Luke does not introduce our Lord's comparison between Jew and Gentile, and the promises to the latter. This last point is characteristic—the rejection of the Jews is not dwelt upon when the Gospel is preached to the Gentiles. This might be further illustrated from the Acts.

5. *a centurion*] i.e. a captain or commander of a century—a company normally composed of a hundred men, the sixtieth part of a legion in the Roman army. This centurion was probably an officer in the army of Herod Antipas, which would be modelled after the Roman fashion.

6. *my servant*] or "slave;" the Greek word is a more affectionate term than the word translated servant in *v.* 9.

the palsy] i.e. paralysis, a disease often free from acute suffering, but

mented. And Jesus saith unto him, I will come and heal 7
him. The centurion answered and said, Lord, I am not 8
worthy that thou shouldest come under my roof: but speak
the word only, and my servant shall be healed. For I am 9
a man under authority, having soldiers under me: and I
say to this *man*, Go, and he goeth; and to another, Come,
and he cometh; and to my servant, Do this, and he doeth
it. When Jesus heard *it*, he marvelled, and said to them 10
that followed, Verily I say unto you, I have not found so
great faith, no not in Israel. And I say unto you, That 11
many shall come from the east and west, and shall sit down
with Abraham, and Isaac, and Jacob, in the kingdom of
heaven. But the children of the kingdom shall be cast out 12
into outer darkness: there shall be weeping and gnashing
of teeth. And Jesus said unto the centurion, Go thy way; 13
and as thou hast believed, *so* be it done unto thee. And
his servant was healed in the selfsame hour.

14—17. *The Cure of Peter's Mother-in-law of a Fever.*

And when Jesus was come into Peter's house, he saw his 14

when it is accompanied by contraction of the muscles, the pain, as in this case, is very grievous. St Luke does not name the nature of the disease.

8. *The centurion answered*] The argument lies in a comparison between the centurion's command and the authority of Jesus. "If I who am under authority command others, how much more hast thou power to command who art under no authority? If I can send my soldiers or my slave to execute my orders, how much more canst thou send thy ministering spirits to do thy bidding?" The centurion was doubtless acquainted with the Jewish belief on the subject of angels, their subordination and their office as ministers of God.

9. *my servant*] Rather, **slave**. Observe the centurion's orders, his *soldiers* come and go, i.e. march when he bids them. His *slave* he orders to do this, i.e. perform any servile work.

Mark this as the first contact of Jesus with slavery. With such relations between master and slave as these slavery would soon pass away.

It was no express enactment of Christ, but the Spirit of Christ, which this centurion had caught, that abolished slavery.

11. *sit down*] i.e. recline at a feast. The image of a banquet is often used to represent the joy of the kingdom of heaven. Luke xiv. 15, xxii. 29, 30; Rev. xix. 9.

12. *outer darkness*] i.e. the darkness outside the house in which the banquet is going on.

15 wife's mother laid, and sick of a fever. And he touched
her hand, and the fever left her: and she arose, and minis-
16 tered unto them. When the even was come, they brought
unto him many *that were* possessed with devils: and he
cast out the spirits with *his* word, and healed all that were
17 sick: that it might be fulfilled which was spoken by Esaias
the prophet, saying, Himself took our infirmities, and
bare our sicknesses.

18—22. *Fitness for Discipleship.*

18 Now when Jesus saw great multitudes about him, he gave
19 commandment to depart unto the other side. And a certain scribe came, and said unto him, Master, I will follow
20 thee whithersoever thou goest. And Jesus saith unto him,
The foxes have holes, and the birds of the air *have* nests;

14—17. THE CURE OF PETER'S MOTHER-IN-LAW OF A FEVER, Mark i. 29—31; Luke iv. 38, 39.

St Luke's description bears special marks of scientific accuracy.

14. *Peter's house*] From John i. 44 we learn that Bethsaida was the city of Andrew and Simon Peter. Either then (i) they had changed their home to Capernaum, or (2) Bethsaida was close to Capernaum. One theory is that Bethsaida was the port of Capernaum.

laid, and sick of a fever] St Luke uses a technical term, "great fever," the symptoms of which were those of typhus fever.

laid] Literally, **struck down**, an expression which denotes the great and sudden prostration which characterises typhus fever.

15. *the fever left her*] The completeness and suddenness of the cure prove the miraculous nature of it.

ministered unto them] Eager, as good housewives are to return to their work.

unto them] There is high MS. authority for "unto Him."

16. *with his word*] not by a touch, as in the case of leprosy and fever. Christ never laid his hand on demoniacs.

17. Isaiah liii. 4.

18—22. FITNESS FOR DISCIPLESHIP. Luke ix. 57—62.

St Luke names three instances, and places the scene of the incident in Samaria.

The instances are typical of the way in which Jesus deals with different characters. To one attracted by the promises of the Gospel and full of eagerness, Jesus presents the darker side—the difficulties of the Christian life; the half-hearted discipleship of the other is confronted with the necessity of absolute self-renunciation.

19. We are not told whether this scribe, thus brought face to face with privation and hardship, was daunted like the young ruler (ch. xix. 16), or persevered like the sons of Zebedee (ch. xx. 22).

but the Son of man hath not where to lay *his* head. And 21
another of his disciples said unto him, Lord, suffer me first
to go and bury my father. But Jesus said unto him, Follow 22
me; and let the dead bury their dead.

23—27. *The Storm on the Lake.*

And when he was entered into a ship, his disciples fol- 23

20. *the Son of man*] The origin of this expression as a Messianic title is found in Dan. vii. 13: "I saw in the night visions, and, behold, one like the Son of man came with(in) the clouds of heaven, and came to the Ancient of days, and they brought him before him." Hence to the Jews it would be a familiar designation of the Messiah—the King whose "everlasting dominion" is described in the next verse (Dan. vii. 14). (See Dr Pusey, *On Daniel*, Lecture II.)

The Hebraism may be considered in the light of similar expressions, "sons of light," "son of perdition," "son of peace," &c., in all of which the genitive denotes a quality inherent in the subject. Sons of light = the spiritually enlightened, sons of wisdom = the wise. By the Son of man then is meant He who is essentially man, who took man's nature upon Him, who is man's representative before God, shewing the possibilities of purified human nature, and so making atonement practicable.

The title "Son of man," so frequently used by our Lord of Himself, is not applied to Him except by Stephen (Acts vii. 56), "I see the heavens opened, and the Son of man standing on the right hand of God." It occurs also in the Vision of St John with a direct reference to the words of Daniel (Rev. i. 13, xiv. 14).

21. *to go*] Rather, **to go away, depart.**

22. *let the dead bury their dead*] Or, **their own dead.** The exact force of this is not quite clear. The word "dead" is used first in a figurative, secondly, in a literal sense. In a figurative sense by the "dead" are intended those who are outside the kingdom, who are dead to the true life. Perhaps a brother or brothers of the disciple had rejected Christ, "let them bury their father." Another way of understanding the proverb is: Let those who are dead in Christ, dead to the world, bury their dead—their affections and lusts, all that connects them with that dead past. St Luke, after "let the dead bury their dead," adds, "but go thou and preach the kingdom of God." Perhaps no incident marks more decisively the height of self-abandonment required by Jesus of His followers. In this instance the disciple is called upon to renounce for Christ's sake the last and most sacred of filial duties. The unswerving devotion to Christ is illustrated in the parallel passage (Luke ix. 62) by "the man who puts his hand to the plough."

23—27. THE STORM ON THE LAKE. Mark iv. 35—41; Luke viii. 22—25.

St Mark, as usual, adds some interesting details: "it was evening—there were other little ships—a great storm of wind—the waves beat

24 lowed him. And behold, there arose a great tempest in
the sea, insomuch that the ship was covered with the waves:
25 but he was asleep. And his disciples came to *him*, and
26 awoke him, saying, Lord, save us: we perish. And he
saith unto them, Why are ye fearful, O ye of little faith?
Then he arose, and rebuked the winds and the sea; and
27 there was a great calm. But the men marvelled, saying,
What manner *of man* is this, that even the winds and the
sea obey him?

28—34. *The Gadarene Demoniacs.*

28 And when he was come to the other side into the country
of the Gergesenes, there met him two possessed with devils,

into the ship—He was asleep on *a pillow* in the hinder part of the ship."

With all these points of difference in seven short verses, how can it be said that St Mark's Gospel is an abridgment of St Matthew's?

23. *a ship*] Rather, the ship or fishing-boat, i.e. the boat which Jesus always used.

24. *he was asleep*] The expression in the original is very impressive. He, the Master, continued to sleep. It is the only place where the sleep of Jesus is named.

26. *faith* = "trust," "confidence."

27. *the men*] the disciples, and other fishermen who were also on the Lake: see account in Mark.

28—34. THE GADARENE DEMONIACS. St Mark v. 1—20; St Luke viii. 26—39.

St Mark and St Luke make mention of one demoniac only. St Mark relates the incident at greater length and with more particularity. St Matthew omits the impossibility of binding him with chains, the absence of clothing, the wild cries night and day, the name "legion," the prayer not to be sent into the "abyss" (Luke), the request of one of the demoniacs to be with Jesus, and the charge which Jesus gives him to tell his friends what great things the Lord had done for him.

28. *Gergesenes*] The readings vary between Gerasenes, Gadarenes and Gergesenes. Gerasa and Gergesa are forms of the same name. Gadara was some distance to the south of the Lake. It was, however, the capital of Peræa, and the more important place; possibly Gergesa was under its jurisdiction. Gergesa is identified with the modern Khersa; in the neighbourhood of which "rocks with caves in them very suitable for tombs, a verdant sward with bulbous roots on which the swine might feed" (Macgregor, *Rob Roy*), and a steep descent to the verge of the Lake, exactly correspond with the circumstances of the miracle. (See Map.)

coming out of the tombs, exceeding fierce, so that no *man*
might pass by that way. And behold, they cried out, say- 29
ing, What have we to do with thee, Jesus, *thou* Son of God?
art thou come hither to torment us before the time? And 30
there was a good way off from them a herd of many swine
feeding. So the devils besought him, saying, If thou cast 31
us out, suffer us to go away into the herd of swine. And 32
he said unto them, Go. And when they were come out,
they went into the herd of swine: and behold, the whole
herd of swine ran violently down a steep place into the sea,
and perished in the waters. And they that kept *them* fled, 33
and went their ways into the city, and told every *thing*, and
what was befallen to the possessed of the devils. And be- 34
hold, the whole city came out to meet Jesus: and when
they saw him, they besought *him* that he would depart out
of their coasts.

1—8. *Cure of a Man afflicted with Paralysis.*

And he entered into a ship, and passed over, and came 9
into his own city. And behold, they brought to him a man 2

tombs hewn out of the mountain-sides formed convenient dwelling-places for the demoniacs.

29. *What have we to do with thee*] Not "what is there in common between you and us?" but "what cause of war is there between us?" The same expression occurs in this sense 2 Chron. xxxv. 21.

31. *devils*] The Greek word here and in the parallel passages is a masculine and not a neuter form. The same word occurs in two other passages (Rev. xvi. 14 and xviii. 2), and nowhere else in N. T.

32. *a steep place*] Translate, the *steep place*. The slope of Gergesa, familiar to Matthew and to the readers of his Gospel.

33. *they that kept them*] It does not appear whether these were Jews or Gentiles, more probably the latter; if the former, they were transgressing the law.

(1) This narrative may be regarded as a signal instance of *Metanoia*, or change from the old evil state to the new life. (2) It recalls the connection between sin and disease. The majority of cases of *mania* may be traced to sins of impurity; the impurity expelled, the man becomes sound in body as well as in mind. (3) The destruction of the swine should present no difficulty. The same God, who, for purposes often hidden, allows men to die by thousands in war or by pestilence, here, by the destruction of a herd of swine, enforces a moral lesson which the world has never forgotten.

34. *that he would depart*] The motive for the request was fear lest a greater disaster should follow (Meyer).

sick of the palsy, lying on a bed: and Jesus seeing their
faith said unto the sick of the palsy; Son, be of good cheer;
3 thy sins be forgiven thee. And behold, certain of the scribes
4 said within themselves, This *man* blasphemeth. And Jesus
knowing their thoughts said, Wherefore think ye evil in your
5 hearts? For whether is easier, to say, *Thy* sins be forgiven
6 thee; or to say, Arise, and walk? But that ye may know
that the Son of man hath power on earth to forgive sins,
(then saith he to the sick of the palsy,) Arise, take up thy
7 bed, and go unto thine house. And he arose, and departed

CHAP. IX. 1—8. CURE OF A MAN AFFLICTED WITH PARALYSIS. Mark ii. 1—12; Luke v. 18—26.

Both St Mark and St Luke notice the crowding of the people to hear Jesus, and narrate the means by which the sufferer was brought into His presence.

1. *a ship*] As ch. viii. 23, **the boat.**

his own city] Capernaum.

2. *sick of the palsy*] not "grievously tormented" (see ch. viii. 6), therefore suffering from a less severe type of paralysis.

lying] The same word and tense translated "laid," ch. viii. 6, where see note.

their faith] The faith of those who brought him, as well as his own. Cp. Mark ix. 23, 24.

Son, be of good cheer] Bengel infers from this that the sufferer was a young man.

thy sins be forgiven thee] Translate, **have been** *forgiven thee.* Christ assigns sin as the cause of this paralytic seizure. Paralysis is not uncommonly the result of sinful indulgence.

2—6. When Jesus said "Thy sins have been forgiven thee" the young man did not immediately rise (see *v.* 7). Instantly the scribes thought with a sneer "this fellow blasphemes," i.e. pretends to a divine power which he does not possess. They said in their hearts it is easy to say, "Thy sins have been forgiven," let him say, "Arise, and walk," then we shall discover his blasphemy. Jesus answers their thoughts. His words are not "*whether*," as in E.V., but "*why* is it easier to say, Thy sins have been forgiven thee, than to say, Arise, and walk?" In truth it was not easier to say "Thy sins have been forgiven" as Jesus says those words, for to say them implied the cure of soul and of body too; but in order to convince the Scribes of His power He adds the words, "Arise, and walk;" and implicitly bids them infer that the inner work of forgiveness had as surely followed the first words as the outward and visible result followed the command to rise and walk.

6. *take up thy bed*] The Oriental frequently spreads a mat upon the ground and sleeps in the open air, in the morning he rolls up his mat and carries it away.

to his house. But when the multitudes saw *it*, they mar- 8
velled, and glorified God, which had given such power unto
men.

9. *The Call of St Matthew.*

And as Jesus passed forth from thence, he saw a man, 9
named Matthew, sitting at the receipt of custom: and he
saith unto him, Follow me. And he arose, and followed
him.

10—13. *A Meal in the Evangelist's House.*

And it came to pass, as Jesus sat at meat in the house, 10
behold, many publicans and sinners came and sat down
with him and his disciples. And when the Pharisees saw 11
it, they said unto his disciples, Why eateth your Master
with publicans and sinners? But when Jesus heard *that*, he 12
said unto them, They that be whole need not a physician,

9. THE CALL OF ST MATTHEW. Mark ii. 14; Luke v. 27, 28.

St Mark has "Levi, the son of Alphæus," St Luke "a publican named Levi." The identification of Matthew with Levi can scarcely be seriously disputed. The circumstances of the call are precisely similar as narrated by the Synoptists; and it was too usual for a Jew to have more than one name for this difference to be a difficulty. Probably the name Matthew, "Gift of God," was adopted by the Apostle when he became a follower of Jesus.

the receipt of custom] Rather, **the toll- or custom-house.** For a longer notice of the call of St Matthew, see Introduction.

10—13. A MEAL IN THE EVANGELIST'S HOUSE. Mark ii. 15—17; Luke v. 29—32.

10. *in the house*] St Luke says "and Levi made him a great feast," which makes it clear that the meal was in Levi's house.

11. *when the Pharisees saw it*] The Pharisees were not guests, but came into the house,—a custom still prevalent in the East. A traveller writes from Damietta, "In the room where we were received, besides the divan on which we sat, there were seats all round the walls. Many came in and took their place on those side-seats, uninvited and yet unchallenged. They spoke to those at table on business, or the news of the day, and our host spoke freely to them. We afterwards saw this custom at Jerusalem...first one and then another stranger opened the door and came in, taking seats by the wall. They leaned forward and spoke to those at table." *Scripture Manners and Customs*, p. 185.

12. *They that be whole*, &c.] There is a touch of irony in the words. They that are "whole" are they who think themselves whole. So below, the "righteous" are those who are righteous in their own eyes.

13 but they that are sick. But go ye and learn what *that*
meaneth, I will have mercy, and not sacrifice: for I
am not come to call *the* righteous, but sinners to repentance.

14—17. *A Question about Fasting.*

14 Then came to him the disciples of John, saying, Why do
we and the Pharisees fast oft, but thy disciples fast not?
15 And Jesus said unto them, Can the children of the bridechamber mourn, as long as the bridegroom is with them?
but the days will come, when the bridegroom shall be taken
16 from them, and then shall they fast. No *man* putteth a

13. *I will have mercy*] i.e. *I* desire *mercy*. I require mercy rather than sacrifice, Hosea vi. 6. It is a protest by the prophet against the unloving, insincere formalist of his day. It is closely parallel to our Lord's injunction, ch. v. 23, 24. Sacrifice without mercy is no acceptable sacrifice. To love sinners is a better fulfilling of the law than to stand aloof from them. See note ch. xii. 7, where our Lord again quotes these words.

The words "to repentance" are omitted in the leading MSS.

14—17. A QUESTION ABOUT FASTING. Mark ii. 18—22; Luke v. 33—39.

It is not quite clear whether this further incident took place at Levi's feast. St Luke leads us to draw that inference.

15. *the children of the bridechamber*] See note, *v.* 6. "The children of the bridechamber" were the bridegroom's friends or groomsmen who went to conduct the bride from her father's house (see note, ch. xxv. 1). The procession passed through the streets, gay with festive dress, and enlivened with music and joyous shouts, and with the brilliant light of lamps and flambeaux. With the same pomp and gladness the bride was conducted to her future home, where the marriage-supper was prepared.

the bridegroom] The Jews symbolized the "congregation" or "church" by the image of a bride. Jesus sets himself forth as the Bridegroom of the Christian Church. See Herschell, *Sketch of the Jews*, pp. 92—97.

shall be taken from them] For the first time Jesus alludes to His death.

then shall they fast] Herschell (quoted in *Scripture Manners and Customs*) observes that many Jews who keep voluntary fasts, if invited to a marriage are specially exempted from the observance of them. Jesus first gives a special answer to the question about fasting. There is a time of sorrow in store for my disciples when fasting will have a real meaning, *now* in my presence they can but rejoice. Note that fasting and mourning are regarded as quite synonymous. This they are to the perfectly sincere only. The words of Jesus are true also of

piece of new cloth unto an old garment; for that which is
put in to fill it up taketh from the garment, and the rent is
made worse. Neither do *men* put new wine into old bottles: 17
else the bottles break, and the wine runneth out, and the
bottles perish: but they put new wine into new bottles, and
both are preserved.

18—26. *The Daughter of Jairus. The Woman cured of an Issue of Blood.*

While he spake these *things* unto them, behold, there came 18

Christian experience. There are joyous times when the presence of Christ is felt to be near. Then fasting would be out of harmony. But there are also seasons of despondency and depression, when Christ seems to be taken away, when fasting is natural and appropriate.

16. *No man*] Rather, **but** no man. The particle δέ (but) is omitted in E. V.; it marks a turn in the argument which is indicated still more clearly in Luke (v. 36), "And (but) He spake also a parable unto them." The words of Jesus here take a wider range. He says in effect to John's disciples: "Your question implies ignorance of my teaching. My doctrine is not merely a reformed Judaism like the teaching of John and Pharisaism, it is a new life to which such questions as these concerning ceremonial fasting are quite alien."

new] Literally, **uncarded, raw.** The old garment is Judaism. Christianity is not to be pieced on to Judaism to fill up its deficiencies. This would make the rent—the divisions of Judaism—still more serious. The word translated "rent" is used of the "schisms" in the Corinthian Church, 1 Cor. i. 10, and has so passed into ecclesiastical language; it is the English "schism."

17. *new wine into old bottles*] The Oriental bottles are skins of sheep or goats. Old bottles would crack and leak. This may be regarded as a further illustration of the doctrine taught in the preceding verse. But it is better to give it an individual application. The new wine is the new law, the freedom of Christianity. The new bottles are those fitted to live under that law. The old wine is Judaism, the old bottles those, who trained in Judaism, cannot receive the new law, who say "the old is better" (or "good"), Luke v. 39.

Our Lord's answer then is threefold, (1) specially as to fasting, (2) as to Christianity in regard to Judaism, (3) as to individuals trained in Judaism.

(1) This is a joyous time, not a season for fasting, which is a sign of sorrow.

(2) Christianity is not a sect of Judaism, or to be judged according to rules of Judaism.

(3) It is not every soul that is capable of receiving the new and spiritual law. The new wine of Christianity requires new vessels to contain it.

a *certain* ruler, and worshipped him, saying, My daughter is
even now dead: but come and lay thy hand upon her, and
19 she shall live. And Jesus arose, and followed him, and *so*
20 *did* his disciples. (And behold, a woman, which was diseased with an issue of blood twelve years, came behind *him*,
21 and touched the hem of his garment: for she said within
herself, If I may but touch his garment, I shall be whole.
22 But Jesus turned him about, and when he saw her, he said,
Daughter, be of good comfort; thy faith hath made thee
whole. And the woman was made whole from that hour.)
23 And when Jesus came into the ruler's house, and saw the
24 minstrels and the people making a noise, he said unto them,
Give place: for the maid is not dead, but sleepeth. And

18—26. The Daughter of Jairus, 18, 19 and 23—26; Mark v. 22—24 and 35—43. Luke viii. 41, 42 and 49—56.

The Woman cured of an Issue of Blood, 20—22. Mark v. 25—34; Luke viii. 43—48.

Related with more detail by St Mark and St Luke. She had spent all her living on physicians. Jesus perceives that virtue has gone out of him. The woman tells all the truth before the people.

18. *a certain ruler*] From Mark and Luke we learn that he was chief ruler of the synagogue, Jairus by name.

My daughter] "My little daughter," (Mark); "one only daughter, about twelve years of age," (Luke).

is even now dead] "lieth at the point of death," (Mark); "lay a-dying," (Luke).

20. *hem of his garment*] See ch. xiv. 36 and xx ii. 5.

21. *she said*] The imperfect tense of the original; denotes intensity of feeling, "she kept saying over and over to herself."

22. *thy faith hath made thee whole*] Rather, "thy faith hath saved thee," and not the external act of touching my garment. True faith—spiritual insight—will be accepted by Jesus in spite of ignorance.

23. St Mark and St Luke mention the message to Jairus on the way, that his daughter was already dead, and name the three disciples whom Jesus permits to enter the house with him.

the minstrels and the people making a noise] The minstrels are mentioned by St Matthew only. Cp. 2 Chron. xxxv. 25, "all the singing men and the singing women spake of Josiah in their lamentations to this day." Lane (*Modern Egyptians*) says "the women of the family raise the cries of lamentations called '*welweleh*' or '*wilwal;*' uttering the most piercing shrieks and calling upon the name of the deceased."

24. *is not dead, but sleepeth*] These words are reported without variation by the three Synoptists; it is open to question whether they ought not to be taken literally. The word for sleepeth (καθεύδει) does

they laughed him to scorn. But when the people were put 25
forth, he went in, and took her by the hand, and the maid
arose. And the fame hereof went abroad into all that 26
land.

27—31. *A Cure of two Blind Men.*

And when Jesus departed thence, two blind men followed 27
him, crying, and saying, *Thou* Son of David, have mercy on
us. And when he was come into the house, the blind men 28
came to him: and Jesus saith unto them, Believe ye that I
am able to do this? They said unto him, Yea, Lord. Then 29
touched he their eyes, saying, According to your faith be it
unto you. And their eyes were opened; and Jesus straitly 30
charged them, saying, See *that* no *man* know *it*. But they, 31
when they were departed, spread abroad his fame in all that
country.

32—34. *Cure of a Dumb Man possessed by an evil spirit.*

As they went out, behold, they brought to him a dumb 32
man possessed with a devil. And when the devil was cast 33
out, the dumb spake: and the multitudes marvelled, saying,

not bear the metaphorical force of κοιμᾶσθαι; and the statement of Jesus is very explicit.

27—31. A Cure of two Blind Men.

Peculiar to St Matthew. Archbp. Trench alludes to the fact that cases of blindness are far more numerous in the East than in Western countries. "The dust and flying sand enter the eyes, causing inflammations......the sleeping in the open air, and the consequent exposure of the eyes to the noxious nightly dews, is another source of this malady."

27. *Son of David*] See note ch. i. 1. The thought of the kingdom of heaven had been closely linked with the reign of a Son of David, but doubtless with many Jews the glory of the Asmonean dynasty (the Maccabees) and the established power of the Herods had tended to obscure this expectation. To have clung to it was an act of faith.

30. *straitly charged*] The word in the original is a remarkable one, Literally, **to roar**, then (1) "to charge with vehement threats," then (2) "to enjoin strictly," (here and Mark i. 43); (3) to be loudly indignant (Mark xiv. 5); (4) "to groan in the spirit;" said of our Lord at the grave of Lazarus (John xi. 33, 38).

34 It was never so seen in Israel. But the Pharisees said, He
casteth out the devils through the prince of the devils.

35—38. *The Preaching of Jesus. The Harvest of the World.*

35 And Jesus went about all the cities and villages, teaching
in their synagogues, and preaching the gospel of the kingdom, and healing every sickness and every disease among
36 the people. But when he saw the multitudes, he was moved
with compassion on them, because they fainted, and were
37 scattered abroad, as sheep having no shepherd. Then saith
he unto his disciples, The harvest truly is plenteous, but the
38 labourers *are* few; pray ye therefore the Lord of the harvest,
that he will send forth labourers into his harvest.

Summer Term 1912

1—4. *The Mission of the Twelve*; 5—42, *and the Charge to them.*

10 And when he had called unto *him* his twelve disciples,
he gave them power against unclean spirits, to cast them

32—34. Cure of a Dumb Man possessed by an Evil Spirit. St Luke xi. 14, 15.

34. *He casteth out the devils through the prince of the devils*] The answer to this charge is given, ch. xii. 25—30.

35—38. The Preaching of Jesus. The Harvest of the World.

35. See ch. iv. 23. All diseases, acute as well as chronic.

36. *fainted*] The word in the received text has no MS. authority; read **harassed.**

scattered abroad] Rather, perhaps, *neglected*, *set at nought*, rejected by the national teachers.

37. *The harvest truly is plenteous*, &c.] The same expression occurs Luke x. 2 on the occasion of sending forth the Seventy, cp. also John iv. 35, "Lift up your eyes and look on the fields, for they are white already to harvest."

38. *send forth*] The original word is more forcible, implying a strong impulse; it is used Mark i. 12. "The spirit *driveth* him into the wilderness;" and frequently of casting out evil spirits, also of casting into outer darkness (ch. xxv. 30).

Chap. X. The Mission of the Twelve **1—4**, and the Charge to them, **5—42.** Mark iii. 14—19, and vi. 7—13. Luke vi. 12—16; ix. 1—6.

1. *his twelve disciples*] The first passages in St Mark and St Luke record the *choice* or *calling* of the Twelve, this chapter and Mark vi.

out, and to heal all *manner of* sickness and all *manner of*
disease. Now the names of the twelve apostles are these; 2
The first, Simon, who is called Peter, and Andrew his
brother; James, the *son* of Zebedee, and John his brother;

and Luke ix. narrate *the* mission or *a* mission of the disciples. Possibly they were sent forth more than once.

sickness...disease] See note ch. iv. 23, and ix. 35.

2. *apostles*] the only passage in this Gospel where the word occurs. The Greek word lit. = "sent forth," "envoys." This sense, though scarcely recognised by classical authors, was not new. It seems to have been a "title borne by those who were despatched from the mother city by the rulers of the race on any foreign mission, especially such as were charged with collecting the tribute paid to the temple service." (Lightfoot, *Gal.* p. 90). The title of "apostles" was given in a special sense to the Twelve, but was not confined to them. Matthias was added to the number of the twelve, Paul was "called to be an apostle," James the Lord's brother, and Barnabas, are designated by the same title. It had even a wider signification: cp. among other passages Rom. xvi. 7. The name is applied to Jesus Christ, Heb. iii. 1, "The Apostle and High Priest of our profession, Christ Jesus." He came to do the will of Him that sent Him.

There are four lists of the Apostles recorded, one by each of the Synoptic Evangelists, one in the Acts of the Apostles. No two of these lists perfectly coincide. This will be seen from the tabular view below.

	Matt. x. 3.	*Mark* iii. 16.	*Luke* vi. 14.	*Acts* i. 13.
1.	Simon Peter.	Simon Peter.	Simon Peter.	Peter.
2.	Andrew.	James the son of Zebedee.	Andrew.	James.
3.	James the son of Zebedee.	John the brother of James.	James.	John.
4.	John his brother.	Andrew.	John.	Andrew.
5.	Philip.	Philip.	Philip.	Philip.
6.	Bartholomew.	Bartholomew.	Bartholomew.	Thomas.
7.	Thomas.	Matthew.	Matthew.	Bartholomew.
8.	Matthew the Publican.	Thomas.	Thomas.	Matthew.
9.	James the son of Alphæus.	James son of Alphæus.	James the son of Alphæus.	James son of Alphæus.
10.	Lebbæus surnamed Thaddæus.	Thaddæus.	Simon Zelotes.	Simon Zelotes.
11.	Simon the Cananite.	Simon the Cananite.	Judas (son) of James.	Judas (son) of James.
12.	Judas Iscariot.	Judas Iscariot.	Judas Iscariot.	

It will be observed from a comparison of these lists that the twelve names fall into three divisions, each containing four names which remain in their respective divisions in all the lists. Within these divisions however, the order varies. But Simon Peter is placed first, and Judas Iscariot last, in all. Again, Philip invariably heads the second, and James the son of Alphæus the third division.

3 Philip, and Bartholomew; Thomas, and Matthew the publican; James the *son* of Alpheus, and Lebbeus, whose sur-
4 name was Thaddeus; Simon the Canaanite, and Judas
Iscariot, who also betrayed him.

Andrew, a Greek name; see John xii. 21, 22, where the Greeks in the temple address themselves to Philip, "Philip cometh and telleth Andrew and Andrew and Philip tell Jesus." An incident that points to some Greek connection besides the mere name.

3. Philip, also a Greek name prevalent at the time, partly through the influence of the Macedonian monarchy, whose real founder was Philip, father of Alexander the Great.

Lebbæus, Thaddæus, Jude the [son] of James, are all names of one and the same person. He was the son in all probability of a James or Jacob, not, as usually translated, brother of James. The name "Lebbæus" = "courageous" from a Hebrew word signifying "heart."

This Jude or Judas must not be confused with Jude or Judas the "brother" of our Lord; nor must James the son of Alphæus be confused with James the brother of our Lord. The "brethren of the Lord" believed not on Him, and could not have been among His apostles. James and Judas were both common names, and the variety of names seems to have been small at this epoch. According to this theory there are four persons named James—(1) the son of Zebedee, (2) the son of Alphæus, (3) the father of Jude, (4) "The less" or rather "the little," the brother of the Lord: and three named Judas—(1) the brother of the Lord, (2) the apostle, son of James, (3) Iscariot.

Matthew or Levi also was son of an Alphæus, but there is no evidence or hint that he was connected with James son of Alphæus.

Bartholomew=son of Tolmai, probably to be identified with Nathanael. (1) St John, who twice mentions the name of Nathanael, never mentions that of Bartholomew; (2) the three Synoptists mention Bartholomew but not Nathanael. (3) Philip is closely connected with Nathanael and also with Bartholomew. (4) Lastly, Nathanael is mentioned with six other disciples as if like them he belonged to the Twelve.

4. Simon the *Cananæan* (not Canaanite), or *Zelotes*, equivalent terms. The fierce party of the Zealots professed a rigid attachment to the Mosaic law; they acknowledged no king save God. Under Judas the Gaulonite they rose in rebellion at the time of the census.

We hear of a Theudas (which is another form of Thaddæus) who rose in rebellion (Acts v. 36). Is it not possible that this Lebbæus or Jude may owe his third name to this *patriot*, as a Galilæan might regard him? It may be observed that Simon (Joseph. *Ant.* XVII. 10, 5) and Judas (*Ant.* XVIII 1, 1) were also names of zealous patriots who rose against the Roman government.

Iscariot] Man of Kerioth, in the tribe of Judah; accordingly (if this be the case) the only non-Galilæan among the Apostles. For other accounts of the name see *Dict. of Bible.*

The choice of the disciples is an instance of the winnowing of Christ,

5—42. *Christ's Charge to the Apostles.*

These twelve Jesus sent forth, and commanded them, 5
saying, Go not into the way of the Gentiles, and into *any*
city of the Samaritans enter ye not: but go rather to 6
the lost sheep of the house of Israel. And as ye go, 7
preach, saying, The kingdom of heaven is at hand. Heal 8
the sick, cleanse the lepers, raise the dead, cast out devils:

the sifting of the wheat from the chaff. In these men the new life had manifested itself. Their faith, or at least their capacity for faith, was intense, and sufficient to bear them through the dangers that confronted them by their Master's side. [*Editor's notes on Greek text of St Luke's Gospel.*]

5—42. CHRIST'S CHARGE TO THE APOSTLES.

This discourse falls naturally into two divisions; of which the first (*vv.* 5—15) has reference to the immediate present, the second relates rather to the church of the future. The subdivisions of the first part are: (1) Their mission field, 5, 6. (2) Their words and works, 7, 8. (3) Their equipment, 9, 10. (4) Their approach to cities and houses, 11—15.

5. *Go not into the way of the Gentiles*] For the expression "way of the Gentiles" cp. ch. iv. 15, "the way of the sea."

This prohibition is not laid on the Seventy (St Luke x. 1—16), they are expressly commissioned to carry tidings of the gospel to cities and places which our Lord Himself proposed to visit.

any city of the Samaritans] The Samaritans were foreigners descended from the alien population introduced by the Assyrian king (probably Sargon), 2 Kings xvii. 24, to supply the place of the exiled Israelites. In Luke xvii. 18, our Lord calls a Samaritan "this stranger," i. e. this man of alien or foreign race. The bitterest hostility existed between Jew and Samaritan, which has not died out to this day. The origin of this international ill-feeling is related Ezra iv. 2, 3. Their religion was a corrupt form of Judaism. For being plagued with lions, the Samaritans summoned a priest to instruct them in the religion of the Jews. Soon, however, they lapsed from a pure worship, and in consequence of their hatred to the Jews, purposely introduced certain innovations. Their rival temple on Mount Gerizim was destroyed by John Hyrcanus about 129 B.C. See Nutt's "*Sketch of the Samaritans,*" p. 19.

About twenty years previous to our Lord's ministry the Samaritans had intensified the national antipathy by a gross act of profanation. During the celebration of the Passover they stole into the Temple Courts when the doors were opened after midnight and strewed the sacred enclosure with dead men's bones (Jos. *Ant.* XVIII. 2, 2). Even after the siege of Jerusalem, when the relations between Jews and Samaritans were a little less hostile, the latter were still designated by the Jews as the "Proselytes of the lions," from the circumstance mentioned above.

9 freely ye have received, freely give. Provide neither gold,
10 nor silver, nor brass in your purses; nor scrip for *your*
journey, neither two coats, neither shoes, nor yet staves:
11 for the workman is worthy of his meat. And into whatsoever city or town ye shall enter, inquire who in it is
12 worthy; and there abide till ye go thence. And when
13 ye come into a house salute it. And if the house be worthy,

8. *cleanse the lepers*] Leprosy is not classed with the other diseases. As especially symbolical of a sin-stricken man, the leper requires cleansing or purification.

raise the dead] These words are omitted in a large number of important MSS. but not in the two most ancient Codices.

9. *Provide neither gold, &c.*] The disciples must not furnish themselves with the ordinary equipment of an Eastern traveller.

gold ...silver...brass] Of the three metals named the brass or copper represents the native currency. The coinage of Herod the Great was copper only. But Greek and Roman money was also current. The Roman *denarius*, a silver coin, is frequently mentioned (ch. xviii. 28, xx. 2). The farthing, *v.* 29, is the Roman *as* the 16th part of a denarius; the Greek *drachma* of nearly the same value as a denarius, and the *stater* (ch. xvii. 27) were also in circulation. See *Student's O. T. History*, p. 596.

in] Rather, **for.**

purses] Literally, **girdles** or **money-belts**, cp. "Ibit eo quo vis qui zonam perdidit," Hor. *Ep.* ii. 2. 40. Sometimes a fold of the tunic held up by the girdle served for a purse, "quando | major avaritiæ patuit sinus?" Juv. *Sat.* I. 88.

10. *scrip*] A wallet such as David wore when he went to meet Goliath. It was fastened to the girdle. Cp.

"Though not with bag and baggage, yet with *scrip* and scrippage."
Shakspeare.

"And in requital ope his leathern *scrip.*" Milton.

two coats]=two tunics. See ch. v. 40. In like manner the philosopher Socrates wore one tunic only, went without sandals, and lived on the barest necessaries of life. Xen. *Mem.* i. 6. 2.

shoes] Rather, **sandals.**

12. *when ye come into a house*] Translate, *when ye* **are entering** *into* **the** *house*, i.e. the house of him who is indicated as "worthy." The injunction to remain in the same house was, perhaps, partly to avoid feasting from house to house, partly for the sake of secrecy—a necessary precaution in after times. Such "worthy" hosts of the Church afterwards were Lydia at Philippi ("If ye have judged me to be faithful to the Lord, come into my house and abide there." Acts xvi. 15), Jason at Thessalonica, Gaius perhaps at Derbe, see Rom. xvi. 23. This kind of general hospitality is still recognised as a duty in the East, where indeed it may be regarded as a necessity.

let your peace come upon it: but if it be not worthy, let
your peace return to you. And whosoever shall not receive 14
you, nor hear your words, when ye depart out of that house
or city, shake off the dust of your feet. Verily I say unto 15
you, It shall be more tolerable for the land of Sodom and
Gomorrha in the day of judgment, than for that city.

16—42. *The Church of the Future.*

Behold, I send you forth as sheep in the midst of wolves: 16
be ye therefore wise as serpents, and harmless as doves. But 17
beware of men: for they will deliver you up to the councils,
and they will scourge you in their synagogues; and ye shall 18

salute it] Saying "Peace be unto you," (*shalom l'cha,*) the usual salutation at this day.

14. *shake off the dust of your feet*] as St Paul did at Antioch in Pisidia, Acts xiii. 51. The cities of Israel that rejected the Gospel should be regarded as heathen. The very dust of them was a defilement as the dust of a heathen land. See Lightfoot, *ad loc.*

15. Comp. ch. xi. 24.

16—42. The Church of the Future.

(1) The Apostolic character, 16. (2) Persecution, 17—25. (3) Consolation—the care of the Father, 26—31. (4) The reward, 32. (5) The Christian choice, 33—39. (6) The hosts of the Church, 40—42.

16. *as sheep in the midst of wolves*] Clemens Rom., who quotes these words, adds to them: "Then Peter answered and said, If then the wolves rend the sheep? but Jesus said to Peter, Let not the sheep fear the wolves after death."

wise as serpents, and harmless as doves] The qualities required for the safety of the unarmed traveller. Prudence and harmlessness are the defence of the weak. *Wise*="prudent," full of precaution, possessing such "practical wisdom" as Paul had when he claimed the rights of Roman citizenship at Philippi. The wisdom of a serpent is to escape notice.

The expression in Rom. xvi. 19, which this passage recalls, is not quite parallel. St Paul is there speaking of the Christian character; our Lord is giving instructions for a special occasion. The word translated *wise* in Romans is not the same Greek word which is here rendered *wise*.

17. *beware of men*] Perhaps with a reference to the serpents and the doves, which shun the approach of men; but comp. ch. xvii. 22, "The Son of Man shall be betrayed into the hands of men."

councils] i.e. provincial synagogue-tribunals. See note, ch. iv. 23.

be brought before governors and kings for my sake, for a
19 testimony against them and the Gentiles. But when they
deliver you up, take no thought how or what ye shall speak:
for it shall be given you in that *same* hour what ye shall
20 speak. For it is not ye that speak, but the Spirit of your
21 Father which speaketh in you. And the brother shall deliver up the brother to death, and the father the child: and
the children shall rise up against *their* parents, and cause
22 them to be put to death. And ye shall be hated of all *men*
for my name's sake: but he that endureth to the end shall
23 be saved. But when they persecute you in this city, flee ye
into another: for verily I say unto you, Ye shall not have
gone over the cities of Israel, till the Son of man be come.

18. *governors*] Such as Felix and Festus at Cæsarea, the Prætors or Duumviri at Philippi (Acts xvi. 20), the Politarchs at Thessalonica (Acts xvii. 6).

kings] As Herod Agrippa or the Roman Emperor.

19. *take no thought how or what ye shall speak*] Curiously enough this has been quoted as if it justified want of preparation for sermons or addresses to a Christian congregation. The direction points definitely to the Christian 'apologies,' of which specimens have come down to us.

20. *the Spirit of your Father*] The Christian "apologist" shall not stand alone. The same Spirit instructs him which inspires the universal Church. St Paul experienced this consolation: "At my first answer no man stood with me......notwithstanding the Lord stood with me and strengthened me." 2 Tim. iv. 16, 17.

21. *the father the child*] The history of persecutions for religion affords many instances of this. It is true even of civil disputes. Thucydides, describing the horrors of the Corcyrean sedition, says (iii. 82), "The ties of relationship became weaker than those of party."

22. *he that endureth to the end shall be saved*] The parallel expression in Luke xxi. 18 is made clear by this verse; "by your patience win for yourselves your souls," i.e. win your true life by enduring to the end. Comp. Rom. v. 4, 5, "we glory in tribulation also, knowing that tribulation worketh patience, and patience experience, and experience hope."

23. *when they persecute you*] Such words indicate that these "instructions" have a far wider range than the immediate mission of the Apostles. They are prophetic, bringing both warning and consolation to all ages of the Church.

till the Son of man be come] The passage in Luke xxi., which is to a great extent parallel to this, treats of the destruction of Jerusalem; and no one who carefully weighs our Lord's words can fail to see that in a real sense He came in the destruction of Jerusalem. That

The disciple is not above *his* master, nor the servant above 24
his lord. *It is* enough for the disciple that he be as his 25
master, and the servant as his lord. If they have called the
master of the house Beelzebub, how much more *shall they*
call them of his household? Fear them not therefore: for 26
there is nothing covered, that shall not be revealed; and
hid, that shall not be known. What I tell you in darkness, 27
that speak ye in light: and what ye hear in the ear, *that*
preach ye upon the housetops. And fear not them which 28
kill the body, but are not able to kill the soul: but rather
fear him which is able to destroy both soul and body in hell.

event was in truth the judgment of Christ falling on the unrepentant nation. In this sense the Gospel had not been preached to all the cities of Israel before Christ came. But all these words point to a more distant future. The work of Christian missions is going on, and will still continue until Christ comes again to a final judgment.

24. *The disciple is not above his master*] The disciples of Jesus can expect no other treatment than that which befell their Master Christ. The same proverb occurs in a different connection Luke vi. 40, where Christ is speaking of the responsibility of the Apostles as *teachers;* "as they are, their disciples shall be."

25. *Beelzebub*] The MSS. vary between Beelzebul and Beelzebub.

Beelzebub, or Baal Zebub = "Lord of flies," i. e. "averter of flies," a serious plague in hot countries. By a slight change of letter the Jews threw contempt on their enemies' god, calling him Baal Zebel—"Lord of mire"—and lastly identified him with Satan. The changes from Bethel ("House of God") to Bethaven ("House of naught or evil"), (Hos. iv. 15), from Nahash ("serpent") to Nehushtan (2 Kings xviii. 4), and from the name Barcochab ("Son of a star"), assumed by a false Messiah, to Barcozab ("Son of a lie"), are instances of the same quaint humour.

Another derivation of Beelzebul makes it equivalent to "Lord of the dwelling," i.e. of the abode of evil spirits. This meaning would be very appropriate in relation to "the master of the house;" and the form Baalzebul is a nearer approach to the Greek word in the text than Baalzebel.

26. *for there is nothing covered*, &c.] Two reasons against fear are implied: (1) If you fear, a day will come which will reveal your disloyalty; (2) Fear not, for one day the unreality of the things that terrify you will be made manifest.

27. *what ye hear in the ear*] Lightfoot (*Hor. Heb.*) refers this to a custom in the "Divinity School" of the synagogue (see ch. iv. 23), where the master whispered into the ear of the interpreter, who repeated in a loud voice what he had heard.

upon the housetops] Travellers relate that in the village districts of Syria proclamations are frequently made from the housetops at the present day.

29 Are not two sparrows sold for a farthing? and one of them
30 shall not fall on the ground without your Father. But the
31 very hairs of your head are all numbered. Fear ye not
32 therefore, ye are of more value than many sparrows. Whosoever therefore shall confess me before men, him will I
33 confess also before my Father which is in heaven. But
whosoever shall deny me before men, him will I also deny
before my Father which is in heaven.
34 Think not that I am come to send peace on earth: I
35 came not to send peace, but a sword. For I am come to
set a man at variance against his father, and the
daughter against her mother, and the daughter in
36 law against her mother in law. And a man's foes
37 *shall be* they of his own household. He that loveth
father or mother more than me is not worthy of me: and he
that loveth son or daughter more than me is not worthy of

28. *him which is able to destroy*] Either (1) God, whose power extends beyond this life. Clemens Rom. (*Ep.* II. 4) with a probable reference to this passage says, "We ought not to fear man but God." Or (2) Satan, into whose power the wicked surrender themselves.

in hell] Literally, **in Gehenna**. See note, ch. v. 22.

29. *one of them shall not fall on the ground without your Father*] Two deductions may be drawn—(1) That human life is more precious in God's sight than the life of the lower animals (*v.* 31); (2) That kindness to animals is part of God's law.

The word translated *sparrow* means any kind of small bird.

32. *shall confess me*] Literally, confess **in** me: make me the central point and object of his confession.

34. *not to send peace, but a sword*] The contrast is rather between union and division than between peace and war. The "sifting" of Christ causes division or perplexity, and conflict of opinion, both in the thoughts of the individual and between man and man. The same idea is illustrated by the husbandman's fan, the refiner's fire, and the shepherd's separation of his flocks. History shews that religion has been the great separating influence in the world.

35. *to set...at variance*] The Greek word occurs here only in the New Testament, and is rare elsewhere. The root is the same as that of the word translated to "cut asunder." The word is used by Plato of a scientific distinction. Here the thought of the dividing sword is carried on. Comp. Micah vii. 6, where see Dr Pusey's note, who quotes Tertullian to shew how true Christ's words proved in the second century.

37. The connection is this: there will be divisions in families; My disciples must not hesitate to side with *Me* rather than with father or mother, or son or daughter. The new life changes the old relation-

me. And he that taketh not his cross, and followeth after 38
me, is not worthy of me. He that findeth his life shall lose 39
it: and he that loseth his life for my sake shall find it.

40—42. *The Reception of the Apostles and Ministers of Jesus Christ.*

He that receiveth you receiveth me, and he that receiveth 40
me receiveth him that sent me. He that receiveth a pro- 41
phet in the name of a prophet shall receive a prophet's
reward; and he that receiveth a righteous *man* in the name
of a righteous *man* shall receive a righteous *man's* reward.
And whosoever shall give to drink unto one of these little 42

ships: everything is viewed now in reference to Christ, to whom His followers are related as mother and sisters and brethren.

38. *he that taketh not his cross*] A further advance in the devotion and self-abandonment required in the disciples of Jesus. These are deeply interesting and solemn words. The cross is named for the first time by the Saviour. The expression recurs ch. xvi. 24, following upon the announcement of the Passion to the disciples. By the Roman custom criminals were compelled to bear the cross to the place of execution. The Galilæans would know too well what was meant by "taking the cross." Many hundreds had paid that forfeiture for rebellion that had not prospered under Judas the Gaulonite and others. (See Introduction, Chapter IV.)

39. *He that findeth his life shall lose it*] The Greek word for life (ψυχή) embraces every form of life from mere vegetative existence to the highest spiritual life of the soul. Sometimes this variety of meaning is found within the limits of a single sentence—"He that findeth the life of external comfort and pleasure, shall lose the eternal life of spiritual joy."

40—42. THE RECEPTION OF THE APOSTLES AND MINISTERS OF JESUS CHRIST.

40. *receiveth*] In the sense of receiving as a teacher, and of welcoming as a guest, see *v.* 14. Whoever welcomes the Apostles and listens to them, listens to the voice of Jesus Christ and of God the Father Himself, and They "will make their abode with him," John xiv. 23.

41. *in the name of*]=for the sake of, out of regard to the prophet's character.

a prophet's reward] Such reward as a prophet or preacher of the gospel hath.

righteous] Those who fulfil the requirements of the *Christian* law (comp. ch. i. 19), true members of the Christian Church—the saints.

42. *one of these little ones*] The reference may be to the disciples. But there appears to be a gradation in the lowest step of which are

ones a cup of cold *water* only in the name of a disciple, verily I say unto you, he shall in no wise lose his reward.

1. *Jesus preaches the Gospel probably unaccompanied by the Twelve.*

2—19. *Concerning John the Baptist.*

11 And it came to pass, when Jesus had made an end of
commanding his twelve disciples, he departed thence to
2 teach and to preach in their cities. Now when John had
heard in the prison the works of Christ, he sent two of his
3 disciples, and said unto him, Art thou he that should come,

"*these* little ones." Possibly some children standing near were then addressed, or, perhaps, some converts less instructed than the Apostles had gathered round. "The little ones" then would mean the young disciples, who are babes in Christ. The lowest in the scale—apostles—prophets—the saints—the young disciples. The simplest act of kindness done to one of Christ's little ones *as such* shall have its reward.

CH. XI. 1. JESUS PREACHES THE GOSPEL PROBABLY UNACCOMPANIED BY THE TWELVE.

2—19. CONCERNING JOHN THE BAPTIST.

His message to Jesus 2—6. His position as a Prophet 7—14. His relation to Jesus and to his contemporaries 15—19.

St Luke vii. 18—35.

2. *in the prison*] At Machærus. See note, ch. xiv. 3. For "two of his disciples" read, on the best MS. authority, *by means of his disciples*.

3. *he that should come*] Literally, **He that cometh.** One of the designations of the Messiah; in every age the prophet said "He cometh."

It is often disputed whether John sent this message (1) from a sense of hope deferred and despondency in his own soul; he would ask himself: (*a*) Is this the Christ whom I knew and whom I baptized? (*b*) Are these works of which I hear, the works of the promised Messiah? or (2) to confirm the faith of his disciples, or (3) to induce Jesus to make a public profession of His Messiahship. (1) The first motive is the most natural and the most instructive. In the weariness and misery of the prison the faith of the strongest fails for a moment. It is not doubt, but faith wavering: "Lord, I believe; help Thou mine unbelief." (2) The second has been suggested and found support rather from the wish to uphold the consistency of the Baptist's character than because it is the clearest inference from the text. (3) The third motive would have been hardly less derogatory to John's faith than the first. And would not our Lord's rebuke *v.* 6 have taken a different form, as when He said to Mary, "Mine hour is not yet come"?

or do we look for another? Jesus answered and said unto 4
them, Go and shew John again *those things* which ye do hear
and see: the blind receive their sight, and the lame walk, 5
the lepers are cleansed, and the deaf hear, the dead are
raised up, and the poor have the gospel preached to them.
And blessed is *he*, whosoever shall not be offended in me. 6
And as they departed, Jesus began to say unto the mul- 7
titudes concerning John, What went ye out into the wilderness to see? A reed shaken with the wind? But what went 8
ye out for to see? A man clothed in soft raiment? behold,
they that wear soft *clothing* are in kings' houses. But what 9
went ye out for to see? A prophet? yea, I say unto you,
and more than a prophet. For this is *he*, of whom it is 10
written, Behold, I send my messenger before thy face,
which shall prepare thy way before thee. Verily I say 11
unto you, Among *them that are* born of women there hath

5. Comp. Isaiah xxxv. 5 and lxi. 1. The first passage describes the work of God, who "*will come* and save you."

the poor have the gospel preached to them] In earthly kingdoms envoys are sent to the rich and great. Compare the thought implied in the disciple's words, "Who then can be saved?" If it is difficult for the rich to enter the kingdom, how much more for the poor?

6. *And blessed is he*] Blessed are all who see that these works of mine are truly the works of the Messiah. Some had thought only of an avenging and triumphant Christ.

blessed] A term that denotes spiritual insight and advance in the true life.

7. *A reed shaken with the wind*] If the first suggestion (*v.* 3) be adopted, the words have a corroborative force. It was no waverer that ye went out to see—his message was clear, his faith was strong *then*.

Others give the words a literal sense—the reeds on the banks of Jordan—and observe a climax, a reed—a man—a prophet—more than a prophet—the greatest of them.

8. *A man clothed in soft raiment*] Mr Plumptre (Smith's *Bib. Dic.* I. 1166) suggests that there may be a historical allusion in these words. A certain Menahem, who had been a colleague of the great teacher Hillel, "was tempted by the growing power of Herod, and with a large number of his followers entered the king's service...they appeared publicly in gorgeous apparel, glittering with gold." (See Lightfoot, *Hor. Hebr.*, on Matt. xxii. 16.)

9. *more than a prophet*] Other prophets foresaw the Messiah, the Baptist beheld Him, and ushered in His kingdom: he was the herald of the King. Further, John was himself the subject of prophecy.

10. *Behold, I send*, &c.] Quoted from the Hebrew of Mal. iii. 1. The LXX. rendering of the passage is different.

not risen a greater than John the Baptist: notwithstanding
he that is least in the kingdom of heaven is greater than he.
12 And from the days of John the Baptist until now the kingdom of heaven suffereth violencc, and the violent take it by
13 force. For all the prophets and the law prophesied until
14 John. And if ye will receive *it*, this is Elias, which was for
15 to come. He that hath ears to hear, let him hear.
16 But whereunto shall I liken this generation? It is like
unto children sitting in the markets, and calling unto their
17 fellows, and saying, We have piped unto you, and ye have
not danced; we have mourned unto you, and ye have not
18 lamented. For John came neither eating nor drinking, and
19 they say, He hath a devil. The Son of man came eating
and drinking, and they say, Behold a man gluttonous, and a
winebibber, a friend of publicans and sinners. But wisdom
is justified of her children.

11. *he that is least in the kingdom of heaven*] Literally, **he that is less**, either (1) than John or (2) than others. Those who are in the kingdom, who are brought nearer to God and have clearer spiritual knowledge of God, have higher privileges than the greatest of those who lived before the time of Christ.

12. *And from*] Translate **but from**: another point shewing the greatness of John, and also the beginning of the Kingdom: it was from the time of John's preaching that men began to press into the kingdom, and the earnest won their way in. For the preaching of John was the epoch to which all prophecy tended.

suffereth violence] **is forced, broken into,** as a ship enters a harbour by breaking the boom stretched across the harbour's mouth. John's preaching was the signal for men to press into the kingdom—to adopt eagerly the new rule and life heralded by John and set forth by Christ.

the violent take it by force] The eager and enthusiastic followers of Christ seize the kingdom—win it as a prize of war.

13. *For*] gives the reason why the wonderful growth of the kingdom should be witnessed *now*.

14. *if ye will receive it*] The present unhappy circumstances in which John was placed seemed inconsistent with such a view of his mission (Meyer).

16. *But whereunto shall I liken this generation?*] The children who complain of their companions are the Jews who are satisfied neither with Jesus nor with John. This generation is out of sympathy with the prophets in whatever guise they come. They blamed John for his too great austerity, Jesus for neglect of Pharisaic exclusiveness and of ceremonial fasting.

19. *But wisdom is justified of her children*] Wisdom = "divine

20—24. *The Cities that repented not.*

Then began he to upbraid the cities wherein most of his 20
mighty works were done, because they repented not. Woe 21
unto thee, Chorazin, woe unto thee, Bethsaida: for if the
mighty works which were done in you, had been done in
Tyre and Sidon they would have repented long ago in sack-
cloth and ashes. But I say unto you, It shall be more 22
tolerable for Tyre and Sidon at the day of judgment, than
for you. And thou, Capernaum, which art exalted unto 23
heaven, shalt be brought down to hell: for if the mighty
works, which have been done in thee, had been done in
Sodom, it would have remained until this day. But I say 24

wisdom"—God regarded as the All Wise. Justified = "is accounted righteous"—"is acquitted of folly." Of her children = "by the divinely wise." The spiritual recognise the wisdom of God, both in the austerity of John and in the loving mercy of Jesus who condescends to eat with publicans and sinners.

The word translated *but* should be *and*. Either the adversative force lies rather in the whole sentence than in the particle, or the Greek *καὶ* is put for the Hebrew connecting particle *vau*, which is sometimes adversative.

20—24. The Cities that repented not.

St Luke x. 13—15, where the words form part of the charge to the seventy disciples. It is instructive to compare the connection suggested by the two evangelists. In St Matthew the link is the rejection of Christ by the Jews—then by these favoured cities; in St Luke, the rejection of the Apostles as suggestive of the rejection of Jesus.

21. *Chorazin*] is identified with Kerazeh, two and a half miles N. of Tell Hum. The ruins here are extensive and interesting; among them a synagogue built of hard black basalt and houses with walls still six feet high. *Recovery of Jerusalem*, p. 347.

Bethsaida] (House of Fish) called Julias in honour of Julia daughter of Augustus, was rebuilt and beautified by Herod Philip, in whose dominions the town was situated.

23. *Capernaum*] See map. Although Capernaum was truly exalted unto heaven in being our Lord's "own city," the thought is rather of self-exaltation. The expressions recall Isaiah xiv. 13—15. Capernaum has exalted herself like Babylon—like Babylon she shall be brought low. Possibly too Capernaum was on a height at Tell Hum or Khan Minyeh. This would give force to the expression in the text.

According to the Sinaitic and Vatican MSS. this verse should be read: "Capharnaum, shalt thou be exalted unto heaven? Thou shalt be brought down to hell."

unto you, that it shall be more tolerable for the land of Sodom in the day of judgment, than for thee.

25—27. *The revelation to "Babes."*

25 At that time Jesus answered and said, I thank thee, O
Father, Lord of heaven and earth, because thou hast hid
these *things* from the wise and prudent, and hast revealed
26 them unto babes. Even so, Father: for so it seemed good
27 in thy sight. All *things* are delivered unto me of my Father:
and no *man* knoweth the Son, but the Father; neither
knoweth any *man* the Father, save the Son, and *he* to
whomsoever the Son will reveal *him*.

28—30. *Rest for the heavy laden.*

28 Come unto me, all *ye* that labour and are heavy laden,
29 and I will give you rest. Take my yoke upon you, and
learn of me; for I am meek and lowly in heart: and ye

25—27. The revelation to "Babes."

St Luke x. 21—22, where the words are spoken on the return of the Seventy.

25. *answered and said*] A Hebraism = "spake and said."

prudent] Rather, **intelligent, acute**. The secrets of the kingdom are not revealed to those who are wise in their own conceit, but to those who have the meekness of infants and the child-like eagerness for knowledge. In a special Jewish sense "the wise and prudent" are the Scribes and Pharisees.

26. *Even so, Father: for*] Translate: "**yea Father [I thank thee] that, &c.**"

27. *are delivered*] Rather, **were delivered.**

28—30. Rest for the heavy laden.

These words of Jesus are preserved by St Matthew only. The connecting thought is, those alone shall know who desire to learn, those alone shall have rest who feel their burden. The babes are those who feel ignorant, the laden those who feel oppressed.

28. *Come unto me*] Jesus does not give rest to all the heavy laden, but to those of them who show their want of relief by coming to Him.

29. *learn of me*] i.e. "become my disciples;" an idea also conveyed by the word "yoke," which was used commonly among the Jews for the yoke of instruction. Stier quotes from the Mishna, "Take upon you the yoke of the holy kingdom." Men of Belial = "Men without the yoke," "the uninstructed."

for (or, *because*) *I am meek and lowly in heart*] The character of Jesus described by Himself; cp. 2 Cor. x. 1, "the meekness and gentle-

shall find rest unto your souls. For my yoke *is* easy, 30
and my burden is light.

1—13. *The Observance of the Sabbath.*

At that time Jesus went on the sabbath day through the 12
corn; and his disciples were a hungred, and began to pluck
the ears of corn, and to eat. But when the Pharisees saw *it*, 2
they said unto him, Behold, thy disciples do *that* which is
not lawful to do upon the sabbath day. But he said unto 3
them, Have ye not read what David did, when he was a
hungred, and they that were with him; how he entered into 4
the house of God, and did eat the shewbread, which was

ness of Christ." It is this character that brings rest to the soul, and therefore gives us a reason why men should become His disciples.

rest unto your souls] Cp. Jer. vi. 16, "Thus saith the Lord, Stand ye in the ways, and see, and ask for the old paths, where is the good way, and walk therein, and ye shall find rest for your souls. But they said, We will not walk therein."

unto your souls] Not relief from *external* bodily toil.

my burden is light] Contrast with this the burden of the Pharisees, ch. xxiii. 4, "heavy burdens and grievous to be borne."

CH. XII. **1—13.** THE OBSERVANCE OF THE SABBATH.

1. The disciples pluck ears of corn on the Sabbath. 2. A man with a withered hand cured on the Sabbath.

St Mark ii. 23—28, iii. 1—5; St Luke vi. 1—11.

1. *began to pluck the ears of corn*] The Pharisees, who seem to have been watching their opportunity, make the objection as soon as the disciples *began* what by Pharisaic rules was an unlawful act.

2. *that which is not lawful to do upon the sabbath day*] This prohibition is a Pharisaic rule not found in the Mosaic Law. It was a principle with the Pharisees to extend the provisions of the Law and make minute regulations over and beyond what Moses commanded, in order to avoid the possibility of transgression. To pluck ears of corn was in a sense, the Pharisees said, to reap, and to reap on the Sabbath day was forbidden and punishable by death. These regulations did in fact make void the Law; e.g. the result of this particular prohibition was to contravene the intention or *motive* of the Sabbath. If sabbatical observances prevented men satisfying hunger, the Sabbath was no longer a blessing but an injury to man.

3. Ahimelech, the priest at Nob, gave David and his companions five loaves of the shewbread (1 Sam. xxi. 1—7).

4. *the shewbread*] Literally, **bread of setting forth**, i.e. bread that was set forth in the sanctuary. It was also called "continual bread" as

not lawful for him to eat, neither for them which were with
5 him, but only for the priests? Or have ye not read in the
law, how that on the sabbath days the priests in the temple
6 profane the sabbath, and are blameless? But I say unto you,
7 That in this place is *one* greater than the temple. But if ye
had known what *this* meaneth, I will have mercy, and
not sacrifice, ye would not have condemned the guiltless.
8 For the Son of man is Lord even of the sabbath day.
9 And when he was departed thence, he went into their
10 synagogue: and behold, there was a man which had *his*
hand withered. And they asked him, saying, Is it lawful to
heal on the sabbath days? that they might accuse him.
11 And he said unto them, What man shall there be among
you, that shall have one sheep, and if it fall into a pit on
the sabbath day, will he not lay hold on it, and lift *it* out?
12 How much then is a man better than a sheep? Wherefore it
13 is lawful to do well on the sabbath days. Then saith he to

being set forth perpetually before the Lord, hence the Hebrew name, "bread of the presence." Twelve loaves or cakes were placed in two "piles" (rather than "rows," Lev. xxiv. 6) on the "pure table" every Sabbath. On each pile was put a golden cup of frankincense. See Exod. xxv. 30; Lev. xxiv. 6—8; Josephus, *Ant.* III. 10. 7.

5. *the priests in the temple profane the sabbath*] by labour in removing the shewbread, preparing fire for the sacrifice, and performing the whole temple service. "Not merely does the sacred *history* relate exceptional instances of *necessity*, but the *Law* itself ordains labour on the Sabbath as a duty" (Stier).

7. *I will have mercy, and not sacrifice*] Quoted a second time, see ch. ix. 13. There is something more binding than the Law, and that is the principle which underlies the Law. The Law rightly understood is the expression of God's love to man. That love allowed the act of David, and the labour of the priests. "Shall it not permit My disciples to satisfy their hunger?"

10. *his hand withered*] i.e. paralysed or affected by atrophy. St Luke has "his *right* hand."

11. In the other Synoptic Gospels the argument is different. "Is it lawful to do good on the Sabbath days, or to do evil? to save life or to kill? St Matthew states the argument that bears specially on the Jewish Law. St Luke, however, mentions the application of the same argument by our Lord on a different occasion, ch. xiv. 5. Our Lord's answer is thrown into the form of a syllogism, the minor premiss and conclusion of which are left to be inferred in St Luke *loc. cit.*

12. *How much then is a man better than a sheep?*] Cp. "ye are of more value than many sparrows," ch. x. 31.

the man, Stretch forth thine hand. And he stretched *it* forth; and it was restored whole, *like* as the other.

14—21. *The Pharisees plot against Jesus, who retires.*

Then the Pharisees went out, and held a council against 14
him, how they might destroy him. But when Jesus knew *it*, 15
he withdrew himself from thence: and great multitudes followed him, and he healed them all, and charged them that 16
they should not make him known: that it might be fulfilled 17
which was spoken by Esaias the prophet, saying, Behold 18
my servant, whom I have chosen; my beloved, in
whom my soul is well pleased: I will put my spirit
upon him, and he shall shew judgment to the Gentiles. He shall not strive, nor cry; neither shall 19
any *man* hear his voice in the streets. A bruised 20
reed shall he not break, and smoking flax shall he
not quench, till he send forth judgment unto victory.
And in his name shall the Gentiles trust. 21

14—21. The Pharisees plot against Jesus, who retires.
Mark iii. 6—12; Luke vi. 11, 12.

14. *held a council against him*] St Mark adds that the Herodians joined the Pharisees.

how they might destroy him] By argument and other means, if necessary by force.

15. *he withdrew himself from thence*] See ch. x. 23. Jesus follows the principle which He laid down for His disciples' guidance.

17. *spoken by Esaias the prophet*] Is. xlii. 3. The original is not accurately followed; the words are probably quoted from memory.

18. *my servant*] Israel as a nation is called the servant of Jehovah, Isaiah xli. 8. Here the same title is given to Jesus, as the representative of the nation.

judgment] The Hebrew word is used in a wider sense to denote "religion as the rule of life;" hence *judgment* may mean (1) "the law of Christ," "the Gospel," or (2) adhering to the strict meaning of the Greek word, "the divine sentence or decree."

to the Gentiles] Possibly our Lord in His retirement addressed Himself more especially to the Gentiles—the Greeks, Phœnicians, and others, settled near the Lake. "They about Tyre and Sidon, a great multitude,...came unto him," Mark iii. 8.

19, 20. These verses describe the gentleness and forbearance of Christ. He makes no resistance or loud proclamation like an earthly prince. The bruised reed and the feebly-burning wick may be referred to the failing lives which Jesus restores and the sparks of faith which He revives.

22, 23. *Cure of a Blind and Dumb Man.*
24—30. *The Charge, "He casteth out devils by Beelzebub." The Answer of Jesus.*

22 Then was brought unto him one possessed with a devil,
blind, and dumb: and he healed him, insomuch that the
23 blind and dumb both spake and saw. And all the people
24 were amazed, and said, Is this the son of David? But when
the Pharisees heard *it*, they said, This *fellow* doth not cast
25 out devils, but by Beelzebub the prince of the devils. And
Jesus knew their thoughts, and said unto them, Every kingdom divided against itself is brought to desolation; and
every city or house divided against itself shall not stand:
26 and if Satan cast out Satan, he is divided against himself;
27 how shall then his kingdom stand? And if I by Beelzebub
cast out devils, by whom do your children cast *them* out?
28 therefore they shall be your judges. But if I cast out devils
by the Spirit of God, then the kingdom of God is come unto
29 you. Or else how can one enter into a strong *man's* house,
and spoil his goods, except he first bind the strong *man?*

20. *till he send forth judgment unto victory*] **Until** He shall make (1) the Gospel or (2) His judgment victorious.

21. *in his name*] The original Hebrew has "in his law."
shall...trust] Rather, **shall hope.**

22, 23. CURE OF A BLIND AND DUMB MAN.

Luke xi. 14—16.

24—30. THE CHARGE, "HE CASTETH OUT DEVILS BY BEELZEBUB." THE ANSWER OF JESUS.

Mark iii. 22—27; Luke xi. 17.

24. *Beelzebub*] See ch. x. 25.

25. *Every kingdom divided against itself is brought to desolation*] Not that civil disputes destroy a nation, but a nation disunited, rent by factions, in the presence of a common enemy must fall. Here Satan's kingdom is regarded as warring against the kingdom of God.

27. *by whom do your children cast them out?*] The children are the disciples of the Pharisees, who either really possessed the power of casting out evil spirits, or pretended to have that power. In either case the argument of Jesus was unanswerable.

28. *is come unto you*] Literally, **surprised you by coming, came upon you unawares.**

29. Not only is Satan not an ally, but he is an enemy and a vanquished enemy.

and then he will spoil his house. He that is not with me is 30
against me; and he that gathereth not with me scattereth
abroad.

31—37. *Blaspheming against the Holy Ghost.*

Wherefore I say unto you, All *manner of* sin and 31
blasphemy shall be forgiven unto men: but the blasphemy
against the *Holy* Ghost shall not be forgiven unto men.
And whosoever speaketh a word against the Son of man, it 32
shall be forgiven him: but whosoever speaketh against the
Holy Ghost, it shall not be forgiven him, neither in this
world, neither in the *world* to come. Either make the tree 33
good, and his fruit good; or else make the tree corrupt, and
his fruit corrupt: for the tree is known by *his* fruit. O gene- 34
ration of vipers, how can ye, being evil, speak good *things?*
for out of the abundance of the heart the mouth speaketh.

30. *He that is not with me is against me*] The thought of the contest between Christ and Satan is continued. Satan is not divided against himself, neither can Christ be. Neutrality is impossible in the Christian life. It must be for Christ or against Christ. The metaphor of gathering and scattering may be from collecting and scattering a flock of sheep, or from gathering and squandering wealth, money, &c.

31—37. Blaspheming against the Holy Ghost.

31. *Wherefore*] The conclusion of the whole is—you are on Satan's side, and *knowingly* on Satan's side, in this decisive struggle between the two kingdoms, and this is blasphemy against the Holy Ghost—an unpardonable sin.

32. *whosoever speaketh against the Holy Ghost*] To speak against the Holy Ghost is to speak against the clear voice of the Holy Ghost within the heart—wilful sin against knowledge. Jesus, who saw the heart, knew that the Pharisees were insincere in the charge which they brought against Him. They were attributing to Satan what they knew to be the work of God. Their former attacks against the Son of man had excuse; for instance, they might have differed conscientiously on the question of Sabbath observance, now they have no excuse.

33. *Either make the tree good,* &c.] The meaning and connection are; "Be honest for once; represent the tree as good, and its fruit as good, or the tree as evil and its fruit as evil; either say that I am evil and that my works are evil, or, if you admit that my works are good, admit that I am good also and not in league with Beelzebub."

34. *generation of vipers*] Cp. ch. iii. 7.

abundance] The same Greek word is translated, "that which was left," Mark viii. 8. Words are, as it were, the overflow of the heart.

35 A good man out of the good treasure of the heart bringeth
forth good *things:* and an evil man out of the evil treasure
36 bringeth forth evil *things*. But I say unto you, That every
idle word that men shall speak, they shall give account
37 thereof in the day of judgment. For by thy words thou
shalt be justified, and by thy words thou shalt be condemned.

38—42. *The Pharisees ask for a Sign.*

38 Then certain of the scribes and of the Pharisees answered,
39 saying, Master, we would see a sign from thee. But he answered and said to them, An evil and adulterous generation
seeketh after a sign; and there shall no sign be given to it,
40 but the sign of the prophet Jonas: for as Jonas was three
days and three nights in the whale's belly; so shall the Son
of man be three days and three nights in the heart of the
41 earth. *The* men of Nineveh shall rise in judgment with this

35. *treasure*] Rather, **treasury** or **storehouse**: for a similar use of the Greek word see ch. ii. 11.

36. *idle*] Rather, useless, ineffectual for good. Words must be not only not evil, but they must be actively good. The same principle rules the decisionat the final judgment (ch. xxv. 45).

37. *by thy words*] i. e. thy words shall be the *ground* of thy acquittal or condemnation. Character shews itself by words. We often say of a friend, "We know what he will *say* when he hears this or that."

38—42. The Pharisees ask for a Sign.

St Luke xi. 16, 29—32. St Luke omits, or at least does not state explicitly, the special application of the sign given in *v.* 40, to understand which required a knowledge of the Jewish prophets which would be lacking to St Luke's readers.

38. *we would see a sign from thee*] This is the second expedient taken by the Pharisees after their resolution to destroy Jesus.

39. *adulterous*] estranged from God; a figure often used by the Prophets to express the defection of Israel from Jehovah.

40. Jonah is a sign (1) as affording a type of the Resurrection, (2) as a preacher of righteousness to a people who needed repentance as this generation needs it.

the whale's belly] The Greek word translated "whale" means "a sea monster." The O. T. rendering is more accurate "the fish's belly" (Jonah ii. 1), "a great fish" (Jonah i. 17). It is scarcely needful to note that there are no whales in the Mediterranean.

41. *in judgment with*] More exactly, **stand up in the judgment**, i. e. in the day of judgment, **beside**. When on the day of judgment the

generation, and shall condemn it: because they repented at
the preaching of Jonas; and behold, a greater than Jonas *is*
here. *The* queen of the south shall rise up in the judgment 42
with this generation, and shall condemn it: for she came
from the uttermost parts of the earth to hear the wisdom of
Solomon; and behold, a greater than Solomon *is* here.

43—45. *A Figure to illustrate the surpassing Wickedness of the day.*

When the unclean spirit is gone out of a man, he walketh 43
through dry places, seeking rest, and findeth none. Then 44
he saith, I will return into my house from whence I came
out; and when he is come, he findeth *it* empty, swept, and
garnished. Then goeth he, and taketh with himself seven 45
other spirits more wicked than himself, and they enter in
and dwell there: and the last *state* of that man is worse than
the first. *Even* so shall it be also unto this wicked generation.

Ninevites stand side by side with the men of that generation, they will by their penitence condemn the impenitent Jews..

42. *The queen of the south*] So correctly and not *a* queen of the South as some translate. The absence of the definite article in the original is due to the influence of the Hebrew idiom. The queen of Sheba, Southern Arabia, 1 Kings x. 1.

43—45. A FIGURE TO ILLUSTRATE THE SURPASSING WICKEDNESS OF THE DAY.

Luke xi. 24—26, where the connection is different. St Luke, as usual, omits the direct application to Israel.

The connection is not clearly marked. It seems to be this: Christ has been speaking of "this generation;" He now contrasts it with past generations. The Jews of former times were like a man possessed by a demon, the Jews of this day are like a man possessed by many demons.

43. *dry places*] The waterless desert uninhabited by man was regarded by the Jews as the especial abode of evil spirits.

44. *empty*] Properly, at leisure. To have cast out a sin does not make a man safe from sin, there must be no leisure in the Christian life.

45. *Even so shall it be also unto this wicked generation*] Israel had cast forth the demon of idolatry—the sin of its earlier history, but worse demons had entered in—the more insidious and dangerous sins of hypocrisy and hardness of heart.

46—50. *Jesus is sought by His Mother and Brethren. The true Mother and Brethren of Jesus.*

46 While he yet talked to the people, behold, *his* mother and
his brethren stood without, desiring to speak with him.
47 Then one said unto him, Behold, thy mother and thy bre-
48 thren stand without, desiring to speak with thee. But he
answered and said unto him that told him, Who is my
49 mother? and who are my brethren? And he stretched
forth his hand toward his disciples, and said, Behold my
50 mother and my brethren. For whosoever shall do the will
of my Father which is in heaven, the same is my brother,
and sister, and mother.

1—9. *Jesus teaches in Parables. The Parable of the Sower.*

13 The same day went Jesus out of the house, and sat by the
2 sea side. And great multitudes were gathered together unto

46—50. Jesus is sought by His Mother and Brethren. The true Mother and Brethren of Jesus.

Mark iii. 31—35; Luke viii. 19—21.

The account is given with very slight variation by the three Synoptists. But see Mark iii. 21 and 30, 31, where a *motive* is suggested—"When his friends heard of it, they went out to lay hold on him: for they said, He is beside himself" (*v.* 21). Comp. the *then* = therefore, of *v.* 31. It would seem that the Pharisees, on the pretext that Jesus had a demon, had persuaded His friends to secure Him. This was another device to destroy Jesus, see *vv.* 14 and 38.

47. *thy brethren*] It is a point of controversy whether these were (1) the own brothers of Jesus, sons of Joseph and Mary, or (2) sons of Joseph by a former marriage, or (3) cousins, sons of a sister of Mary. Their names are given ch. xiii. 55, where see note.

49. *Behold my mother and my brethren*] The new life subverts the old relationships. By the spiritual birth new ties of kindred are established.

50. *whosoever shall do the will of my Father*] "These which hear the word of God and do it" (Luke viii. 21).

Ch. XIII. **1—9.** Jesus teaches in Parables. The Parable of the Sower.

Mark iv. 1—9; Luke viii. 4—9.

1. *sat*] The usual position of a Jewish teacher.

by the sea side] At the N. end of the Lake of Gennesaret there are small creeks or inlets "where the ship could ride in safety only a few

him, so that he went into a ship, and sat; and the whole
multitude stood on the shore. And he spake many *things* 3
unto them in parables, saying, Behold, a sower went forth to
sow; and when he sowed, some *seeds* fell by the way side, 4
and the fowls came and devoured them up: some fell upon 5
stony *places*, where they had not much earth: and forthwith
they sprung up, because *they* had no deepness of earth: and 6
when the sun was up, they were scorched; and because *they*
had not root, they withered away. And some fell among 7
thorns; and the thorns sprung up, and choked them: but 8
other fell into good ground, and brought forth fruit, some an
hundred*fold*, some sixty*fold*, some thirty*fold*. Who hath ears 9
to hear, let him hear.

feet from the shore, and where the multitudes seated on both sides and before the boat could listen without distraction or fatigue. As if on purpose to furnish seats, the shore on both sides of these narrow inlets is piled up with smooth boulders of basalt." Thomson, *Land and Book*, p. 356.

2. *a ship*] According to the received Greek text, the ship or boat.

3. *in parables*] Up to this time Jesus had preached repentance, proclaiming the kingdom, and setting forth the laws of it in direct terms. He now indicates by parables the reception, growth, characteristics, and future of the kingdom. The reason for this manner of teaching is given below, *vv.* 10—15.

A parable (Hebr. *mashal*) = "a likeness" or "comparison." Parables differ from fables in being pictures of possible occurrences—frequently of actual daily occurrences,—and in teaching *religious* truths rather than *moral* truths.

4. *by the way side*] i. e. along the narrow footpath dividing one field from another.

5. *stony places*] Places where the underlying rock was barely covered with earth. The hot sun striking on the thin soil and warming the rock beneath would cause the corn to spring up rapidly and then as swiftly to wither.

7. *thorns sprung up*] The scholar will remember that Vergil mentions among the "plagues" of the wheat,

> "Ut mala culmos
> Esset robigo segnisque horreret in arvis
> Carduus." *Georg.* I. 150—153.

8. *some an hundredfold*, &c.] The different kinds of fertility may be ascribed to different kinds of grain; barley yields more than wheat, and "white maize sown in the neighbourhood often yields several hundredfold." See Thomson's *Land and Book*, p. 83.

10—17. *The Reason why Jesus teaches in Parables.*

10 And the disciples came, and said unto him, Why speakest
11 thou unto them in parables? He answered and said unto
them, Because it is given unto you to know the mysteries of
12 the kingdom of heaven, but to them it is not given. For
whosoever hath, to him shall be given, and he shall have
more abundance: but whosoever hath not, from him shall be
13 taken away even that he hath. Therefore speak I to them
in parables: because they seeing see not; and hearing they
14 hear not, neither do they understand. And in them is fulfilled the prophecy of Esaias, which saith, By hearing ye
shall hear, and shall not understand; and seeing ye
15 shall see, and shall not perceive: for this people's
heart is waxed gross, and *their* ears are dull of hearing, and their eyes they have closed; lest at any
time they should see with *their* eyes, and hear with

10—17. The Reason why Jesus teaches in Parables.

Mark iv. 10—12; Luke viii. 10.

10. *parables*] The parable is suited (1) to the uninstructed, as being attractive in form and as revealing spiritual truth exactly in proportion to the capacity of the hearer; and (2) to the divinely wise as wrapping up a secret which he can penetrate by his spiritual insight. In this it resembles the Platonic myth; it was the form in which many philosophers clothed their deepest thoughts. (3) It fulfils the condition of all true knowledge. He alone who seeks finds. In relation to Nature, Art, God Himself, it may be said the dull "seeing see not." The commonest and most obvious things hide the greatest truths. (4) The divine Wisdom has been justified in respect to this mode of teaching. The parables have struck deep into the thought and language of men (not of Christians only), as no other teaching could have done; in proof of which it is sufficient to name such words and expressions as "talents," "dispensation," "leaven," "prodigal son," "light under a bushel," "building on sand."

11. *the mysteries of the kingdom of heaven*] Secrets known only to the initiated—the inner teaching of the gospel. St Paul regards as "mysteries," the spread of the gospel to the Gentiles, Eph. iii. 3, 4, 9; the doctrine of the resurrection, 1 Cor. xv. 51, the conversion of the Jews, Rom. xi. 25.

12. Cp. ch. xxv. 29.

14. Isaiah vi. 9, 10. The words form part of the mission of Isaiah.

15. *this people's heart is waxed gross*] The heart was regarded as the seat of intelligence. *Gross*, literally, **fat**, so **stolid**, **dull**, like *pinguis* in Latin.

their ears, and should understand with *their* heart,
and should be converted, and I should heal them.
But blessed *are* your eyes, for they see: and your ears, for 16
they hear. For verily I say unto you, That many prophets 17
and righteous *men* have desired to see *those things* which ye
see, and have not seen *them;* and to hear *those things* which
ye hear, and have not heard *them.*

18—23. *The Parable of the Sower is explained.*

Hear ye therefore the parable of the sower. When 18
any one heareth the word of the kingdom, and under- 19
standeth *it* not, then cometh the wicked one, and catcheth
away that which was sown in his heart. This is he which
received seed by the way side. But he that received 20
the seed into stony *places*, the same is he that heareth
the word, and anon with joy receiveth it; yet hath he 21
not root in himself, but dureth for a while: for when
tribulation or persecution ariseth because of the word,
by and by he is offended. He also that received seed 22
among the thorns is he that heareth the word; and the care
of this world, and the deceitfulness of riches, choke the

16. *blessed are your eyes*] The disciples have discernment to understand the explanation which would be thrown away on the uninstructed multitude.

18—23. THE PARABLE OF THE SOWER IS EXPLAINED.
Mark iv. 14—20; Luke viii. 11—15.

19. On some the word of God makes no *impression*, as we say; some hearts are quite unsusceptible of good.

20. *anon*]=*immediately;* the same Greek word is translated *by and by* in the next verse. Cp. "Then I will come to my mother by and by." Shaksp. *Hamlet*, Act III. sc. 2.

21. *when tribulation or persecution ariseth*] Jesus forecasts the persecution of Christians, and the time when "the love of many shall wax cold," ch. xxiv. 12.

is offended] See note, ch. v. 29. All things are not so smooth as he expected. The prospect of the cross took all enthusiasm away from Judas. Perhaps even Mark was "offended" for the moment at Perga.

22. *the care of this world, and the deceitfulness of riches*] St Mark adds "the lusts of other things," St Luke, "the pleasures of this life." These things destroy the "singleness" of the Christian life. Compare with this the threefold employment of the world as described by Christ, at the

23 word, and he becometh unfruitful. But he that received
seed into the good ground is he that heareth the word, and
understandeth *it:* which also beareth fruit, and bringeth
forth, some an hundred*fold*, some sixty, some thirty.

24—30. *The Parable of the Tares.*

24 Another parable put he forth unto them, saying, The
kingdom of heaven is likened unto a man which sowed good
25 seed in his field: but while men slept, his enemy came and
26 sowed tares among the wheat, and went his way. But
when the blade was sprung up, and brought forth fruit, then
27 appeared the tares also. So the servants of the householder
came and said unto him, Sir, didst not thou sow good seed
28 in thy field? from whence then hath it tares? He said unto
them, An enemy hath done this. The servants said unto
29 him, Wilt thou then *that* we go and gather them up? But
he said, Nay; lest while ye gather up the tares, ye root up

time of the Flood, at the destruction of Sodom and Gomorrah, and at the coming of the Son of man. (Luke xvii. 26—30.)

24—30. The Parable of the Tares. Confined to St Matthew.

25. *while men slept*] i.e. during the night. The expression is not introduced into the Lord's explanation of the parable.

sowed tares] Travellers mention similar instances of spiteful conduct in the East, and elsewhere, in modern times.

tares] Probably the English "darnel;" Latin, *lolium;* in the earlier stages of its growth this weed very closely resembles wheat, indeed can scarcely be distinguished from it. This resemblance gives an obvious point to the parable. The good and the evil are often undistinguishable in the visible Church. The Day of Judgment will separate. Men have tried in every age to make the separation beforehand, but have failed. For proof of this read the history of the Essenes or the Donatists. The Lollards—as the followers of Wyckliffe were called—were sometimes by a play on the word *lolium* identified by their opponents with the tares of this parable. A friend suggests the reflection: "How strange it was that the very men who applied the word 'Lollard' from this parable, acted in direct opposition to the great lesson which it taught, by being persecutors."

The parable of the Tares has a sequence in thought on the parable of the Sower. The latter shews that the kingdom of God will not be co-extensive with the world; all men have not the capacity to receive the word. This indicates that the kingdom of God—the true Church—is not co-extensive with the visible Church. Some who seem to be subjects of the Kingdom are not really subjects.

also the wheat with them. Let both grow together until the 30
harvest: and in the time of harvest I will say to the reapers,
Gather ye together first the tares, and bind them in bundles
to burn them: but gather the wheat into my barn.

31—33. (1) *The Parable of the Mustard Seed.* (2) *The Parable of the Leaven which leavened the Meal.*

Another parable put he forth unto them, saying, The 31
kingdom of heaven is like unto a grain of mustard seed,
which a man took, and sowed in his field: which indeed is 32
the least of all seeds: but when it is grown, it is the greatest
among herbs, and becometh a tree, so that the birds of the
air come and lodge in the branches thereof.
Another parable spake he unto them; The kingdom of 33
heaven is like unto leaven, which a woman took, and hid in

31—33. (1) THE PARABLE OF THE MUSTARD SEED. (2) THE PARABLE OF THE LEAVEN WHICH LEAVENED THE MEAL.
(1) Mark iv. 30—32. (1) and (2) Luke xiii. 18—21.

The "mystery" or secret of the future contained in these two parables has reference to the growth of the Church; the first regards the growth in its external aspect, the second in its inner working.

31. *which a man took, and sowed*] "Which when it is sown," St Mark, who thus does not name an agent, the planter of the seed.

in his field] "into his (own) garden," St Luke, with special reference to the land of Israel.

32. *the least of all seeds*] Not absolutely the least, but least in proportion to the plant that springs from the seed. Moreover the mustard seed was used proverbially of anything excessively minute.

lodge in the branches] i.e. settle for the purpose of rest or shelter or to eat the seeds of which goldfinches and linnets are very fond (Tristram, *Nat. Hist. of Bible*, p. 473). *Lodge*, literally **dwell in tents.** If we think of the leafy huts constructed for the feast of tabernacles the propriety of the word will be seen. The mustard plant does not grow to a very great height, so that St Luke's expression "waxed a great tree" must not be pressed. Dr Thomson (*Land and Book*) mentions as an exceptional instance that he found it on the plain of Akkar as tall as a horse and its rider.

33. *leaven*] Except in this one parable, leaven is used of the working of evil; cp. "A little leaven leaveneth the whole lump," Gal. v. 9; 1 Cor. v. 6; and "purge out therefore the old leaven," 1 Cor. v. 7. So, too, in the Rabbinical writings. This thought probably arose from the prohibition of leaven during the paschal season. But the secrecy and the all-pervading character of leaven aptly symbolize the growth of Christianity, (1) as a society penetrating everywhere by a subtle and

34 three measures of meal, till the whole was leavened. All
these *things* spake Jesus unto the multitude in parables; and
35 without a parable spake he not unto them: that it might be
fulfilled which was spoken by the prophet, saying, I will
open my mouth in parables; I will utter *things which
have been* kept secret from the foundation of the
world.

36—43. *Explanation of the Parable of the Tares.*

36 Then Jesus sent the multitude away, and went into the
house: and his disciples came unto him, saying, Declare
37 unto us the parable of the tares of the field. He answered
and said unto them, He that soweth the good seed is the
38 Son of man; the field is the world; the good seed are the
children of the kingdom; but the tares are the children of
39 the wicked one; the enemy that sowed them is the devil;
the harvest is the end of the world; and the reapers are *the*
40 angels. As therefore the tares are gathered and burnt in
41 the fire; so shall it be in the end of this world. The Son of

mysterious operation until in this light—as a secret brotherhood—it appeared dangerous to the Roman empire; (2) as an influence unfelt at *first* growing up within the human soul.

Compare Sir Bartle Frere on *Indian Missions*, p. 9; speaking of the gradual change wrought by Christianity in India, he says, in regard to religious innovations in general: "They are always subtle in operation, and generally little noticeable at the outset in comparison with the power of their ultimate operation."

three measures] Literally, *three* **seahs**. In Gen. xviii. 6, Abraham bids Sarah "make ready three 'seahs' of fine meal, knead it and make cakes upon the hearth."

35. Ps. lxxviii. 2. The quotation does not agree verbally with the LXX. It is a direct translation of the Hebrew. The psalm which follows these words is a review of the history of Israel from the Exodus to the reign of David. This indicates the somewhat wide sense given to "parables" and "dark sayings."

36—43. EXPLANATION OF THE PARABLE OF THE TARES, in St Matthew only.

39. *the end of the world*] Literally, **the completion of this æon**, "the point where one æon ends and another begins." The expression is found also in *vv.* 40 and 49 of this chapter, and in ch. xxiv. 3, xxviii. 20, and in Hebr. ix. 26, "the completion of the æons," not elsewhere in N. T.

man shall send forth his angels, and they shall gather out of
his kingdom all things that offend, and them which do
iniquity; and shall cast them into a furnace of fire: there 42
shall be wailing and gnashing of teeth. Then shall the 43
righteous shine forth as the sun in the kingdom of their
Father. Who hath ears to hear, let him hear.

44. *The Parable of the Hid Treasure.*

Again, the kingdom of heaven is like unto treasure hid in 44
a field; the which when a man hath found, he hideth, and
for joy thereof goeth and selleth all that he hath, and buyeth
that field.

45, 46. *The Parable of the Pearl of Great Price.*

Again, the kingdom of heaven is like unto a merchant 45
man, seeking goodly pearls: who, when he had found one 46

43. *Then shall the righteous shine forth as the sun*] Cp. Dan. xii. 3, "Then they that be wise shall shine as the brightness of the firmament."

44. THE PARABLE OF THE HID TREASURE, in this Gospel only.

In ancient times, and in an unsettled country like Palestine, where there were no banks, in the modern sense, it was a common practice to conceal treasures in the ground. Even at this day the Arabs are keenly alive to the chance of finding such buried stores. The dishonesty of the purchaser must be excluded from the *thought* of the parable. The *unexpected* discovery, the consequent excitement and joy, and the eagerness to buy at any sacrifice, are the points to be observed in the interpretation.

when a man hath found] Here the kingdom of heaven presents itself unexpectedly, "Christ is found of one who sought Him not." The woman of Samaria, the jailer at Philippi, the centurion by the Cross.

selleth all that he hath] This is the renunciation which is always needed for the winning of the kingdom, cp. ch. x. 38. Thus Paul gave up position, Matthew wealth, Barnabas lands.

buyeth that field] Puts himself in a position to attain the kingdom.

45, 46. THE PARABLE OF THE PEARL OF GREAT PRICE, in St Matthew only.

Here the story is of one who succeeds in getting what he strives to obtain. The Jewish or the Greek "seekers after God," possessing many pearls, but still dissatisfied, sought others yet more choice, and finding one, true to the simplicity in Christ, renounce all for that; the one his legalism, the other his philosophy.

pearl of great price, went and sold all that he had, and bought it.

47—50. *The Parable of the Net.*

47 Again, the kingdom of heaven is like unto a net, *that was*
48 cast into the sea, and gathered of every kind: which, when
it was full, they drew to shore, and sat down, and gathered
49 the good into vessels, but cast the bad away. So shall it be
at the end of the world: the angels shall come forth, and
50 sever the wicked from among the just, and shall cast them
into the furnace of fire: there shall be wailing and gnashing
of teeth.

51, 52. *The Scribes of the Kingdom of Heaven.*

51 Jesus saith unto them, Have ye understood all these
52 *things?* They say unto him, Yea, Lord. Then said he unto
them, Therefore every scribe *which is* instructed unto the

47—50. The Parable of the Net, in St Matthew only.

47. *a net, that was cast into the sea*] The reference is to the large drag-net or *seine* [Greek σαγήνη—the word in the text—hence *sagena* (Vulgate) and English *sean* or *seine*]. One end of the *seine* is held on the shore, the other is hauled off by a boat and then returned to the land. In this way a large number of fishes of all kinds is enclosed. Seine-fishing is still practised on the coasts of Devonshire and Cornwall.

The teaching of this parable partly coincides with that of the parable of the Tares (*vv.* 24—30). In both are exhibited the mixture of good and evil in the visible Church, and the final separation of them. But here the thought is specially directed to the ingathering of the Church. The ministers of Christ will of necessity draw converts of diverse character, good and evil, and actuated by different motives. From the parable of the Tares we learn not to reject any from within the Church, in the hope of expelling the element of evil. It is a parable of the settled Church. This is a missionary parable. It teaches that as a matter of history or of fact, no barrier or external test will serve to exclude the unworthy convert.

51, 52. The Scribes of the Kingdom of Heaven.

52. *instructed unto the kingdom of heaven*] The new law requires a new order of Scribes who shall be instructed unto the kingdom of heaven—instructed in its mysteries, its laws, its future—as the Jewish Scribes are instructed in the observances of the Mosaic law.

kingdom of heaven is like unto a man *that is* a householder, which bringeth forth out of his treasure *things* new and old.

53—58. *The Prophet in his own Country.*

And it came to pass, *that* when Jesus had finished these 53
parables, he departed thence. And when he was come into 54
his own country, he taught them in their synagogue, insomuch that they were astonished, and said, Whence hath this
man this wisdom, and *these* mighty works? Is not this the 55
carpenter's son? is not his mother called Mary? and his
brethren, James, and Joses, and Simon, and Judas? And 56
his sisters, are they not all with us? Whence then hath
this *man* all these *things*? And they were offended in him. 57

things new and old] (1) Just as the householder brings from his stores or treasury precious things which have been heir-looms for generations, as well as newly acquired treasures; the disciples following their Master's example will exhibit the true teaching of the old law, and add thereto the new lessons of Christianity. (2) Another interpretation finds a reference to Jewish sacrificial usage by which sometimes the newly-gathered fruit or corn, sometimes the produce of a former year furnished the offering. The wise householder was ready for all emergencies. So the Christian teacher will have an apt lesson on each occasion.

53—58. THE PROPHET IN HIS OWN COUNTRY. Mark vi. 1—6. where the incident is placed between the cure of Jairus' daughter and the mission of the Twelve, Luke iv. 16—30, where our Lord's discourse in the synagogue is given at length. But many commentators hold with great probability that St Luke's narrative refers to a different and earlier visit to Nazareth.

54. *his own country*] Nazareth and the neighbourhood.

55. *the carpenter's son*] "Is not this the carpenter?" (Mark). As every Jew was taught a trade there would be no improbability in the carpenter's son becoming a scribe. But it was known that Jesus had not had the ordinary education of a scribe.

his brethren] Probably the sons of Joseph and Mary. It is certain that no other view would ever have been propounded except for the assumption that the blessed Virgin remained ever-virgin.

Two theories have been mooted in support of this assumption. (1) The "brethren of the Lord" were His cousins, being sons of Clopas (or Alphæus), and Mary, a sister of the Virgin Mary. (2) They were sons of Joseph by a former marriage.

Neither of these theories derives any support from the direct words of Scripture, and some facts tend to disprove either. The second theory is the least open to objection on the ground of language, and of the facts of the gospel.

But Jesus said unto them, A prophet is not without honour,
58 save in his own country, and in his own house. And he did
not many mighty works there, because of their unbelief.

1—12. *Herod the Tetrarch puts to death John the Baptist.*

14 At that time Herod the tetrarch heard of the fame of
2 Jesus, and said unto his servants, This is John the Baptist;

CH. XIV. **1—12.** HEROD THE TETRARCH PUTS TO DEATH JOHN THE BAPTIST.

Mark vi. 14—29, where the further conjectures as to the personality of Jesus are given, "Elias, a [or the] prophet, or as one of the prophets," and the whole account is narrated in the vivid dramatic manner of St Mark. St Luke relates the cause of the imprisonment, iii. 19, 20; the conjectures as to Jesus, ix. 7—9.

1. *At that time*] During the missionary journey of the Twelve. See Mark loc. cit.

Herod] Herod Antipas, tetrarch of Galilee and Peræa. He was a son of Herod the Great, and Malthakè, a Samaritan, who was also the mother of Archelaus and Olympias. He was thus of Gentile origin, and his early associations were Gentile, for he was brought up at Rome with his brother Archelaus. He married first a daughter of Aretas, king of Arabia, and afterwards, while his first wife was still living, he married Herodias, wife of his half-brother Philip,—who was living in a private station, and must not be confused with Philip the tetrarch of Iturea. Cruel, scheming, irresolute, and wicked, he was a type of the worst of tyrants. He intrigued to have the title of tetrarch changed for the higher title of king; very much as Charles the Bold, of Burgundy, endeavoured to change his dukedom into a kingdom. In pursuance of this scheme Antipas went to Rome "to receive for himself a kingdom and return" (Luke xix. 12). He was however foiled in this attempt by the arts of his nephew Agrippa, and was eventually banished to Lyons, being accused of confederacy with Sejanus, and of an intention to revolt. Herodias was his worst enemy: she advised the two most fatal errors of his reign: the execution of John Baptist, which brought him into enmity with the Jews, and the attempt to gain the royal title, the result of which was his fall and banishment. But there is a touch of nobility in the determination she took to share her husband's exile as she had shared his days of prosperity. For Herod's designs against our Lord, see Luke xiii. 31; and for the part which he took in the Passion, see Luke xxiii. 6—12.

the tetrarch] Literally, the ruler of a fourth part or district into which a province was divided; afterwards the name was extended to denote generally a petty king, the ruler of a provincial district. Deiotarus, whose cause Cicero supported, was tetrarch of Galatia. He is called king by Appian, just as Herod Antipas is called king, *v.* 9, and Mark vi. 14.

he is risen from the dead; and therefore mighty works do
shew forth themselves in him. For Herod had laid hold on 3
John, and bound him, and put *him* in prison for Herodias'
sake, his brother Philip's wife. For John said unto him, It 4
is not lawful for thee to have her. And when he would 5
have put him to death, he feared the multitude, because they
counted him as a prophet. But when Herod's birthday was 6
kept, the daughter of Herodias danced before them, and

2. *he*] The Greek is emphatic, "he himself," "in his own person."

risen from the dead] A proof that Herod did not hold the Sadducean doctrine, that there is no resurrection.

and therefore] In consequence of having risen from the dead he is thought to be possessed of larger powers. Alford remarks that this incidentally confirms St John's statement (ch. x. 41), that John wrought no miracle while living.

mighty works do shew forth themselves] Literally, **works of power are active in him.**

3. *in prison*] At Machærus, in Peræa, on the eastern side of the Dead Sea, near the southern frontier of the tetrarchy. Here Antipas had a palace and a prison under one roof, as was common in the East. Cp. Nehemiah iii. 25, "The tower which lieth out from the king's high house that was by the court of the prison." It was the ordinary arrangement in feudal castles. At Machærus, now M'khaur, remains of buildings are still visible. These are probably the ruins of the Baptist's prison. Herod was living in this border fortress in order to prosecute the war with his offended father-in-law, Aretas. He was completely vanquished—a disaster popularly ascribed to his treatment of John the Baptist.

4. *It is not lawful for thee to have her*] St Luke adds, iii. 19, that Herod was also reproved "for all the evil which he had done." "Boldly to rebuke vice" is fixed upon as the leading characteristic of the Baptist in the collect for St John the Baptist's day.

to have her] i. e. "to **marry** her," a force which the word in the original bears, cp. 1 Cor. v. 1.

5. *when he would*] In modern language "although he was willing." From St Mark we learn that Herodias was eager to kill John, while Herod, partly from fear of his prisoner, partly from interest in him, refused to take away his life. St Mark's narrative gives a picture of the inner court intrigues, and bears evidence of keen questioning of some eye-witness as to facts. Possibly some of Herod's own household were secret adherents of John.

feared the multitude, &c.] The same motive that held the tyrant's hand, checked the arguments of the Pharisees, ch. xxi. 26.

6. *the daughter of Herodias*] Salome; she was afterwards married to her uncle Herod-Philip, the tetrarch, and on his death to Aristobulus, grandson of Herod the Great.

danced before them] Some sort of pantomimic dance is meant. Horace

7 pleased Herod. Whereupon he promised with an oath to
8 give her whatsoever she would ask. And she, being before
instructed of her mother, said, Give me here John Baptist's
9 head in a charger. And the king was sorry: nevertheless
for the oaths' sake, and them which sat with him at meat, he
10 commanded *it* to be given *her*. And he sent, and beheaded
11 John in the prison. And his head was brought in a charger,
and given to the damsel: and she brought *it* to her mother.
12 And his disciples came, and took up the body, and buried
it, and went and told Jesus.

13—21. *Jesus retires to a Desert Place, where He feeds Five Thousand.*

13 When Jesus heard *of it*, he departed thence by ship into a
desert place apart: and when the people had heard *thereof*,

notes as one of the signs of national decay that even highborn maidens learnt the voluptuous dances of the East. Herod would recall similar scenes at Rome. See note *v.* 1.

8. *instructed*] Rather, **impelled, instigated.**

a charger] The original word = "a flat wooden trencher" on which meat was served. This appears to have been the meaning of the old English word "charger," which is connected with *cargo* and with French *charger*, and signified originally that on which a load is placed, hence a dish.

9. *for the oaths' sake*] "Because of the *oaths*;" he had sworn repeatedly.

11. *brought it to her mother*] The revenge of Herodias recalls the story of Fulvia, who treated with great indignity the head of her murdered enemy Cicero, piercing the tongue once so eloquent against her. Both are instances of "furens quid femina possit."

12. *his disciples came, and took up the body, and buried it*] There is in this some proof of forbearance, if not of kindness, on Herod's part. He did not persecute John's disciples, or prevent them paying the last offices to their master.

13—21. Jesus retires to a Desert Place, where He feeds Five Thousand.

Mark vi. 31—44; Luke ix. 10—17; John vi. 5—14.

This is the only miracle narrated by all the Evangelists. In St John it prepares the way for the memorable discourse on the "Bread of Life." St John also mentions, as a result of this miracle, the desire of the people "to take Him by force and make Him a king." There is a question as to the locality of the miracle. St Luke says (ch. ix. 10) that Jesus "went aside privately into a desert place *belonging to a city called Bethsaida*." St Mark (ch. vi. 45) describes the disciples as crossing to

they followed him on foot out of the cities. And Jesus went 14
forth, and saw a great multitude, and was moved with compassion toward them, and he healed their sick. And when 15
it was evening, his disciples came to him, saying, *This* is a
desert place, and the time is now past; send the multitude
away, that they may go into the villages, and buy themselves
victuals. But Jesus said unto them, They need not depart; 16
give ye them to eat. And they say unto him, We have here 17
but five loaves, and two fishes. He said, Bring them hither 18
to me. And he commanded the multitude to sit down on 19
the grass, and took the five loaves, and the two fishes, and
looking up to heaven, he blessed, and brake, and gave the
loaves to *his* disciples, and the disciples to the multitude.
And they did all eat, and were filled: and they took up of 20
the fragments that remained twelve baskets full. And they 21

Bethsaida after the miracle. The general inference has been that there were two Bethsaidas; Bethsaida Julias, near the mouth of the Jordan (where the miracle is usually said to have taken place), and another Bethsaida, mentioned in the parallel passage in St Mark and possibly John i. 44. But the Sinaitic MS. omits the words in italics from Luke, and at John vi. 23 reads, "When, therefore, the boats came from Tiberias, which was nigh unto the place where they did eat bread." If these readings be accepted, the scene of the miracle must be placed near Tiberias; the Bethsaida of Mark, to which the disciples crossed, will be the well-known Bethsaida Julias, and the other supposed Bethsaida will disappear even from the researches of travellers.

15. *And when it was evening*] In the Jewish division of the day there were two evenings. According to the most probable view the space of time called "between the evenings" (Ex. xii. 6) was from the ninth to the eleventh hour. Hence the first evening ended at 3 o'clock, the second began at 5 o'clock. In this verse the first evening is meant, in *v.* 23 the second.

19. *to sit down on the grass*] Rather, **grassy places.** St Mark and St Luke mention that they sat in companies "by hundreds and by fifties" (Mark), "by fifties" (Luke). St John notes the time of year; "the passover, a feast of the Jews, was nigh."

20. *they took up of the fragments*] The Greek word for fragments is connected with the verb "to break" in the preceding verse. The true meaning of the word is therefore "the portions broken off for distribution."

twelve baskets] The same word *kophinoi* is used for baskets in the four accounts of this miracle, and also by our Lord, when He refers to the miracle (ch. xvi. 9); whereas a different word is used in describing the feeding of four thousand and in the reference made to that event by our Lord (ch. xvi. 10). The Roman poet Juvenal describes a large provision-basket of this kind, together with a bundle of hay, as being

that had eaten were about five thousand men, beside women and children.

22—33. *The Disciples cross from the Scene of the Miracle to Bethsaida.*

22 And straightway Jesus constrained his disciples to get
into a ship, and to go before him unto the other side, while
23 he sent the multitudes away. And when he had sent the
multitudes away, he went up into a mountain apart to pray:
24 and when the evening was come, he was there alone. But
the ship was now in the midst of the sea, tossed with waves:
25 for the wind was contrary. And in the fourth watch of the
26 night Jesus went unto them, walking on the sea. And when
the disciples saw him walking on the sea, they were troubled,
27 saying, It is a spirit; and they cried out for fear. But straightway Jesus spake unto them, saying, Be of good cheer; it is

part of the equipment of the Jewish mendicants who thronged the grove of Egeria at Rome. The motive for this custom was to avoid ceremonial impurity in eating or in resting at night.

22—33. The Disciples cross from the Scene of the Miracle to Bethsaida.

Mark vi. 45—52; John vi. 15—21.

St Matthew alone narrates St Peter's endeavour to walk on the sea.

22. *a ship*] **the** ship or **their** ship.

23. *when the evening was come*] See *v.* 15.

he was there alone] This is a simple but sublime thought:—the solitary watch on the lonely mountain, the communion in prayer with the Father throughout the beautiful Eastern night.

24. *tossed with waves*] The expression in the original is forcible, "tortured by the waves," writhing in throes of agony, as it were. These sudden storms are very characteristic of the Lake of Gennesaret.

25. *in the fourth watch*] i.e. early in the morning. Cp. "Et jam quarta canit venturam buccina lucem," Propert. IV. 4. 63. At this time the Jews had adopted the Greek and Roman custom of four night watches. Formerly they divided the night into three watches, or rather according to Lightfoot (*Hor. Heb.*) the Romans and Jews alike recognised four watches, but with the Jews the fourth watch was regarded as morning, and was not included in the three watches of "deep night." The four watches are named (Mark xiii. 35) 1 Even; 2 Midnight; 3 Cockcrowing; 4 Morning. St John states that they had rowed 25 or 30 furlongs.

Jesus went unto them] Mark adds "He would have passed by them."

I, be not afraid. And Peter answered him and said, Lord, 28
if it be thou, bid me come unto thee on the water. And he 29
said, Come. And when Peter was come down out of the
ship, he walked on the water, to go to Jesus. But when he 30
saw the wind boysterous, he was afraid; and beginning to
sink, he cried, saying, Lord, save me. And immediately 31
Jesus stretched forth *his* hand, and caught him, and said
unto him, O thou of little faith, wherefore didst thou doubt?
And when they were come into the ship, the wind ceased. 32
Then they that were in the ship came and worshipped him, 33
saying, Of a truth thou art the Son of God.

34—36. *Jesus cures sick folk in the Land of Gennesaret.*

And when they were gone over, they came into the land 34
of Gennesaret. And when the men of that place had know- 35
ledge of him, they sent out into all that country round about,
and brought unto him all that were diseased; and besought 36
him that they might only touch the hem of his garment: and
as many as touched were made perfectly whole.

29. *And he said, Come*] The boat was so near that the voice of Jesus could be heard even through the storm, though the wind was strong and the oarsmen labouring and perhaps calling out to one another. The hand of the Saviour was quite close to the sinking disciple.

33. *the Son of God*] See note, ch. iv. 6.

34—36. Jesus cures sick folk in the Land of Gennesaret.

Mark vi. 53—56, where the stir of the neighbourhood and eagerness of the people are vividly portrayed.

34. *the land of Gennesaret*] By this is meant the plain of Gennesaret, two miles and a half in length and about one mile in breadth. Modern travellers speak of "its charming bays and its fertile soil rich with the scourings of the basaltic hills." Josephus describes the district in glowing terms (*B. J.* III. 10. 8). See *Recovery of Jerusalem*, p. 351.

36. *the hem of his garment*] The hem of the garment had a certain sanctity attached to it. It was the distinguishing mark of the Jew: cp. Numbers xv. 38, 39, "that they add to the fringes of the borders (or corners) a thread of blue." At each corner of the robe there was a tassel; each tassel had a conspicuous blue thread symbolical of the heavenly origin of the Commandments. The other threads were white.

as many as touched were made perfectly whole] Cp. the case of the woman with an issue of blood, ch. ix. 20—22.

1—20. *The True Religion and the False. A Discourse to the Pharisees, the People, and the Disciples.*

15 Then came to Jesus scribes and Pharisees, which were of
2 Jerusalem, saying, Why do thy disciples transgress the tradition of the elders? for they wash not their hands when they
3 eat bread. But he answered and said unto them, Why do
you also transgress the commandment of God by your tra-
4 dition? For God commanded, saying, Honour thy father
and mother: and, He that curseth father or mother,
5 let him die the death. But ye say, Whosoever shall say
to *his* father or *his* mother, *It is* a gift, *by* whatsoever thou
6 mightest be profited by me; and honour not his father
or his mother, *he shall be free.* Thus have ye made the
7 commandment of God of none effect by your tradition. *Ye*

CH. XV. 1—20. THE TRUE RELIGION AND THE FALSE. A DISCOURSE TO THE PHARISEES, THE PEOPLE, AND THE DISCIPLES. Mark vii. 1—23.

These twenty verses sum up the great controversy of the N. T., that between the religion of the letter and external observances and the religion of the heart, between what St Paul calls "the righteousness which is of the law and the righteousness which is of God by (or grounded upon) faith," Phil. iii. 9.

1. *scribes and Pharisees, which were of Jerusalem*] Probably a deputation from the Sanhedrin, such as was commissioned to question John the Baptist. Cp. John i. 19.

2. *the tradition of the elders*] The elders, or presbyters, were the Jewish teachers, or scribes, such as Hillel and Shammai. The traditions were the rules or observances of the unwritten law, which they enjoined on their disciples. Many of these were frivolous; some actually subversive of God's law; and yet one Rabbinical saying was, "The words of the law are weighty and light, but all the words of the scribes are weighty."

when] Rather, **whenever**.

4. *For God commanded*] "For Moses said" (Mark).

5. *It is a gift*] Rather, **Let it be a gift**, or "devoted to sacred uses," which the Jews expressed by the word *corban*, found in Mark vii. 11. The scribes held that these words, even when pronounced in spite and anger against parents who needed succour, excused the son from his natural duty; and, on the other hand, did not oblige him really to devote the sum to the service of God or of the temple.

6. *he shall be free*] These words do not occur in the original, either here or in the parallel passage in Mark. It is as if the indignation of Jesus did not allow him to utter the words of acquittal. The silence is more eloquent than the utterance.

hypocrites, well did Esaias prophesy of you, saying, This 8
people draweth nigh unto me with their mouth, and
honoureth me with *their* lips; but their heart is far
from me. But in vain they do worship me, teaching 9
for doctrines the commandments of men.

And he called the multitude, and said unto them, Hear, 10
and understand: not that which goeth into the mouth 11
defileth a man; but that which cometh out of the mouth,
this defileth a man. Then came his disciples, and said 12
unto him, Knowest thou that the Pharisees were offended,
after they heard *this* saying? But he answered and said, 13
Every plant, which my heavenly Father hath not planted, shall
be rooted up. Let them alone: they be blind leaders of the 14
blind. And if the blind lead the blind, both shall fall into
the ditch. Then answered Peter and said unto him, Declare 15
unto us this parable. And Jesus said, Are ye also yet 16
without understanding? Do not ye yet understand, that 17

7. *well did Esaias prophesy*] A common Jewish formula for quoting a saying of the prophets.

8, 9. Isaiah xxix. 13. The quotation does not follow precisely either the LXX. version or the Hebrew text.

10. *he called the multitude*] The moment our Lord turns to the people, His teaching is by parables.

This appeal to the multitude as worthier than the Pharisees to receive the divine truths is significant of the popular character of the Kingdom of heaven.

11. *defileth*] Literally, **maketh common**; cp. "common or unclean," Acts x. 14. "The Pharisees esteemed 'defiled' men for '*common* and vulgar' men; on the contrary, a religious man among men is 'a *singular* man.'" Lightfoot *ad loc.*

12. *the Pharisees were offended*] A proof of the influence of the Pharisees. The disciples believed that Christ would be concerned to have offended those who stood so high in popular favour.

13. *Every plant*] Not a wild flower, but a cultivated plant or tree; the word occurs here only in N. T.; in LXX. version of O. T. it is used of the vine, the most carefully cultivated plant; 2 Kings xix. 29; Ezek. xvii. 7; Mic. i. 6; and in one other passage, Gen. xxi. 33, of the tamarisk. Here the plant cultivated by human hands—the vine that is not the true vine of Israel—is the doctrine of the Pharisees.

14. *blind leaders of the blind*] The proverb which follows is quoted in a different connection, Luke vi. 39; cp. also ch. xxiii. 16.

fall into the ditch] Palestine abounded in dangers of this kind, from unguarded wells, quarries, and pitfalls; it abounded also in persons afflicted with blindness. See note ch. ix. 27.

whatsoever entereth in at the mouth goeth into the belly,
18 and is cast out into the draught? But those *things* which
proceed out of the mouth come forth from the heart; and
19 they defile the man. For out of the heart proceed evil
thoughts, murders, adulteries, fornications, thefts, false
20 witness, blasphemies: these are *the things* which defile a
man: but to eat with unwashen hands defileth not a man.

21—28. *The Daughter of a Canaanite Woman is cured.*

21 Then Jesus went thence, and departed into the coasts of
22 Tyre and Sidon. And behold, a woman of Canaan came
out of the same coasts, and cried unto him, saying, Have

16. *without understanding*] Cp. the "spiritual understanding," Col. i. 9, and "knowledge in the mystery of Christ," Ephes. iii. 4.

19. *For out of the heart proceed*] The enumeration follows the order of the Commandments. Evil thoughts—harmful reasonings—form a class under which the rest fall, indicating, too, that the transgression of the Commandments is often in thought, by Christ's law, not in deed only. For "blasphemies," which may be thought to sum up the first table, St Mark, whose order differs slightly, has "covetousness," thus completing the decalogue, and adds to the list in the text "wickedness, deceit, lasciviousness, an evil eye, pride, foolishness."

The plurals "murders, adulteries," &c., as Meyer points out, denote the different instances and kinds of murder and adultery. Murder includes far more than the act of bloodshed.

21—28. THE DAUGHTER OF A CANAANITE WOMAN IS CURED.
Mark vii. 24—30.

This narrative of faith without external observance or knowledge of the Law affords a suggestive contrast to the preceding discourse.

21. *the coasts*] The neighbourhood, district, not the sea-shore, as might be thought.

22. *a woman of Canaan*] Called in Mark "a Greek, a Syrophœnician by nation." The two expressions are identical, for the land of Canaan, literally, the **low lands** or **netherlands**, at first applicable to the whole of Palestine, was confined in later times to the maritime plain of Phœnicia. In Joshua v. 12 "the land of Canaan" appears in the LXX. version as the "land of the Phœnicians." The important point is that this woman was a foreigner and a heathen—a descendant of the worshippers of Baal. She may have heard and seen Jesus in earlier days. Cp. Mark iii. 8, "they about Tyre and Sidon...came unto him."

out of the same coasts] Literally, **those coasts**. Jesus did not himself pass beyond the borders of Galilee, but this instance of mercy extended to a Gentile points to the wide diffusion of the Gospel beyond the Jewish race.

mercy on me, O Lord, *thou* Son of David; my daughter is
grievously vexed with a devil. But he answered her not a 23
word. And his disciples came and besought him, saying,
Send her away; for she crieth after us. But he answered 24
and said, I am not sent but unto the lost sheep of the house
of Israel. Then came she and worshipped him, saying, 25
Lord, help me. But he answered and said, It is not meet 26
to take the children's bread, and to cast *it* to dogs. And 27
she said, Truth, Lord: yet the dogs eat of the crumbs which
fall from their masters' table. Then Jesus answered and 28
said unto her, O woman, great *is* thy faith: be it unto thee

Have mercy on me] Identifying herself with her daughter. Cp. the prayer of the father of the lunatic child: "Have compassion on *us* and help *us*," Mark ix. 22.

Son of David] A title that proves the expectation that the Messiah should spring from the house of David. It is the particular Messianic prophecy which would be most likely to reach foreign countries.

23. *answered her not a word*] Jesus, by this refusal, tries the woman's faith, that he may purify and deepen it. Her request must be won by earnest prayer, "lest the light winning should make light the prize."

Observe that Christ first refuses by silence, then by express words.

Send her away] By granting what she asks, by yielding, like the unjust judge, to her importunity.

24. *I am not sent but unto the lost sheep of the house of Israel*] Jesus came to save all, but His personal ministry was confined, with few exceptions, to the Jews.

The thought of Israel as a flock of sheep lost on the mountains is beautifully drawn out, Ezekiel xxxiv.; "My flock was scattered upon all the face of the earth, and none did search or seek after them," (*v.* 6.) Read the whole chapter.

26. *to take the children's bread, and to cast it to dogs*] The "children" are the Jews; the "dogs" are the Gentiles. This was the name applied by the Jews to all outside the chosen race, the dog being in the East a symbol of impurity. St Paul, regarding the Christian Church as the true Israel, terms the Judaizing teachers "dogs," Phil. iii. 2. Christ's words, as reported by St Mark (ch. vii. 27), contain a gleam of hope, "Let the children first be filled."

27. *yet the dogs eat of the crumbs*] "Yet," of the E. V., is misleading. Translate "**for even**;" the woman takes Jesus at his word, accepts the name of reproach, and claims the little share that falls even to the dogs. No need to cast the children's bread to the dogs, for even the dogs have crumbs from the Master's hands.

the crumbs] Probably as in E. V., not, as Trench suggests, the pieces of bread used by the guests to wipe their hands on and then thrown to the dogs.

even as thou wilt. And her daughter was made whole from
that *very* hour.

29—31. *Jesus returns to the high land of Galilee, and cures many Blind, Dumb, and Lame.*

29 And Jesus departed from thence, and came nigh unto
the sea of Galilee; and went up into a mountain, and
30 sat down there. And great multitudes came unto him,
having with them *those that were* lame, blind, dumb,
maimed, and many others, and cast them *down* at Jesus'
31 feet; and he healed them: insomuch that the multitude
wondered, when they saw the dumb to speak, the maimed
to be whole, the lame to walk, and the blind to see: and
they glorified the God of Israel.

32—38. *Four thousand Men, besides women and children, are miraculously fed.*

32 Then Jesus called his disciples unto *him*, and said, I have
compassion on the multitude, because they continue with
me now three days, and have nothing to eat: and I will not
33 send them away fasting, lest they faint in the way. And his
disciples say unto him, Whence should we have so much
34 bread in the wilderness, as to fill so great a multitude? And
Jesus saith unto them, How many loaves have ye? And
35 they said, Seven, and a few little fishes. And he com-
36 manded the multitude to sit down on the ground. And he
took the seven loaves and the fishes, and gave thanks, and
brake *them*, and gave to his disciples, and the disciples to

their masters' table] The "Masters" must be interpreted to mean God, not, as by some, the Jewish people.

29—31. JESUS RETURNS TO THE HIGH LAND OF GALILEE, AND CURES MANY BLIND, DUMB, AND LAME.

Mark vii. 31—37, where, not content with the general statement, the Evangelist describes one special case of healing.

29. *a mountain*] Rather, the *mountain country*; the high land, as distinguished from the low land, which He had left.

32—38. FOUR THOUSAND MEN, BESIDES WOMEN AND CHILDREN, ARE MIRACULOUSLY FED.

Mark viii. 1—9.

36. *gave to his disciples*] St Matthew uses the aorist, St Mark the more vivid imperfect "kept giving."

the multitude. And they did all eat, and were filled: and 37
they took up of the broken *meat* that was left seven baskets
full. And they that did eat were four thousand men, beside 38
women and children.

39—XVI. 4. *Jesus at Magdala, or Magadan, is tempted to give a Sign.*

And he sent away the multitude, and took ship, and came 39
into the coasts of Magdala. The Pharisees also with the 16
Sadducees came, and tempting desired him that *he* would
shew them a sign from heaven. He answered and said 2
unto them, When it is evening, ye say, *It will be* fair

37. *seven baskets*] *Spurides*, see note ch. xiv. 20, and Acts ix. 25, where St Paul is said to have been let down from the wall of Damascus in a *spuris*, probably a large basket made of rope-net, possibly a fisherman's basket. Why the disciples brought different kinds of baskets on the two occasions we cannot determine.

the broken meat that was left] See ch. xiv. 20. One side of the lesson is the lavishness of Providence. God gives even more than we require or ask for. But the leading thought is a protest against waste.

39—XVI. 4. JESUS AT MAGDALA, OR MAGADAN, IS TEMPTED TO GIVE A SIGN. Mark viii. 10—12; Luke xii. 54—57.

took ship] Literally, **went on board the ship.**

the coasts of Magdala] The MSS. vary between Magdala and Magadan. The latter reading, however, has by far the highest authority in its favour. It is probable that the familiar Magdala supplanted in the text the more obscure Magadan. Magdala or Migdol (a watch tower) is identified with the modern *Mejdel*, a collection of ruins and squalid huts at the S.E. corner of the plain of Gennesaret, opposite to K'hersa or Gergesa. This is the point where the lake is broadest. Prof. Rawlinson thinks that this Magdala may be the Magdolus of Herodotus, II. 159; unless indeed by a confusion curiously similar to that in the text, Herodotus has mistaken Migdol for Megiddo. Magdala was probably the home of Mary Magdalene.

xvi. 1. *The Pharisees also with the Sadducees*] "The Pharisees" (Mark). The coalition between these opposing sects can only be accounted for by the uniting influence of a strong common hostility against Jesus.

a sign from heaven] They could not perceive the inner beauty of Christ's teaching, but they would follow the rules of a Rabbi who, like one of the ancient prophets, should give an external sign—a darkening of the glowing sky—a flash of light—a peal of thunder. The answer of Christ teaches that the signs of the times, the events of the day, are the signs of God, the signs that Christ gives.

3 weather: for the sky is red. And in the morning, *It will
be* foul weather to day: for the sky is red and lowring. O
ye hypocrites, ye can discern the face of the sky; but can ye
4 not *discern* the signs of the times? A wicked and adulterous
generation seeketh after a sign; and there shall no sign be
given unto it, but the sign of the prophet Jonas. And he
left them, and departed.

5—12. *The Leaven of the Pharisees and of the Sadducees.*

5 And when his disciples were come to the other side, they
6 had forgotten to take bread. Then Jesus said unto them,
Take heed and beware of the leaven of the Pharisees and
7 *of the* Sadducees. And they reasoned among themselves,
8 saying, *It is* because we have taken no bread. *Which* when
Jesus perceived, he said unto them, O ye of little faith, why
reason ye among yourselves, because ye have brought no
9 bread? Do ye not yet understand, neither remember the
five loaves of the five thousand, and how many baskets ye

3. *the face of the sky*] Perhaps Jesus and his questioners were looking across the lake towards the cliffs of Gergesa, with the sky red from the reflected sunset. In Luke the signs are "a cloud rising in the west" and the blowing of the "south wind."

the signs of the times] Which point in many ways to the fulfilment of prophecy, and to the presence of Christ among men.

4. *adulterous*] See ch. xii. 39.

the sign of the prophet Jonas] See ch. xii. 39—41. The words in Mark viii. 12 are "there shall no sign be given unto this generation," i. e. no such sign as they demanded.

5—12. THE LEAVEN OF THE PHARISEES AND OF THE SADDUCEES. Mark viii. 14—21, where the rebuke of Christ is given more at length in stirring language; and Luke xii. 1, where the context is different.

7. *It is because we have taken no bread*] "Neither had they more than one loaf" (Mark). It is possible that Jesus may have employed figurative language even more than was usual with Eastern teachers; certainly this special metaphorical use of leaven was new. See Lightfoot *ad loc.* Again, the Pharisees had rules of their own as to what kind of leaven it was lawful to use, and what kind it was right to avoid. Hence it was not strange that the disciples should imagine that their Master was laying down similar rules for their guidance.

The error of the disciples was twofold; (1) they took "leaven" in a literal sense, (2) they thought Jesus intended a rebuke to their forgetfulness. The first (1) implied a want of spiritual insight; the second (2) a want of trust.

took up? Neither the seven loaves of the four thousand, 10
and how many baskets ye took up? How *is it that* ye do 11
not understand that I spake *it* not to you concerning bread,
that *ye* should beware of the leaven of the Pharisees and *of*
the Sadducees? Then understood they how that he bade 12
them not beware of the leaven of bread, but of the doctrine
of the Pharisees and *of the* Sadducees.

13—20. *The great Confession of St Peter, and the Promise given to him.*

When Jesus came into the coasts of Cesarea Philippi, he 13
asked his disciples, saying, Whom do men say that I the Son
of man am? And they said, Some *say that thou art* John the 14
Baptist: some, Elias; and others, Jeremias, or one of the
prophets. He saith unto them, But whom say ye that I 15
am? And Simon Peter answered and said, Thou art the 16

12. *Then understood they*] The Greek word and its derivative is used specially of spiritual intelligence.

13—20. THE GREAT CONFESSION OF ST PETER, AND THE PROMISE GIVEN TO HIM.

Mark viii. 27—30: The question is put "while they were on the way," the words "the Son of the living God" are omitted, as also the blessing on Peter. Luke ix. 18—20: Jesus was engaged in prayer alone; the words of the confession are "the Christ of God;" the blessing on Peter is omitted.

13. *Cesarea Philippi*] The most northerly point reached by our Lord. The city was rebuilt by Herod-Philip, who called it by his own name to distinguish it from Cæsarea Stratonis on the sea coast, the seat of the Roman government, and the scene of St Paul's imprisonment.

The Greek name of this Cæsarea was Paneas, which survives in the modern Banias. Cæsarea was beautifully placed on a rocky terrace under Mount Hermon, a few miles east of Dan, the old frontier city of Israel. The cliffs near this spot, where the Messiah was first acknowledged, bear marks of the worship of Baal and of Pan. See *Recovery of Jerusalem*, and Tristram's *Land of Israel.*

Son of man] See note ch. viii. 20. The question of Jesus is: In what sense do the people believe me to be the Son of man? In the sense which Daniel intended or in a lower sense? Observe the antithesis in Peter's answer:—the Son of man is the Son of God.

14. *Jeremias*] Named by St Matthew only. He is mentioned as a representative of the Prophets, because in the Jewish Canon the book of Jeremiah came first of the Prophets, following the books of Kings. See Lightfoot, on ch. xxvii. 9.

17 Christ, the Son of the living God. And Jesus answered
and said unto him, Blessed art thou, Simon Bar-jona: for
flesh and blood hath not revealed *it* unto thee, but my
18 Father which is in heaven. And I say also unto thee, That
thou art Peter, and upon this rock I will build my church;

16. *Thou art the Christ, the Son of the living God*] This confession not only sees in Jesus the promised Messiah, but in the Messiah recognises the divine nature. He is more than one of the old prophets risen from the dead.

17. *Bar-jona*] "son of Jonah"; in John i. 42, "son of John," R.V. Bar is Aramaic for son; cp. Bar-abbas, Bar-tholomew, Bar-nabas.

for flesh and blood, &c.] Not man, but God; "flesh and blood" was a common Hebrew expression in this contrast.

18. *Thou art Peter, and upon this rock I will build my church*] Cp. Isaiah xxviii. 16, from which passage probably the expression is drawn. There is a play on the words "Peter" and "rock" which is lost in the E.V. It may be seen in a French rendering, "Tu es Pierre et sur cette pierre je bâtirai mon Eglise."

On these words mainly rest the enormous pretensions of the Roman pontiff. It is therefore important (1) To remember that it is to Peter with the great confession on his lips that the words are spoken. The Godhead of Christ is the keystone of the Church, and Peter is for the moment the representative of the belief in that truth among men. (2) To take the words in reference: (*a*) to other passages of Scripture. The Church is built on the foundation of the Apostles and Prophets, Eph. ii. 20, on Christ Himself, 2 Cor. iii. 11. (*b*) To history; Peter is not an infallible repository of truth. He is rebuked by Paul for Judaizing. Nor does he hold a chief place among the Apostles afterwards. It is James, not Peter, who presides at the Council at Jerusalem. (*c*) To reason: for even if Peter had precedence over the other Apostles, and if he was Bishop of Rome, which is not historically certain, there is no proof that he had a right of conferring such precedence on his successors.

my church] The word *ecclesia* (Church) occurs twice in Matthew and not elsewhere in the Gospels. See note ch. xviii. 17 where the Jewish *ecclesia* is meant. From the analogy of the corresponding Hebrew word, *ecclesia* in a Christian sense may be defined as the congregation of the faithful throughout the world, united under Christ as their Head. The use of the word by Christ implied at least two things: (1) that He was founding an organized society, not merely preaching a doctrine: (2) That the Jewish *ecclesia* was the point of departure for the Christian *ecclesia* and in part its prototype. It is one among many links in this gospel between Jewish and Christian thought. The Greek word (ἐκκλησία) has passed into the language of the Latin nations; *église* (French), *chiesa* (Italian), *iglesia* (Spanish). The derivation of the Teutonic *Church* is very doubtful. That usually given—*Kuriakon* (the Lord's house)—is abandoned by many scholars. The word is probably

and the gates of hell shall not prevail against it. And I 19
will give unto thee the keys of the kingdom of heaven: and
whatsoever thou shalt bind on earth shall be bound in
heaven: and whatsoever thou shalt loose on earth shall be
loosed in heaven. Then charged he his disciples that they 20
should tell no *man* that he was Jesus the Christ.

21—23. *The Passion is foretold.*

From that time forth began Jesus to shew unto his 21
disciples, how that he must go unto Jerusalem, and suffer
many *things* of the elders and chief priests and scribes, and
be killed, and be raised *again* the third day. Then Peter 22

from a Teutonic root and may have been connected with heathen usages. See *Bib. Dict.* Art. *Church.*

the gates of hell] Lit. "the gates of Hades." The Greek *Hades* is the same as the Hebrew *Sheol*, the abode of departed spirits, in which were two divisions *Gehenna* and *Paradise.* "The gates of Hades" are generally interpreted to mean the power of the unseen world, especially the power of death: cp. Rev. i. 18, "the keys of hell (Hades) and of death."

shall not prevail against it] The gates of Hades prevail over all things human, but the Church shall never die.

19. *the keys of the kingdom of heaven*] This expression was not altogether new. To a Jew it would convey a definite meaning. He would think of the symbolic key given to a Scribe when admitted to his office, with which he was to open the treasury of the divine oracles. Peter was to be a Scribe in the kingdom of heaven. He has received authority to teach the truths of the kingdom.

whatsoever thou shalt bind on earth shall be bound in heaven] To bind (cp. ch. xxiii. 4) is to impose an obligation as binding; to loose is to declare a precept not binding. Such expressions as this were common: "The school of Shammai binds it, the school of Hillel looseth it." The power is over things, not persons. The decisions of Peter as an authorized Scribe of the Kingdom of God will be ratified in heaven.

20. *they should tell no man that he was Jesus the Christ*] Lest the Galilæan enthusiasm should endeavour to make Him a king.

21—23. THE PASSION IS FORETOLD.

Mark viii. 31—33; Luke ix. 22. St Luke omits the rebuke to Peter.

21. *From that time forth*] An important note of time. Now that the disciples have learned to acknowledge Jesus to be the Messiah, He is able to instruct them in the true nature of the Kingdom.

elders and chief priests and scribes] = the Sanhedrin. See ch. ii. 4, and xxvi. 3.

be killed] As yet there is no mention of the Roman judge or of the death upon the cross; this truth is broken gradually, see *v.* 24.

took him, and began to rebuke him, saying, Be it far from
23 thee, Lord: this shall not be unto thee. But he turned,
and said unto Peter, Get thee behind me, Satan: thou art
an offence unto me: for thou savourest not the *things* that
be of God, but *those* that be of men.

24—28. *Self-renouncement required in Christ's followers. Their Reward.*

24 Then said Jesus unto his disciples, If any *man* will
come after me, let him deny himself, and take up his
25 cross, and follow me. For whosoever will save his life
shall lose it: and whosoever will lose his life for my
26 sake shall find it. For what is a man profited, if he
shall gain the whole world, and lose his own soul? or what

be raised again the third day] How can the plainness of this intimation be reconciled with the slowness of the disciples to believe in the Resurrection? Not by supposing that obscure hints of the Passion were afterwards put into this explicit form; but rather (1) partly by the blindness of those who will not see; (2) partly by the constant use of metaphor by Jesus. "Might not," they would argue, "this 'death and rising again' be a symbol of a glorious visible kingdom about to issue from our present debasement?"

22. *Be it far from thee, Lord*] Literally, (1) "*may God pity thee,*" i. e. "*give thee a better fate,*" or (2) "*pity thyself.*"

23. *Get thee behind me, Satan*] Peter takes the place of the tempter, and argues for the false kingdom instead of for the true. If the words of the tempter are in Peter's mouth he is addressed as the tempter; when he speaks the words of truth he is the foundation-stone of the Church.

an offence unto me] Literally, **my stumblingblock**; by suggesting visions of earthly pride.

thou savourest not the things that be of God] The Greek word, literally, **to think**, is often used of political partisanship, "to take a side," "thou art not on God's side but on man's." The English "savourest" is connected with Lat. *sapere* through the French *savoir*.

24—28. SELF-RENOUNCEMENT REQUIRED IN CHRIST'S FOLLOWERS. THEIR REWARD. Mark viii. 34—ix. 1; Luke ix. 23—27.

24. *take up his cross*] St Luke adds "daily." The expression, ch. x. 38, differs slightly, "he that taketh not his cross," where see note.

25. *whosoever will save his life shall lose it*] See note, ch. x. 39. Let Christ's follower lose the lower life on his cross, crucify his earthly affections, and he shall win the higher spiritual life here and hereafter.

will save] Not the mere future, but = "shall resolve to save."

26. *and lose his own soul*] The Greek word translated "life" in the

shall a man give in exchange for his soul? For the Son 27
of man shall come in the glory of his Father with his
angels: and then he shall reward every man according to
his works. Verily I say unto you, There be some standing 28
here, which shall not taste of death, till they see the Son of
man coming in his kingdom.

1—13. *The Transfiguration.*

17 And after six days Jesus taketh Peter, James, and John 1
his brother, and bringeth them up into a high mountain

preceding verse is here translated "soul," which is life in its highest phase.

27. *For*] The reason given why the higher life—the soul—is of priceless value: (1) The Judge is at hand who will condemn self-indulgence and all the works of the lower life, and will reward those who have denied themselves. (2) Further (*v.* 28) this judgment shall not be delayed—it is very near. The same motive for the Christian life is adduced by St Paul, Phil. iv. 5, "Let your moderation be known unto all men. The Lord is at hand." Cp. 1 Cor. xvi. 22.

28. *Taste of death*] Compare

The valiant never taste of death but once. *Jul. Caes.* Act. II. 2.

St Matthew's version of this "hard saying" indicates more plainly than the other Synoptic Gospels, the personal presence of Christ. St Mark has, "till they have seen the kingdom of God come with power;" St Luke, "till they see the kingdom of God;" but the meaning in each case is the same. Various solutions are given. The expression is referred to (1) the Transfiguration, (2) the Day of Pentecost, (3) the Fall of Jerusalem. The last best fulfils the conditions of interpretation—a judicial coming—a signal and visible event, and one that would happen in the lifetime of some, but not of all, who were present.

CH. XVII. 1—13. THE TRANSFIGURATION.
Mark ix. 2—13; Luke ix. 28—36.

1. *after six days*] Within a week of Peter's confession. St Luke has "about an eight days after," according to the common Jewish reckoning, by which each part of a day is counted as a day.

Peter, James, and John] The *three* who *were chosen* to be with their Master on two other occasions, (1) the raising of Jairus' daughter, (2) the agony in the Garden of Gethsemane.

a high mountain] A contrast suggests itself, between this mountain of the Kingdom of God, and the mountain of the kingdoms of the world, ch. iv. 8.

An old tradition placed the scene of the Transfiguration on Mount Tabor. It is known, however, that the summit of Tabor was at this period occupied by a fortress, and there is no hint given of Jesus being in that neighbourhood. Many regard one of the spurs of the snow-capped Hermon as the most likely spot. Cæsarea Philippi, the last named locality, lies under Hermon, and its glittering cone of snow may

2 apart, and was transfigured before them: and his face did
shine as the sun, and his raiment was white as the light.
3 And behold, there appeared unto them Moses and Elias
4 talking with him. Then answered Peter, and said unto
Jesus, Lord, it is good for us to be here: if thou wilt, let us
make here three tabernacles: one for thee, and one for
5 Moses, and one for Elias. While he yet spake, behold, a
bright cloud overshadowed them: and behold a voice out of
the cloud, which said, This is my beloved Son, in whom I am
6 well pleased; hear ye him. And when the disciples heard
7 *it*, they fell on their face, and were sore afraid. And Jesus
came and touched them, and said, Arise, and be not afraid.
8 And when they had lift up their eyes, they saw no *man*,
save Jesus only.

9 And as they came down from the mountain, Jesus charged
them, saying, Tell the vision to no *man*, until the Son of
10 man be risen again from the dead. And his disciples asked
him, saying, Why then say the scribes that Elias must first

have suggested the expression in Mark "exceeding white as snow," if, indeed, the words "as snow" are to be admitted into the text.

2. *was transfigured before them*] St Luke mentions that this was "as He prayed." The glorified change may be illustrated by Mark xvi. 12, "He appeared in *another form* unto two of them." The word implies more than a change of mere outward semblance.

as the light] A hint that the Transfiguration took place at night, which is also rendered probable by the statement of St Luke that the three apostles were "heavy with sleep," that they "kept awake," that they descended "the next day," ch. ix. 32 and 37.

3. *Moses and Elias*] (Elijah). The representatives of the Law and the Prophets. The whole history of the Jewish Church is brought in one glance, as it were, before the Apostles' eyes in its due relation to Christ. St Luke names the subject of converse: they "spake of his decease which he should accomplish at Jerusalem" (ix. 31).

4. *let us make*] Read, with the best MSS., "*let* me *make*." The transition to the singular is in keeping with Peter's temperament; *he* would like to make the tabernacles.—Meyer. By "tabernacles" are meant little huts made out of boughs of trees or shrubs.

This is my beloved Son, in whom I am well pleased] words that recall the baptism of Jesus; ch. iii. 17.

8. *they saw no man, save Jesus only*] Christ, who came to fulfil the Law and the Prophets, is left alone. To His voice alone the Church will listen.

9. *the vision*] = "what things they had seen" (Mark); "those things which they had seen" (Luke).

come? And Jesus answered and said unto them, Elias 11
truly shall first come, and restore all *things*. But I say unto 12
you, That Elias is come already, and they knew him not,
but have done unto him whatsoever they listed. Likewise
shall also the Son of man suffer of them. Then the disciples 13
understood that he spake unto them of John the Baptist.

14—21. *A Lunatic Child is cured.*

And when they were come to the multitude, there came 14
to him a *certain* man, kneeling down to him, and saying,
Lord, have mercy on my son: for he is lunatick, and sore 15
vexed: for ofttimes he falleth into the fire, and oft into the
water. And I brought him to thy disciples, and they could 16

10. *Why then say the scribes that Elias must first come?*] The truth of the resurrection was new to the disciples, see Mark ix. 10. "If thou art the Messiah," they say, "and shalt rise from the dead, surely the scribes are wrong in teaching that Elijah must precede the Messiah."

Jesus shews that the prophecy of Malachi iv. 5 was fulfilled in John the Baptist. Others contend that our Lord's words do not necessarily mean this, but that Malachi's prediction, though partially fulfilled in John the Baptist, should have a more literal accomplishment before Christ's second coming.

11. *restore all things*] To restore is strictly to bring back to a lost perfection, then to develope, raise, to introduce a purer, nobler epoch; here specially to proclaim the kingdom of God. Cp. Acts i. 6, and ch. xix. 28.

12. *knew him not*] did not recognise him as the Elijah prophesied by Malachi.

13. *understood*] See note ch. xvi. 12.

14—21. A Lunatic Child is cured.

Mark ix. 14—29, where the scene and the symptoms of the disease are described with great particularity. Luke ix. 37—42.

14. *when they were come to the multitude*] Some will recall Raphael's great picture of the Transfiguration, in which the contrast is powerfully portrayed between the scene on the mount, calm, bright, and heavenly, and the scene below of suffering, human passions, and failure.

15. *for he is lunatick*] This is the only special instance of cure in the case of a lunatic. They are mentioned as a class, ch. iv. 24. The word literally means "affected by changes of the moon." There appears to be some truth in the notion that there is an access of mania at the time of lunar changes. See Belcher, *Our Lord's Miracles of Healing*, p. 131.

St Mark describes the child as foaming, gnashing with his teeth, and pining away. St Luke mentions that he "crieth out." All these were epileptic symptoms; "the child was a possessed epileptic lunatic."

17 not cure him. Then Jesus answered and said, O faithless
and perverse generation, how long shall I be with you? how
18 long shall I suffer you? bring him hither to me. And Jesus
rebuked the devil; and he departed out of him: and the
19 child was cured from that *very* hour. Then came the disciples to Jesus apart, and said, Why could not we cast him
20 out? And Jesus said unto them, Because of your unbelief:
for verily I say unto you, If ye have faith as a grain of mustard seed, ye shall say unto this mountain, Remove hence
to yonder place; and it shall remove; and nothing shall be
21 unpossible unto you. Howbeit this kind goeth not out but
by prayer and fasting.

22, 23. *The Second Announcement of the Passion.*

22 And while they abode in Galilee, Jesus said unto them,
The Son of man shall be betrayed into the hands of men:
23 and they shall kill him, and the third day he shall be raised
again. And they were exceeding sorry.

24—27. *Jesus pays the half shekel of the Sanctuary.*

24 And when they were come to Capernaum, they that re-

17. *O faithless and perverse generation*] addressed to the scribes and the multitude thronging round, as representing the whole nation. The disciples, if not specially addressed, are by no means excluded from the rebuke.

20. *ye shall say unto this mountain, Remove hence*] Such expressions are characteristic of the vivid imagery of Eastern speech generally. To "remove mountains" is to make difficulties vanish. The Jews used to say of an eminent teacher, he is "a rooter up of mountains." See Lightfoot *ad loc.*

21. *this kind goeth not out but by prayer and fasting*] Those only whose own spiritual life and faith are made strong by self-denial and by communion with God in prayer are able to cast forth this kind of evil spirit.

22, 23. THE SECOND ANNOUNCEMENT OF THE PASSION.
Mark ix. 31; Luke ix. 44.

Both St Mark and St Luke add that the disciples "understood not this saying." It was difficult for them to abandon cherished hopes of an earthly kingdom, and "might not Jesus be speaking in parables of a figurative death and resurrection?" See note, ch. xvi. 21.

24—27. JESUS PAYS THE HALF SHEKEL OF THE SANCTUARY.
Peculiar to St Matthew.

24. *they that received*] i.e. "the collectors of." After the fall of

ceived tribute money came to Peter, and said, Doth not
your master pay tribute? He saith, Yes. And when he 25
was come into the house, Jesus prevented him, saying, What
thinkest thou, Simon? of whom do the kings of the earth
take custom or tribute? of their own children, or of
strangers? Peter saith unto him, Of strangers. Jesus saith 26
unto him, Then are the children free. Notwithstanding, lest 27
we should offend them, go thou to the sea, and cast a hook,
and take up the fish that first cometh up; and when thou
hast opened his mouth, thou shalt find a piece of money:
that take, and give unto them for me and thee.

1—4. *A Lesson in Humility. The Kingdom of Heaven and Little Children.*

At the same time came the disciples unto Jesus, say- 18

Jerusalem and the destruction of the Temple the Jews were obliged to pay the two drachmæ into the Roman treasury. Joseph. *B. J.* VII. 6. 6.

tribute money] Literally, **the two drachmæ**. This was not a tribute levied by Cæsar or by Herod, but the half-shekel (Exod. xxx. 13) paid annually by every Jew into the Temple treasury. The "sacred tax" was collected from Jews in all parts of the world. Josephus (*Ant.* XVI. 6) has preserved some interesting letters from Roman proconsuls and from Augustus himself, to Cyrene, Ephesus, and other communities, directing that the Jews should be allowed to forward their contributions to the Temple without hindrance.

It would be interesting to know whether the Jewish Christians continued to pay the Temple-tax in accordance with this precedent.

25. *prevented*] anticipated him by answering his thoughts. To prevent is (1) to "go before," "to anticipate" then, "to precede" either (2) to aid, or (3) to hinder.

custom or tribute] taxes (1) indirect and (2) direct; on (1) things and on (2) persons.

of their own children, or of strangers?] i.e. of their own sons, or of those who do not belong to the family, namely, subjects and tributaries.

26. *then are the children free*] "the sons are exempt from tribute." The deduction is, "Shall He whom thou hast rightly named the Son of God pay tribute to the Temple of his Father?" The Romans called their sons free (*liberi*), as opposed to slaves.

27. *a piece of money*] Literally, **a stater**; a Greek silver coin equivalent to the Hebrew shekel, or to four drachmæ in Greek money.

CH. XVIII. 1—4. A LESSON IN HUMILITY. THE KINGDOM OF HEAVEN AND LITTLE CHILDREN.

Mark ix. 33—37; Luke ix. 46—48.

1. *At the same time*] "in that hour." The preceding incident and

2 ing, Who is the greatest in the kingdom of heaven? And
Jesus called a little child unto *him*, and set him in the midst
3 of them. And said, Verily I say unto you, Except ye be
converted, and become as little children, ye shall not enter
4 into the kingdom of heaven. Whosoever therefore shall
humble himself as this little child, the same is greatest in
the kingdom of heaven.

5, 6. *Christ's Little Ones.*

5 And whoso shall receive one such little child in my name
6 receiveth me. But whoso shall offend one of these little
ones which believe in me, it were better for him that a
millstone were hanged about his neck, and *that* he were
drowned in the depth of the sea.

7—9. *Of Offences.*

7 Woe unto the world because of offences: for it must needs
be that offences come; but woe to that man by whom the

our Lord's words had again excited hopes of a glorious kingdom on earth.

greatest] Literally, **greater** (than others).

2. *set him in the midst of them*] St Mark adds, "when He had taken him in His arms."

3. *be converted*] Literally, **be turned**. The Greek word is used in a literal sense, except here and Acts vii. 39 and 42.

shall not enter] much less be great therein.

4. *Whosoever therefore shall humble himself*] He who shall be most Christ-like in humility (see Phil. ii. 7—9) shall be most like Christ in glory.

5, 6. CHRIST'S LITTLE ONES. Mark ix. 37.

The thought of Jesus passes from the dispute among His disciples to the care of His little ones, the young in faith, who, if they have the weakness, have also the humility of little children.

whoso shall receive] It is a sacrament of lovingkindness when Christ Himself is received in the visible form of His little ones. *To receive* is to welcome, shew kindness to.

a millstone] Literally, **a millstone turned by an ass**, and so larger than the ordinary millstone. Cp. Ovid (*Fasti* VI. 318): "Et quæ pumiceas versat asella molas."

The manner of death alluded to appears to have been unknown to the Jews. But Plutarch mentions this punishment as being common to Greece and Rome. Cp. Juv. *Sat.* XIV. 16, 17, where, as in other places, it is named rather than the cross as a swift and terrible penalty for crime.

offence cometh. Wherefore if thy hand or thy foot offend 8
thee, cut them off, and cast *them* from thee: it is better for
thee to enter into life halt or maimed, rather than having
two hands or two feet to be cast into everlasting fire. And 9
if thine eye offend thee, pluck it out, and cast *it* from thee:
it is better for thee to enter into life with one eye, rather
than having two eyes to be cast into hell fire.

10—14. *Christ's care for His Little Ones illustrated by a Parable.*

Take heed that ye despise not one of these little ones; 10
for I say unto you, That in heaven their angels do always
behold the face of my Father which is in heaven. For the 11
Son of man is come to save that which was lost. How think 12
ye? if a man have an hundred sheep, and one of them be
gone astray, doth he not leave the ninety and nine, and

7—9. OF OFFENCES. Mark ix. 43—48.

From offences—hindrances to the faith of Christ's little ones—the discourse proceeds to offences in general—every thing that hinders the spiritual life.

8, 9. Cp. note ch. v. 29, 30.

10—14. CHRIST'S CARE FOR HIS LITTLE ONES ILLUSTRATED BY A PARABLE. Luke xv. 3—7.

After a brief digression (*vv.* 7—9), Christ's love for His young disciples again breaks out in words. Let no one despise them. They have unseen friends in the court of heaven, who are ever in the presence of the King himself. There, at any rate, they are not despised. It was for them especially that the Son of Man came to earth.

11. This verse is omitted in the Sinaitic and the Vatican MSS., and is consequently rejected by Lachmann, Tischendorf, and Tregelles. However, it falls in precisely with the train of thought, and is almost required to connect *vv.* 10 and 12.

The expression and the imagery of the parable recall Ezek. xxxiv.; comp. also ch. xv. 24. In Luke the parable is spoken with direct reference to publicans and sinners, whom the Pharisees despised, and who are the "little ones" of these verses. Such differences of context in the Gospels are very instructive; they are, indeed, comments by the Evangelists themselves on the drift and bearing of particular sayings of Christ.

12. This parable is followed in Luke by the parable of the Lost Drachma and that of the Prodigal Son which illustrate and amplify the same thought.

doth he not leave the ninety and nine] St Luke adds "in the wilderness."

goeth into the mountains, and seeketh that which is gone
13 astray? And if so be that he find it, verily I say unto you,
he rejoiceth more of that *sheep*, than of the ninety and nine
14 which went not astray. *Even* so it is not the will of your
Father which is in heaven, that one of these little ones
should perish.

15—35. *Forgiveness of Sins.*

15 Moreover if thy brother shall trespass against thee, go
and tell him his fault between thee and him alone: if he
16 shall hear thee, thou hast gained thy brother. But if he will
not hear *thee*, *then* take with thee one or two more, that in
the mouth of two or three witnesses every word
17 may be established. And if he shall neglect to hear them,
tell *it* unto the church: but if he neglect to hear the church,
let him be unto thee as a heathen *man* and a publican.
18 Verily I say unto you, Whatsoever ye shall bind on earth

13. *of that sheep*] Rather, **over** that sheep.

15—35. Forgiveness of Sins. Luke xvii. 3, 4.

God's forgiveness of sinners suggests the duty of forgiveness among men.

15. *go and tell him his fault between thee and him alone*] See Levit. xix. 17, where the words "not suffer sin upon him," mean "thou shalt not incur sin through him," i.e. by letting him go on unrebuked in his sin. *Tell him his fault*, rather, **convict him**; the same Greek word is translated **rebuke**, Levit. *loc. cit.* St Luke has a different Greek word with a similar meaning.

gained] i.e. won over to a better mind,—to Christ. Cp. 1 Cor. ix. 19—22, and 1 Pet. iii. 1.

17. *tell it unto the church*] The word "church" (Grk. *ekklesia*) is found only here and ch. xvi. 18 in the Gospels. In the former passage the reference to the Christian Church is undoubted. Here either (1) the assembly or congregation of the Jewish synagogue, or rather, (2) the ruling body of the synagogue (collegium presbyterorum, *Schleusner*) is meant. This must have been the sense of the word to those who were listening to Christ. But what was spoken of the Jewish Church was naturally soon applied to the Christian Church.

a heathen man and a publican] Jesus, the friend of publicans and sinners, uses the phrase of His contemporaries. What Jesus says, Matthew the publican records.

18. Taking up the word "Church," Jesus passes from its present meaning—the ruling body in the synagogue—to its meaning in the future. The ruling body is the Christian Church.

shall be bound in heaven: and whatsoever ye shall loose on
earth shall be loosed in heaven. Again I say unto you, That 19
if two of you shall agree on earth as touching any thing that
they shall ask, it shall be done for them of my Father which
is in heaven. For where two or three are gathered together 20
in my name, there am I in the midst of them.
Then came Peter to him, and said, Lord, how oft shall 21
my brother sin against me, and I forgive him? till seven
times? Jesus saith unto him, I say not unto thee, Until 22
seven times: but, Until seventy times seven. Therefore is 23
the kingdom of heaven likened unto a certain king, which
would take account of his servants. And when he had 24
begun to reckon, one was brought unto him, which ought
him ten thousand talents. But forasmuch as he had not to 25

Whatsoever ye shall bind on earth shall be bound in heaven] What was spoken to Peter alone is now spoken to all the disciples, representing the Church. "Whatsoever you as a Church declare binding or declare not binding, that decision shall be ratified in heaven."

19. The slight digression is continued. Christ thinks of His Church. Not only shall your decisions be ratified, but your requests shall be granted, provided ye agree.

20. *two or three*] In the smallest gathering of His followers Christ will be present. A derivative (*synaxis*) of the Greek word in the text came to be used among the early Christians for their assemblies, especially in reference to assembling for the Lord's Supper. *Synaxarium*, derived from the same verb, meant a Service-book.

21. *till seven times?*] The Rabbinical rule was that no one should ask forgiveness of his neighbour more than thrice. Peter, who asks as a scribe a scribe's question, thought he was making a great advance in liberality and shewing himself worthy of the Kingdom of heaven. But the question itself indicates complete misunderstanding of the Christian spirit.

22. *Until seventy times seven*] i.e. an infinite number of times. There is no limit to forgiveness.

23. *a certain king, which would take account of his servants*] The picture is drawn from an Oriental Court. The provincial governors, farmers of taxes, and other high officials are summoned before a despotic sovereign to give an account of their administration.

would] "chose," "resolved:" all is subject to his sole will.

servants] i.e. subjects, for all subjects of an Eastern monarch are "slaves." The scholar will remember how often Demosthenes makes a point of this.

24. *ten thousand talents*] Even if silver talents are meant, the sum is enormous—at least two million pounds of our money. It was probably more than the whole annual revenue of Palestine at this time; see

pay, his lord commanded him to be sold, and his wife, and
children, and all that he had, and payment to be made.
26 The servant therefore fell down, and worshipped him, saying, Lord, have patience with me, and I will pay thee all.
27 Then the lord of that servant was moved with compassion,
28 and loosed him, and forgave him the debt. But the same
servant went out, and found one of his fellowservants, which
ought him an hundred pence: and he laid hands on him,
and took *him* by the throat, saying, Pay me that thou owest.
29 And his fellowservant fell down at his feet, and besought
him, saying, Have patience with me, and I will pay thee all.
30 And he would not: but went and cast him into prison, till
31 he should pay the debt. So when his fellowservants saw
what was done, they were very sorry, and came and told
32 unto their lord all that was done. Then his lord, after that
he had called him, said unto him, O *thou* wicked servant,
I forgave thee all that debt, because thou desiredst me:
33 shouldest not thou also have had compassion on thy fellow-
34 servant, even as I had pity on thee? And his lord was

Joseph. *Ant.* XII. 4. 4. The modern kingdoms of Norway or Greece or Denmark hardly produce a larger national income.

The vast sum implies the hopeless character of the debt of sin.

25. *he had not to pay*] He had wasted in extravagance the provincial revenues, or the proceeds of taxation.

26. *worshipped him*] The imperfect tense in the original denotes persistence.

27. *forgave him the debt*] With the almost reckless generosity of an Eastern Court that delights to exalt or debase with swift strokes. The pardon is free and unconditional.

28. *found*] perhaps, even sought him out.

one of his fellowservants] By this is meant the debt of man to man, offences which men are bound to forgive one another.

an hundred pence] i.e. *denarii.* The *denarius* was a day's wages (ch. xx. 2). The sum therefore is about three months' wages for an ordinary labourer, by no means a hopeless debt as the other was; see note ch. xxvi. 7.

29. *besought*] Not the same word as "worshipped," *v.* 26. The word in the text would be used by an equal addressing an equal.

31. *when his fellowservants saw what was done, they were very sorry*] This seems to point to the common conscience of mankind approving or anticipating the divine sentence.

32. *desiredst*] The same Greek word is translated "besought," *v.* 29.

33. Cp. the Lord's Prayer, where forgiveness of others is put forward as the claim for divine pardon.

wroth, and delivered him to the tormentors, till he should
pay all that was due unto him. So likewise shall my 35
heavenly Father do *also* unto you, if ye from your hearts forgive not every one his brother their trespasses.

1, 2. *Jesus goes to Judæa from Galilee.*

And it came to pass, *that* when Jesus had finished 19
these sayings, he departed from Galilee, and came into the
coasts of Judea beyond Jordan; and great multitudes fol- 2
lowed him; and he healed them there.

3—12. *The Question of Marriage and Divorce.*

The Pharisees also came unto him, tempting him, and 3
saying unto him, Is it lawful for a man to put away his
wife for every cause? And he answered and said unto 4

34. The acquittal is revoked—a point not to be pressed in the interpretation. The truth taught is the impossibility of the unforgiving being forgiven, but the chief lesson is the example of the divine spirit of forgiveness in the act of the king. This example the pardoned slave should have followed.

35. *from your hearts*] A different principle from the Pharisee's arithmetical rules of forgiveness.

their trespasses] The MS. authority is against these words.

CH. XIX.—**1, 2.** JESUS GOES TO JUDÆA FROM GALILEE.
Mark x. i.

1. *came into the coasts of Judea beyond Jordan*] From the parallel passage in Mark we learn that this means: Came into Judæa by the trans-Jordanic route through Peræa, thus avoiding Samaria. It does not mean that any portion of Judæa lay beyond Jordan. St Matthew here omits various particulars, of which some are to be supplied from Luke ix. 51—xvii. 11; others from John—two visits to Jerusalem (vii. 8—10 and x. 22—39); the raising of Lazarus (xi. 1—46); the retirement to Ephraim (xi. 54).

3—12. THE QUESTION OF MARRIAGE AND DIVORCE.
Mark x. 2—9.

vv. 10—12 are peculiar to Matthew. St Mark mentions the part of the conversation contained in *v.* 9 as having taken place "in the house," *vv.* 10—12.

3. *Is it lawful for a man to put away his wife for every cause?*] The words "for every cause" are omitted in Mark. In Matthew they contain the pith of the question: "Is the husband's right to divorce his wife quite unlimited?" The school of Shammai allowed divorce in the case of adultery, the school of Hillel on any trivial pretext.

them, Have ye not read, that he which made *them* at
5 the beginning made them male and female, and said,
For this cause shall a man leave father and
mother, and shall cleave to his wife: and they
6 twain shall be one flesh? Wherefore they are no
more twain, but one flesh. What therefore God hath
7 joined together, let not man put asunder. They say unto
him, Why did Moses then command to give a writing of
8 divorcement, and to put her away? He saith unto them,
Moses because of the hardness of your hearts suffered you
to put away your wives: but from the beginning it was not
9 so. And I say unto you, Whosoever shall put away his
wife, except *it be* for fornication, and shall marry another,
committeth adultery: and whoso marrieth her *which is* put
10 away doth commit adultery. His disciples say unto him, If
the case of the man be so with *his* wife, it is not good
11 to marry. But he said unto them, All *men* cannot receive
12 this saying, save *they* to whom it is given. For there are
some eunuchs, which were so born from *their* mother's
womb: and there are *some* eunuchs, which were made

4. *at the beginning*] An appeal from the law of Moses to a higher and absolute law, which has outlived the law of Moses.

5. *For this cause*] The lesson of Nature is the lesson of God, "Nunquam aliud Natura aliud Sapientia dicit." Juv. *Sat.* XIV. 321.

7. *a writing of divorcement*] See ch. v. 31, 32.

8. *because of the hardness of your hearts*] Literally, **having respect to,** with a view to the hardness of your hearts towards God. So the law was relatively good, not absolutely. A great principle. Even now all are not capable of the higher religious life or of the deepest truths. Some interpret "hardness of heart," of the cruelty of men towards their wives.

9. See ch. v. 32.

and shall marry another] Omitted in the Sinaitic MS.

The reading "causeth her to commit adultery," instead of "committeth adultery," has high MS. authority. The Sinaitic MS. also omits *and whoso...adultery.*

10. *If the case of the man be so with his wife*] If these are the conditions of marriage.

it is not good to marry] Nothing could prove more clearly the revolution in thought brought to pass by Christ than this. Even the disciples feel that such a principle would make the yoke of marriage unbearable.

11. *this saying*] viz. that it is not good to marry.

12. *eunuchs* = "unmarried."

eunuchs of men: and there be eunuchs, which have made themselves eunuchs for the kingdom of heaven's sake. He that is able to receive *it*, let him receive *it*.

13—15. *Little Children are brought to Christ.*

Then were there brought unto him little children, that he 13
should put *his* hands on them, and pray: and the disciples
rebuked them. But Jesus said, Suffer little children, and 14
forbid them not, to come unto me: for of such is the kingdom of heaven. And he laid *his* hands on them, and de- 15
parted thence.

16—22. *The Young Rich Ruler.*

And behold, one came and said unto him, Good Master, 16

12. *for the kingdom of heaven's sake*] In old days some men abstained from marriage in order to devote themselves to the study of the law, in later times men have done so for the furtherance of Christianity.

13—15. LITTLE CHILDREN ARE BROUGHT TO CHRIST.
Mark x. 13—16. Luke xviii. 15—17.

In Luke the incident is placed immediately after the parable of the Pharisee and Publican; there it is an illustration of humility. Here, and in Mark, the connection between the purity of married life and the love of little children cannot be overlooked.

13. *Then were there brought unto him little children*] It appears that it was customary for Jewish infants to be taken to the synagogue to be blessed by the Rabbi. Smith's *Dict. of Bible*, Art. "Synagogue," note E.

14. *of such is the kingdom of heaven*] Love, simplicity of faith, innocence, and above all, humility, are the ideal characteristics of little children, and of the subjects of the kingdom.

15. *laid his hands on them*] No unmeaning act, therefore infants are capable of receiving a blessing, though not *conscious* of an obligation.

16—22. THE YOUNG RICH RULER.
Mark x. 17—22. Luke xviii. 18—23.

From Luke alone we learn that he was a "*ruler;*" from Matthew alone that he was *young*. Each of the three Synoptists states that "he was very rich" (Luke); "had great possessions" (Matthew and Mark).

16. *one came*] "Came one running, and kneeled to him" (Mark). "A certain ruler," i.e. one of the rulers of the synagogue, like Jairus. The "decemvirate" (see ch. iv. 23) of the synagogue were chosen from "men of leisure" (Hebr. *Batlanin*, cp. our "*scholars*"), who were free from the necessity of labour, and could devote themselves to the duties

what good *thing* shall I do, that I may have eternal life?
17 And he said unto him, Why callest thou me good? *there is*
none good but one, *that is*, God: but if thou wilt enter into
18 life, keep the commandments. He saith unto him, Which?
Jesus said, Thou shalt do no murder, Thou shalt
not commit adultery, Thou shalt not steal, Thou
19 shalt not bear false witness, Honour thy father
and *thy* mother: and, Thou shalt love thy neigh-
20 bour as thyself. The young man saith unto him, All
these *things* have I kept from my youth up: what lack
21 I yet? Jesus said unto him, If thou wilt be perfect, go *and*
sell that thou hast, and give to the poor, and thou shalt

of the synagogue, and to study; of these the first three were called "Rulers of the Synagogue."

Good Master] According to good MS. authority simply "Master."

what good thing shall I do] In this question 'what shall I *do*' the ruler touches the central error of the Pharisaic system—that goodness consisted in exact conformity to certain external rules of conduct. Jesus shews that it is not by *doing* anything whatever that a man can inherit eternal life, but by *being* something; not by observing Pharisaic rules, but by being childlike.

17. *Why callest thou me good?*] Here, but not in the parallel passages in Mark and Luke, the leading MSS. read, "Why askest thou me about what is good? He who is good is one." With either reading the drift of our Lord's answer is to cause reflection. "In a single breath thou hast twice used the word good; think what good really means. Am *I* then the one good?" Jesus refuses the conventional title of "good master;" and leads the questioner to think of the only One who could be called "good" in a high and true sense.

18. *Which?*] Accurately "what sort of commandments."

Comp. this enumeration with that in ch. xv. 19. Here, as there, the commandments proceed in order from the 6th to the 9th. Here, as there, the enumeration stops at covetousness—the rich ruler's special failing. Neither St Mark nor St Luke preserve the same order.

20. *All these things have I kept*] Like St Paul he was "touching the righteousness which is in the law, blameless." Phil. iii. 6.

from my youth up] These words which seem unsuitable to the "young man" are omitted here, but not in the parallel passages, by the oldest MSS. They might be translated "from childhood."

21. *If thou wilt be perfect*] i. e. "if thou desirest to be perfect."

go and sell that thou hast] Jesus does indeed bid him do something, but to *do* that would be a proof of *being* perfect, it is *the* test for his special case, not a universal rule. With many it is more difficult to use wealth for Christ than to give it up for Christ. St Mark has the touching words "Jesus beholding him loved him." The incident recalls the parable of the "merchant man seeking goodly pearls" (ch. xiii. 45, 46).

have treasure in heaven: and come *and* follow me. But 22
when the young man heard *that* saying, he went away sorrowful: for he had great possessions.

23—26. *Of Riches, and the Kingdom of God.*

Then said Jesus unto his disciples, Verily I say unto you, 23
That a rich *man* shall hardly enter into the kingdom of
heaven. And again I say unto you, It is easier for a camel 24
to go through the eye of a needle, than for a rich *man* to
enter into the kingdom of God. When his disciples heard 25
it, they were exceedingly amazed, saying, Who then can be
saved? But Jesus beheld *them*, and said unto them, With 26
men this is unpossible; but with God all *things* are possible.

27—30. *The Claim of the Disciples.*

Then answered Peter and said unto him, Behold, we have 27
forsaken all, and followed thee; what shall we have there-

Here is a seeker after good, the pearl is found: will he not sell all that he hath and buy it?

22. *sorrowful*] A conflict of opposite desires vexed his soul. He wished to serve God and mammon. He was sorrowful because he saw that the special sacrifice required to win eternal life was too great for him.

23—26. OF RICHES, AND THE KINGDOM OF GOD.
Mark x. 23—27. Luke xviii. 24—27.

These reflections follow naturally on the last incident.

23. *hardly*] i.e. with difficulty.

24. *easier for a camel to go through the eye of a needle*] An expression familiar to Jews of our Lord's time. The exaggeration is quite in the Eastern style. It is unnecessary to give other explanations, as that *camel* is a Greek word meaning "a rope," or that "the eye of a needle" is a gate so called.

25. *Who then can be saved?*] Salvation seemed to belong by right to the rulers of synagogues and other rich people. It was a notable fact that the gospel should be preached to the poor. The thought of the disciples still lives. Wealth and intellect make men *seem* better, "Sometimes even supplying the absence of real good with what looks extremely like it." See a Sermon by Prof. Mozley, on *The Reversal of Human Judgment*, pp. 85—87.

27—30. THE CLAIM OF THE DISCIPLES.
Mark x. 28—31. Luke xviii. 28—30.

27. *what shall we have therefore*] Peter, still not perfect in the Spirit of Christ, suggests a lower motive for following Christ. The

28 fore? And Jesus said unto them, Verily I say unto you,
That ye which have followed me, in the regeneration, when
the Son of man shall sit in the throne of his glory, ye also
shall sit upon twelve thrones, judging the twelve tribes of
29 Israel. And every one that hath forsaken houses, or brethren, or sisters, or father, or mother, or wife, or children, or
lands, for my name's sake, shall receive an hundredfold,
30 and shall inherit everlasting life. But many *that are* first
shall be last; and *the* last *shall be* first.

1—16. *The Parable of the Labourers in the Vineyard.*

20 For the kingdom of heaven is like unto a man *that is*

answer of Christ shews that all true sacrifice shall have its reward, but all that looks like sacrifice is not really such, therefore "Many that are first shall be last." Among the Twelve there was a Judas.

28. *the regeneration*] "The renewal of things," "the return to a perfect state," otherwise called "the restitution of all things," nearly = the Kingdom of God. Cp. ch. xvii. 11.

29. *hath forsaken*] Bp Thirlwall remarks, "Strange as it may sound, there is a sense in which it is a most certain truth that a man may leave that which he keeps, and keep that which he leaves. And there can be no doubt that this is the sense in which our Lord meant to be understood. For it is clear that He is speaking not of a mere outward act, but of the disposition from which it proceeds."

shall receive an hundredfold] St Mark seems to take the words of Jesus in a more literal sense by naming the earthly goods expressly, and adding "*now in this time*," but he points to the true and spiritual interpretation by subjoining "*with persecutions*."

CH. XX. **1—16.** THE PARABLE OF THE LABOURERS IN THE VINEYARD. Peculiar to St Matthew.

1. *For the kingdom of heaven*, &c.] There are many possible applications of the parable, but the only true explanation of its meaning to the disciples at the time must be reached by considering the question to which it is an answer. The parable is addressed solely to the disciples. The thread of thought may be traced in this way: It is impossible for a rich man, one who trusts in riches, to enter the kingdom of heaven. The disciples, through Peter, say "We at any rate left all and followed thee; what shall we have therefore?" Our Lord's answer is (1) partly encouraging, (2) partly discouraging.

(1) All who have in a *true* sense given up all for Christ shall have a great reward (ch. xix. 28, 29).

(2) But (*v.* 30) priority of time is not everything. The parable is given in explanation of this point. Not only will the disciples not be the only called, but they may not reach a higher place or

a householder, which went out early in the morning to
hire labourers into his vineyard. And when he had agreed 2
with the labourers for a penny a day, he sent them into
his vineyard. And he went out about the third hour, and 3
saw others standing idle in the marketplace, and said unto 4
them; Go ye also into the vineyard, and whatsoever is
right I will give you. And they went their way. Again 5
he went out about the sixth and ninth hour, and did
likewise. And about the eleventh hour he went out, and 6
found others standing idle, and saith unto them, Why
stand ye here all the day idle? They say unto him, Be- 7
cause no *man* hath hired us. He saith unto them, Go ye
also into the vineyard; and whatsoever is right, *that* shall
ye receive. So when even was come, the lord of the vine- 8
yard saith unto his steward, Call the labourers, and give them
their hire, beginning from the last unto the first. And when 9
they came that *were hired* about the eleventh hour, they
received every man a penny. But when the first came, they 10
supposed that they should have received more; and they likewise received every man a penny. And when they had re- 11
ceived *it*, they murmured against the goodman of the house,

a higher reward than some who follow them. Still all who work shall have their reward. But they must beware of a spirit very prevalent among hard workers, and not think too much of their own labours, or be displeased because others are equally rewarded.

labourers into his vineyard] i.e. workers for the Church of Christ.

2. *a penny*] a denarius. See ch. xviii. 28.

4. *whatsoever is right I will give you*] The justice of the award is disputed *v.* 12, on the ground that those who were first called had borne the burden and heat of the day. Man does not here acquiesce in the Judge's decision, as in the parable of the debtors, ch. xviii. What is just does not at first *seem* just, but, as in science many things that seemed untrue are proved to be true, what seems unjust will be proved just when we know all. Further, time is not the only element in service. An act of swift intelligence or of bravery wrought in the space of a single minute has saved an army or a people, and merited higher reward than a lifetime of ordinary service.

6. *the eleventh hour*] The various hours may be referred in the first instance to the call of a Paul, a Barnabas, or a Timothy, who adopted the Cause later than the Twelve. In a secondary and less immediate sense they seem to indicate the successive periods at which the various nations were admitted to the Church of Christ. Was it unjust that European nations should have equal privileges with the Jews in the Church of Christ, or that Paul should be equal to Peter?

12 saying, These last have wrought *but* one hour, and thou hast
made them equal unto us, which have borne the burden and
13 heat of the day. But he answered one of them, and said,
Friend, I do thee no wrong: didst not thou agree with me
14 for a penny? Take *that* thine *is*, and go thy way: I will
15 give unto this last, even as unto thee. Is it not lawful for
me to do what I will with mine own? Is thine eye evil, be-
16 cause I am good? So the last shall be first, and the first
last: for many be called, but few chosen.

17—19. *Jesus going up to Jerusalem foretells His Passion for the third time.*

17 And Jesus going up to Jerusalem took the twelve dis-
18 ciples apart in the way, and said unto them, Behold, we go
up to Jerusalem; and the Son of man shall be betrayed
unto the chief priests and *unto the* scribes, and they shall

12. *which have borne the burden and heat of the day*] This may be regarded as man's estimate of his own merits, which is not the divine estimate. The words echo the tone of "what shall we have?" ch. xix. 27.

13. *Friend*] The Greek word is used of any temporary connection, without the idea of affectionate friendship. It is used by a master to his slave; by a guest to a fellow-guest; as a general address on meeting. Cp. ch. xxii. 12 and xxvi. 50, where it is a term of reproachful rebuke.

15. *Is thine eye evil*] The belief in the evil eye still prevails in the East. The envious or malevolent glance is thought to have an injurious effect. Here the sense is: Art thou envious because I am just?

16. *For many be called, but few chosen*] This clause which occurs in a natural connection in ch. xxii. 14, but is difficult to explain here, is omitted in the best MSS. The words are probably interpolated.

17—19. JESUS GOING UP TO JERUSALEM FORETELLS HIS PASSION FOR THE THIRD TIME.

See chs. xvi. 21, xvii. 22, 23; and Mark x. 32—34; Luke xviii. 31—34. St Mark and St Luke add "shall spit upon him" (Mark); "shall be spitted on" (Luke); St Matthew alone names "crucifixion;" St Luke, who mentions only the share which the Gentiles had in the Passion, adds "they understood none of these things, and this saying was hid from them, neither knew they the things which were spoken."

The disciples, as Jews, still placed their hopes in the present world: "what shall we have?" They still thought Jesus might be using a figure of speech. Jesus was alone in the certainty of His awful secret. He had no sympathy from His followers.

condemn him to death, and shall deliver him to the Gentiles 19
to mock, and to scourge, and to crucify *him:* and the third
day he shall rise again.

20—28. *Salome's Prayer for her sons, and the Answer of Jesus.*

Then came to him the mother of Zebedee's children with 20
her sons, worshipping *him*, and desiring a certain *thing* of
him. And he said unto her, What wilt thou? She saith 21
unto him, Grant that these my two sons may sit, the one on
thy right hand, and the other on the left, in thy kingdom.
But Jesus answered and said, Ye know not what ye ask. 22
Are ye able to drink *of* the cup that I shall drink *of*, and to

18, 19. Observe the exactness of the prediction; the Sanhedrin shall condemn but not kill, the Gentiles shall scourge and crucify.

20—28. Salome's Prayer for her sons, and the Answer of Jesus.

Mark x. 35—41. St Mark begins "And James and John the sons of Zebedee came unto him, saying, &c." For once St Matthew is more graphic and true to detail than St Mark.

20. *the mother of Zebedee's children*] Her name was Salome, as we learn by comparing Matthew xxvii. 56 with Mark xv. 40.

"Among which was Mary Magdalene, and Mary the mother of James and Joses, and the mother of Zebedee's children." Matthew xxvii. 56.

"Among whom was Mary Magdalene, and Mary the mother of James the less and of Joses, and Salome." Mark xv. 40.

worshipping him] The act of prostration before an Eastern King—though the word "crucify" might have suggested a slave's death. The Kingdom of heaven introduces many such contrasts.

desiring a certain thing] She dares not speak until her Lord addresses her.

21. *may sit, the one on thy right hand*] Cp. for the thought ch. xix. 28.

22. *Ye know not*] Observe, Jesus addresses the sons, not the mother.

what ye ask] There is some force in the middle voice of the original, "ask for yourselves," or "cause to be asked."

the cup that I shall drink of] "The destiny in store for me." Cp. among other passages, Is. li. 17, "Thou hast drunken the dregs of the cup of trembling, and wrung them out," and Ps. lxxv. 8; the idea of vengeance, of God's wrath against sin, is paramount in the prophets. When the disciples afterwards recalled the image it would signify to them the mediation of Christ, who by His passion and death drank for

be baptized *with* the baptism that I am baptized *with*?
23 They say unto him, We are able. And he saith unto them,
Ye shall drink indeed *of* my cup, and be baptized *with* the
baptism that I am baptized *with:* but to sit on my right
hand, and on my left, is not mine to give, but *it shall*
24 *be given to them* for whom it is prepared of my Father. And
when the ten heard *it*, they were moved with indignation
25 against the two brethren. But Jesus called them unto *him*,
and said, Ye know that the princes of the Gentiles exercise
dominion over them, and they *that are* great exercise au-
26 thority upon them. But it shall not be so among you: but

man the cup of God's wrath. Maldonatus suggests the thought of "the poison cup," the cup of death. For the image, cp. "quot bella *exhausta* canebat." Verg. *Aen.* IV. 14.

and to be baptized, &c.] These words are omitted in the most ancient MSS. They are probably an insertion from St Mark. The crucifixion was the baptism through which Jesus passed to the new life after the Resurrection. Our Christian baptism is a crucifixion by which the old man dies that the new man may live. See Rom. vi. 6; Gal. v. 24; Col. iii. 3, 5, 10.

23. *Ye shall drink indeed of my cup*] James was slain by the sword of Herod Agrippa I. (Acts xii. 2). John suffered many persecutions, but died a natural death. The rebuke of Jesus is very gentle; His soul knew what suffering was in store for the two brothers.

it shall be given] These words are not in the Greek text, but may be understood from the infinitive "to give" in the first clause. By another interpretation "but" = "except," and the sentence would run, "it is not mine to give except to those," &c., but it is more than doubtful whether the Greek word can have this meaning.

24. *they were moved with indignation*] The indignation of the "Ten" displayed the same spirit and motive as the request of the sons of Zebedee. It seemed as if the jealousies and intrigues of an earthly court were breaking out among the disciples of Jesus.

25. *Jesus called them unto him, and said*] Jesus points out the inversion of earthly ideas in the Kingdom of heaven. The gradation and contrast of the original are hardly brought out in E. V. In the Kingdom of heaven the ambition must be to serve not to reign; that Kingdom is in every way the reverse of the kingdoms of the world. In the latter the gradation of rank is (1) the supreme prince; (2) the nobles (the great); (3) the ministers or attendants; (4) the slaves. In the Kingdom of heaven he that will be the noble must be the minister or attendant; he that will be the monarch must be the slave. What Jesus teaches is the dignity of service in the Kingdom of heaven.

The bearing of such passages as this on the alleviation of slavery in the ancient world should be considered. The influence of this towards the abolition of slavery in modern times might have been still greater

whosoever will be great among you, let him be your minister; and whosoever will be chief among you, let him be 27
your servant: even as the Son of man came not to be mi- 28
nistered unto, but to minister, and to give his life a ransom
for many.

29—34. *Two Men cured of Blindness.*

And as they departed from Jericho, a great multitude 29
followed him. And behold, two blind men sitting by the 30

if the translators had used the word "slave" rather than "servant" in the E. V.

28. *a ransom*] = the price paid for the redemption of a captive from slavery. For the thought cp. Rom. iii. 24; 1 Cor. vi. 20; 1 Pet. i. 19. The English word is derived through the French *rançon* from Lat. *redemptionem*.

for many] Cp. 1 Tim. ii. 6, "Who gave himself a ransom for *all*."

for] Not ὑπέρ, 'on behalf of,' but ἀντί, 'in the place of.'

29—34. Two Men cured of Blindness.
Mark x. 46—52. Luke xviii. 35—43.

There are remarkable divergences in the Synoptic accounts of this miracle. Some indeed have supposed that different miracles are related by the Evangelists. St Mark speaks of one man, "blind Bartimæus, the son of Timæus." St Luke also mentions one only, but describes the incident as taking place "when Jesus came nigh unto Jericho," whereas St Matthew and St Mark state that the miracle was wrought "as they departed from Jericho."

It is of course possible that St Luke narrates a separate miracle. The only other solution is to suppose an inaccuracy in an unimportant detail.

29. *a great multitude*] The caravan of Galilæans and others going up to Jerusalem for the Passover. Their numbers would protect them from attack in the dangerous mountain defiles leading to the capital. *Jericho* was at this time a flourishing city. It was opulent even in the days of Joshua from the fertility of the surrounding plain, its extensive commerce, and from the metals found in the neighbourhood. Levelled to the ground and laid under a curse by Joshua, it was afterwards made a fortified city by Hiel the Bethelite, and regained a portion of its former prosperity. At this period the balsam trade was a principal source of its wealth.

Herod the Great beautified the city with palaces and public buildings, and here he died. After Herod's death Jericho was sacked and burnt, but restored by his son Archelaus.

"Jericho was once more a 'City of Palms' when our Lord visited it. As the city that had so exceptionally contributed to His own ancestry; as the city which had been the first to fall, amidst so much ceremony, before 'the captain of the Lord's host and his servant Joshua,'

way side, when they heard that Jesus passed by, cried out,
31 saying, Have mercy on us, O Lord, *thou* Son of David. And
the multitude rebuked them, because they should hold their
peace: but they cried the more, saying, Have mercy on us,
32 O Lord, *thou* Son of David. And Jesus stood still, and
called them, and said, What will ye *that* I shall do unto
33 you? They say unto him, Lord, that our eyes may be
34 opened. So Jesus had compassion *on them*, and touched
their eyes: and immediately their eyes received sight, and
they followed him.

1—10. *The Royal Entry into Jerusalem.*

21 And when they drew nigh unto Jerusalem, and were
come to Bethphage, unto the mount of Olives, then sent
2 Jesus two disciples, saying unto them, Go into the village
over against you, and straightway ye shall find an ass tied,
and a colt with her: loose *them*, and bring *them* unto me.

we may well suppose that His eyes surveyed it with unwonted interest."—Smith's *Bib. Dict.* Art. "Jericho."

31. *thou Son of David*] An appeal which reflects the thought that especially signalizes this period of our Lord's ministry, the Son of David entering upon His kingdom.

34. *they followed him*] It is probable that very many of those who had received sight and soundness of limb by the word or touch of Jesus followed Him to Jerusalem.

followed] Jesus Himself leads the procession. See Luke xix. 28.

Nisan 9 (*Palm Sunday*).

CH. XXI. **1—10**. THE ROYAL ENTRY INTO JERUSALEM.

Mark xi. 1—11. Luke xix. 29—40. John xii. 12—19. St Luke alone places here the incident of Christ weeping over Jerusalem (xix. 40—44).

1. *were come to Bethphage, unto the mount of Olives*] "Unto Bethphage and Bethany at the mount of Olives" (Mark). "Nigh to Bethphage and Bethany at the mount called the mount of Olives" (Luke). Bethany was about two miles from Jerusalem, at the S.E. base of the mount of Olives. Of Bethphage ("place of green or winter figs") no remains have been discovered, and its exact position is unknown. It was probably west of Bethany, and so near to Jerusalem as to be reckoned part of the Holy City. See Godet on St Luke xix. 28. Some have inferred from the order in which Bethphage and Bethany are named that Bethphage was east of Bethany.

2. *an ass tied, and a colt with her*] "A colt tied whereon never man

And if any *man* say ought unto you, ye shall say, The Lord 3
hath need of them; and straightway he will send them. All 4
this was done, that it might be fulfilled which was spoken
by the prophet, saying, Tell ye the daughter of Sion, Be- 5
hold, thy King cometh unto thee, meek, and sitting upon an ass, and a colt the foal of an ass.
And the disciples went, and did as Jesus commanded them, 6
and brought the ass, and the colt, and put on them their 7
clothes, and they set *him* thereon. And a very great multi- 8
tude spread their garments in the way; others cut down
branches from the trees, and strawed *them* in the way. And 9
the multitudes that went before, and that followed, cried,
saying, Hosanna to the Son of David: Blessed *is* he

sat" (Mark and Luke). St Matthew notes the close correspondence with the words of the prophecy; see *v.* 5.

Oriental travellers describe the high estimation in which the ass is held in the East. The variety of Hebrew names for these animals indicates the many uses to which they are put. "His lot varies as does the lot of those he serves. The rich man's ass is a lordly beast. In size he is far ahead of anything of his kind we see here at home. His coat is as smooth and glossy as a horse's....His livery is shiny black, satiny white or sleek mouse colour. I never saw one of the dingy red of his Poitou brethren." Zincke's *Egypt*.

3. The account leads to the inference that the owner of the ass was an adherent of Jesus who had perhaps not yet declared himself. The number of such secret followers was probably very large.

4. *that it might be fulfilled*] See note ch. i. 22.

5. *Tell ye the daughter of Sion*, &c.] Zech. ix. 9. The prophet is predicting the triumph of Israel and the fall of the neighbouring nations. The prophecy contains three distinct Hebrew words for an "ass." "Sitting upon an ass (*chamâr*, from a root meaning *red*) and a colt (*air*, 'a young male ass') the foal (lit. 'the son') of an ass (*athôn* = 'a she-ass,' from a root meaning 'slow')."

meek] See ch. v. 5.

7. *put on them their clothes*] Their upper garments, the *abbas* of modern Arabs. Cp. with this the throne extemporised for Jehu, 2 Kings ix. 13.

8. *a very great multitude*] Rather, **the greater part of the crowd.**

spread their garments in the way] Instances are recorded of similar acts of respect shewn to Rabbis by their disciples. See Schöttgen, ad loc.

9. *Hosanna*] Hebr. "*hoshiah-na*," "save now," "save I pray." *Na* is a particle of entreaty added to imperatives. They are the first words of Ps. cxviii. 25, "Save now I beseech thee, O Lord; O Lord, I beseech thee, send now prosperity," a verse which was sung in solemn

that cometh in the name of the Lord; Hosanna in
10 the highest. And when he was come into Jerusalem, all the
11 city was moved, saying, Who is this? And the multitude
said, This is Jesus the prophet of Nazareth of Galilee.

12—14. *The Second Cleansing of the Temple.*

12 And Jesus went into the temple of God, and cast out all
them that sold and bought in the temple, and overthrew the
tables of the moneychangers, and the seats of them that sold

procession round the altar at the feast of Tabernacles and on other occasions. The multitude recognise the Messiah in Jesus and address to Him the strains of their most joyous festival. St Luke paraphrases the expression for his Gentile readers, "glory in the highest."

Blessed is he that cometh in the name of the Lord] (Ps. cxviii. 26). "He that cometh" (*Habba*) was a recognised Messianic title. St Mark and St John add "Blessed be the kingdom of our father, David ('the king of Israel,' John), that cometh in the name of the Lord." St Luke has "Blessed be the king that cometh," &c., and mentions that the multitude began to rejoice and praise God *with a loud voice* for all the mighty works that they had seen." These shouts of triumph—which are the "gospel" or heralding of the King—must have sounded across the valley of Kedron up to the precincts and porches of the Temple.

"Bethany stands in a shallow hollow scooped out of the shoulder of the hill. The path follows this till the descent begins at a turn where the first view of the Temple is caught. First appeared the castles and walls of the city of David; and immediately afterwards the glittering roof of the Temple and the gorgeous royal arcade of Herod with its long range of battlements overhanging the southern edge of Moriah."—Tristram's *Topography of Holy Land*.

The entry into Jerusalem must not be regarded as an isolated fact. It was a culminating outburst of feeling. It is clear that the expectation of the kingdom was raised to the highest pitch. The prostration of Salome at the feet of the Prince; the request of her sons; the dispute among the ten; the gathering crowds; the cry of Bartimæus; the triumphal entry, are all signs of this feeling.

For us the Royal Entry is a figure, a parable through external sights and sounds of the true and inner secret kingdom of God.

10. *all the city was moved*] By a census taken in the time of Nero it was ascertained that there were 2,700,000 Jews present at the Passover. We may picture the narrow streets of Jerusalem thronged with eager inquisitive crowds demanding, with Oriental vivacity, in many tongues and dialects, "who is this?"

was moved] The word in the original is forcible, "convulsed" or "stirred" as by an earthquake, or by a violent wind. Cp. ch. xxvii. 51, and Rev. vi. 13, where the same verb is used.

doves, and said unto them, It is written, My house shall 13
be called the house of prayer; but ye have made it a
den of thieves. And *the* blind and *the* lame came to him 14
in the temple; and he healed them.

Monday, Nisan 10.

The events of this day extend to the end of ch. xxv.

12—14. THE SECOND CLEANSING OF THE TEMPLE. Mark xi. 15—18; Luke xix. 45, 46.

It is clear from the other Synoptists that the Cleansing of the Temple took place on Nisan 10, not on the day of the entry. St Mark says (xi. 11) that "when he had looked round about on all things there, the eventide being come he went back to Bethany." In point of time "the cursing of the fig-tree" should precede the "Cleansing of the Temple." St Mark adds to this account "would not suffer that any man should carry any vessel through the temple." St Matthew alone mentions the healing of the lame and the blind, and omits the incident of "the widow's mite," recorded by the other Synoptists. The first "Cleansing of the Temple," at the commencement of our Lord's ministry, is recorded John ii. 13—17.

12. *cast out all them that sold*, &c.] It is probable that a look of divine authority, the enthusiasm of His Galilæan followers, and the consciousness of wrongdoing on the part of the traders, rather than any special exercise of miraculous power, effected this triumph of Jesus in His Father's House.

them that sold and bought in the temple] The traffic consisted in the sale of oxen and sheep, and such requisites for sacrifice as wine, salt, and oil. This merchandise took place in the Court of the Gentiles.

the tables of the moneychangers] The Greek word signifies those who took a small coin (Hebr. *Kolbon*, Grk. κόλλυβος, perhaps a Phœnician word) as a fee for exchanging the money of the worshippers, who were required to pay in Hebrew coin. This exaction of the fee was itself unlawful (Lightfoot). And probably other dishonest practices were rife.

that sold doves] See Luke ii. 24.

13. *My house shall be called the house of prayer*] Is. lvi. 7, "Mine house shall be called a house of prayer for all people," or for all nations, *not* of all nations (Mark).

a den of thieves] Rather, **a cave of robbers or bandits**. Cp. Jer. vii. 11, "Is this house which is called by my name become a den of robbers in your eyes?" The context of these words is strikingly suggestive: "if ye thoroughly amend your ways and your doings...and *shed not innocent blood in this place*...then will I cause you to dwell in this place in the land that I gave to your fathers for ever and ever." The caves of Palestine had always been refuges for the lawless, and in the reign of Herod the Great the robbers dwelling in caves had rebelled against him and resisted his power, Jos. *Ant.* I. 12. Possibly this thought may be

15, 16. *The Children's Praise.*

15 And when the chief priests and scribes saw the wonderful
things that he did, and the children crying in the temple,
and saying, Hosanna to the Son of David; they were sore
16 displeased, and said unto him, Hearest thou what these
say? And Jesus saith unto them, Yea; have ye never
read, Out of the mouth of babes and sucklings
17 thou hast perfected praise? And he left them, and
went out of the city into Bethany; and he lodged there.

18—22. *The Cursing of the Fig-Tree.*

18 Now in the morning as he returned into the city, he hun-
19 gered. And when he saw a fig tree in the way, he came to

present here: "Ye have made my house a stronghold of rebels against God and the Messiah, when it ought to be a garrison of loyal subjects." Also the disputes of the traffickers resembled the wrangling of bandits in their caves.

15, 16. THE CHILDREN'S PRAISE. Peculiar to St Matthew.

15. *the chief priests*] The heads of the twenty-four priestly courses, as well as the high-priest and those who had served that office. See note ch. xxvi. 3.

children crying in the temple] Children were taught at an early age to join in the temple services. These caught the familiar feast-day strain from the Galilæan pilgrims, and unconscious of all that their words meant, saluted Jesus.

16. *Out of the mouths of babes and sucklings thou hast perfected praise*] Rather, *out of* (or **by**) *the mouths of* **children** *and sucklings hast thou* **founded strength**. Ps. viii. 2. The ruling thought of the opening verses is the glory of God set forth in His works. The "scarcely articulate" cry of an infant proves, like the heaven and the stars, the power and providence of God. On all these God builds a stronghold against His adversaries, i.e. convinces them of His might. So also the children in the temple attest the truth of God. See Canon Perowne and *Speaker's Commentary* on the passage quoted.

17. *Bethany*] "House of dates," or, according to Caspari, "Place of shops, or merchant tents," on the S.E. of the Mount of Olives, see note *v.* 9. Here Jesus lodged with Lazarus and his sisters.

18—22. THE CURSING OF THE FIG-TREE.

Mark xi. 12—14, and 20—24. St Mark places this incident before the "Cleansing of the Temple," see note *vv.* 12—14.

19 *a fig tree*] Rather, **a single fig-tree**.

it, and found nothing thereon, but leaves only, and said
unto it, Let no fruit grow on thee henceforward for ever.
And presently the fig tree withered away. And when the dis- 20
ciples saw *it*, they marvelled, saying, How soon is the fig tree
withered away! Jesus answered and said unto them, Verily 21
I say unto you, If ye have faith, and doubt not, ye shall not
only do this which is done to the fig tree, but also if ye shall
say unto this mountain, Be thou removed, and be thou cast
into the sea; it shall be done. And all *things*, whatsoever ye 22
shall ask in prayer, believing, ye shall receive.

23—27. *The Authority of Christ is questioned.*

And when he was come into the temple, the chief priests 23

found nothing thereon, but leaves only] The fig-tree loses its leaves in the winter: indeed it looks particularly bare with its white naked branches. One species, however, puts forth fruit and leaves in the very early spring, the fruit appearing before the leaves. It was doubtless a fig-tree of this kind that Jesus observed, and seeing the leaves expected to find fruit thereon. At the time of the Passover the first leaf-buds would scarcely have appeared on the common fig-tree, while this year's ripe fruit would not be found till four months later.

The teaching of the incident depends on this circumstance (comp. Luke xiii. 6—9). The early fig-tree, conspicuous among its leafless brethren, seemed alone to make a show of fruit and to invite inspection. So Israel, alone among the nations of the world, held forth a promise. From Israel alone could fruit be expected; but none was found, and their harvest-time was past. Therefore Israel perished as a nation, while the Gentile races, barren hitherto, but now on the verge of their spring-time, were ready to burst into blossom and bear fruit.

presently = immediately; cp. French *présentement*.

the fig tree withered away] From St Mark we gather that the disciples observed the effect of the curse on the day after it was pronounced by Jesus.

20. *they marvelled*] It was rather the power and wonder of the act than the deeper significance of it that moved the disciples. The miracle was to them an "act of power" (δύναμις), or a "wonder" (τέρας), rather than a "sign" (σημεῖον). Yet Jesus follows the turn their thoughts take, and teaches that prayer and faith will remove mountains of difficulty, see ch. xvii. 20.

21. *and doubt not*] The Greek verb implies the doubt that follows questioning and discussion. The active voice is used of *discerning* the face of the sky (ch. xvi. 3): from the sense of deciding litigation the meaning passes to disputation in general, and thence in middle voice to its force in the text. The last usage is not classical. The context of Acts x. 20, where the same word is used, illustrates this passage.

and the elders of the people came unto him as he was teaching, and said, By what authority doest thou these *things?*
24 and who gave thee this authority? And Jesus answered and
said unto them, I also will ask you one thing, which if ye tell
me, I in like wise will tell you by what authority I do these
25 *things.* The baptism of John, whence was it? from heaven,
or of men? And they reasoned with themselves, saying, If
we shall say, From heaven; he will say unto us, Why did ye
26 not then believe him? But if we shall say, Of men; we fear
27 the people; for all hold John as a prophet. And they answered Jesus, and said, We cannot tell. And he said unto
them, Neither tell I you by what authority I do these *things.*

28—32. *The Parable of the Two Sons, and the Explanation of it.*

28 But what think you? A *certain* man had two sons; and he

23—27. The Authority of Christ is questioned. Mark xi. 27—33; Luke xx. 1—8.

23. *By what authority doest thou these things? and who gave thee this authority?*] The second question is not a mere repetition of the first, Jesus is asked (1) what kind of authority He possesses—human or divine? (2) By whose agency this authority was bestowed? No one had a right to teach unless "authority" had been conferred upon him by the scribes.

24. *I also will ask you one thing*] This form of argument was usual. The question of the Elders was really an attack. Jesus meets that attack by a counter-question which presented equal difficulties in three ways—whether they said from heaven or of men, or left it unanswered. To say from heaven was equivalent to acknowledging Jesus as Christ, to say from men was to incur the hostility of the people, to be silent was to resign their pretensions as spiritual chiefs of the nation.

28—32. The Parable of the Two Sons, and the Explanation of it. Peculiar to St Matthew.

St Luke omits the parable, perhaps as referring especially to Israel. The parable follows in close connection with the question as to the teaching of John.

The parables and discourses that follow deal no longer with the distant future of the Church, but with an immediate present. The subjects illustrated are—(1) The rejection of the Messiah. (2) The rejection of the Jews as a nation. (3) The Judgment, (*a*) which has already begun; (*b*) which will be enacted terribly at the siege of Jerusalem; and (*c*) finally fulfilled at the end of the world.

Observe throughout the *separation* which is implied in the Judgment —the dividing sword which Christ brings—the Jewish race and the

came to the first, and said, Son, go work to day in my
vineyard. He answered and said, I will not: but afterward 29
he repented, and went. And he came to the second, and 30
said likewise. And he answered and said, I *go*, sir: and went
not. Whether of *them* twain did the will of *his* father? 31
They say unto him, The first. Jesus saith unto them, Verily
I say unto you, That the publicans and the harlots go into
the kingdom of God before you. For John came unto you 32
in the way of righteousness, and ye believed him not: but
the publicans and the harlots believed him: and ye, when
ye had seen *it*, repented not afterward, that *ye* might believe
him.

world, each parted into two great divisions—the two sons—the two parties of husbandmen or of guests—the wise and foolish virgins—the sheep and the goats—the talents used and misused.

It is the last act in a divine drama of surpassing interest and full of contrasts. The nation, and especially the Pharisees, who are the leaders of thought, triumphant to external sight, are hurrying to destruction, impelled by a hidden fate in the face of clear warnings; while Christ the King, Who seems to be vanquished and done to death, is really winning an eternal victory.

28. *two sons*] representing the sinners who first refused to do God's will, but repented at the preaching of John; and the Pharisees who, having "the righteousness which is of the law" (Phil. iii. 9), professed to do God's will but did it not. Both are sons. God still cares for both. The Pharisees may follow the sinners into the kingdom of God (*v.* 31). Paul was still a Pharisee; Nicodemus the Pharisee was still a secret follower of Christ.

29. *repented*] Rather "changed his mind," felt regret but not repentance or *metanoia*, a deeper and more lasting feeling: see ch. iii. 2.

According to a well-supported reading the cases of the two sons are reversed. The first agrees but goes not, the second refuses but afterwards works in the vineyard. The variation is interesting, because it points to an interpretation by which the two sons represent Jew and Gentile.

32. *the way of righteousness*] A Hebrew expression. Cp. "the way of God," ch. xxii. 16; "the way of salvation," Acts xvi. 17. The Christian doctrine was called in a special sense "the way" (Acts xix. 9, 23). The Greek word in the text also signified a philosophical system.

when ye had seen it] viz. that the publicans and the harlots believed him.

repented not afterward] Rather, **did not even change your minds**, much less repented in the deeper sense; see above, *v.* 29.

33—42. *The Wicked Husbandmen.*

33 Hear another parable: There was a certain householder,
which planted a vineyard, and hedged it round about, and
digged a winepress in it, and built a tower, and let it out to
34 husbandmen, and went into a far country: and when the

33—42. The Wicked Husbandmen.

Mark xii. 1—11; Luke xx. 9—18.

No parable interprets itself more clearly than this. Israel is represented by an image which the prophets had made familiar and unmistakeable—the Vineyard of the Lord. The householder who planted the Vineyard and fenced it round signifies God the Father, Who created the nation for Himself—a peculiar and separate people. The husbandmen are the Jews, and especially the Pharisees, the spiritual leaders of the Jews. The servants are the prophets of God, the Son is the Lord Jesus Christ.

33. *planted a vineyard*] Cp. the parable in Isaiah v. 1—7, where the description is very similar to this. See also Ps. lxxx. 8—16; Jer. ii. 21; Ezek. xv. 1—6. The vine was adopted as a national emblem on the Maccabean coins.

hedged it round about] with a stone wall or with a fence of prickly pears. St Luke makes no mention of the separating hedge. Israel was separated throughout her history politically, and even physically, by the natural position of Palestine.

digged a winepress] The winepress was often dug or hewn out of the limestone rock in Palestine. There were two receptacles or vats. The upper one was strictly the press or ληνός (Matthew), the lower one the winefat or ὑπολήνιον (Mark) into which the expressed juice of the grape passed. The two vats are mentioned together only in Joel iii. 13, "The press (*gath*) is full, the fats (*yekabim*) overflow" (quoted in *Bibl. Dict.*, see art. "Winepress").

built a tower] Probably a wooden booth raised on a high platform, in which a watcher was stationed to guard the grapes.

Neither the winepress nor the tower seems to have any special significance in the interpretation of the parable.

let it out to husbandmen] This kind of tenancy prevails in many parts of Europe. It is known as the *metayer* system, the arrangement being that the occupier of the land should pay to the landlord a portion—originally half—of the produce. The system existed in England for about sixty years at the end of the fourteenth century. Before the Revolution of 1790 nearly the whole of the land of France was rented by metayers. At the time of our Lord's ministry it was customary for the Romans to restore conquered lands on condition of receiving a moiety of the produce. Fawcett's *Manual of Political Economy*, p. 223; Rogers' *Political Economy*, p. 168.

went into a far country] Translate, **left his home.** The words "went into a far country" are not in the original text.

time of the fruit drew near, he sent his servants to the husbandmen, that *they* might receive the fruits of it. And the 35
husbandmen took his servants, and beat one, and killed
another, and stoned another. Again, he sent other servants 36
moe than the first: and they did unto them likewise. But 37
last *of all* he sent unto them his son, saying, They will reve-
rence my son. But when the husbandmen saw the son, they 38
said among themselves, This is the heir; come, let us kill
him, and let us seize on his inheritance. And they caught 39
him, and cast *him* out of the vineyard, and slew *him*. When 40
the lord therefore of the vineyard cometh, what will he do
unto those husbandmen? They say unto him, He will mise- 41
rably destroy those wicked *men*, and will let out *his* vineyard
unto other husbandmen, which shall render him the fruits in
their seasons. Jesus saith unto them, Did ye never read in 42
the scriptures, The stone which the builders rejected,

35. *beat one, and killed another, and stoned another*] See ch. xxiii. 35.

38. *let us seize on his inheritance*] This would be impossible in real life, but not more impossible than the thought of the Pharisees that by the death of Jesus they would gain the spiritual supremacy.

39. *cast him out of the vineyard*] Words that recall the crucifixion of Jesus outside the city of Jerusalem.

41. *They say unto him*] An interruption from the listening crowd, which marks the intense interest with which these parables were heard. The indignation of the bystanders is aroused as if it were a tale of actual life.

42. *Did ye never read in the scriptures*] Ps. cxviii. 22 (*v.* 25 of the same psalm is quoted above, *v.* 9, where see note); the psalm "was probably composed for the first celebration of the Feast of Tabernacles after the completion of the Second Temple" (Neh. viii. 13—18). (Canon Perowne.) The original reference was to a stone used in the erection of the second Temple. The "corner stone" is the Jewish nation rejected at first, afterwards restored from captivity. Christ transfers this image to His Church, formed of Jew and Gentile alike (see Meyer), which, though despised at first, was destined to succeed to the spiritual supremacy of Israel.

In Acts iv. 11, Eph. ii. 20, 1 Pet. ii. 6, Christ Himself is the head-corner-stone; but the two applications are not inconsistent, for Christ was the Representative first of the Jewish Nation (ch. iv. 15, ii. 1—11 (3)), then of the Church. Cp. also Isai. xxviii. 16, "I lay in Zion for a foundation a stone, a tried stone, a precious corner stone, a sure foundation."

The stone] Rather, A *stone*. The builders rejected many stones.

the same is become the head of the corner: this is
the Lord's doing, and it is marvellous in our eyes?
43 Therefore say I unto you, The kingdom of God shall be
taken from you, and given to a nation bringing forth the
44 fruits thereof. And whosoever shall fall on this stone shall
be broken: but on whomsoever it shall fall, it will grind him
45 to powder. And when the chief priests and Pharisees had
heard his parables, they perceived that he spake of them.
46 But when they sought to lay hands on him, they feared the
multitude, because they took him for a prophet.

1—14. *The Parable of the Royal Marriage Feast.*

22 And Jesus answered and spake unto them again by
2 parables, and said, The kingdom of heaven is like unto

the head of the corner] The stone that connects the two walls at the top and supports the roof.

44. *whosoever shall fall on this stone*, &c.] Lightfoot, *Hor. Hebr.*, sees here a reference to the custom of stoning: "the place of stoning was twice as high as a man. From the top of this, one of the witnesses striking him on his loins, fells him to the ground: if he died of this, well; if not, another witness threw a stone upon his heart."

But it is better to refer the image to an earthenware vessel (1) falling to the ground when it would be shattered, or (2) crushed by a stone when it would be bruised into atoms.

will grind him to powder] The Greek word lit. = "to winnow." So "cause to disappear," "destroy." Those to whom Jesus is a "rock of offence" (1 Peter ii. 8; Isai. viii. 14) in the days of His humiliation shall have great sorrow: but to incur His wrath when He comes to judge the earth will be utter destruction.

46. *when they sought to lay hands on him*] The Sanhedrin aimed at two things: (1) to seize Jesus quickly, for the Passover (during which no hostile measures could be taken) was close at hand; and because Jesus might be expected to quit Jerusalem after the feast. (2) To seize Him apart from the people; for the Galilæans would suffer no one to lay hands on their King and Prophet. Treachery alone enabled the Jews to secure their end.

CH. XXII. 1—14. THE PARABLE OF THE ROYAL MARRIAGE FEAST. Peculiar to St Matthew.

The parable recorded by St Luke (xiv. 16—24), though similar to this in some respects, differs in its context and special teaching and in many details.

As of the other parables of the Passion, the primary intention of this regards the present and the immediate future. The parable falls into two divisions, (1) *vv.* 1—7; (2) *vv.* 8—14. In the first (1) the servants

a certain king, which made a marriage for his son, and sent 3
forth his servants to call them that were bidden to the wedding: and they would not come. Again, he sent forth other 4
servants, saying, Tell them which are bidden, Behold, I have
prepared my dinner: my oxen and *my* fatlings *are* killed,
and all *things are* ready: come unto the marriage. But they 5
made light of *it*, and went their ways, one to his farm, another to his merchandise: and the remnant took his servants, 6
and entreated *them* spitefully, and slew *them*. But when the 7
king heard *thereof*, he was wroth: and he sent forth his
armies, and destroyed those murderers, and burnt up their
city. Then saith he to his servants, The wedding is ready, 8
but they which were bidden were not worthy. Go ye there- 9
fore into the highways, and as many as ye shall find, bid to
the marriage. So those servants went out into the *high*ways, 10
and gathered together all as many as they found, both bad
and good: and the wedding was furnished with guests. And 11
when the king came in to see the guests, he saw there a
man which had not on a wedding garment: and he saith 12

are John Baptist and the first disciples of Christ; the feast is the Kingdom of God, or the Christian Church; the invited guests, who refuse to come, are the Jews; the vengeance taken was literally fulfilled at the siege of Jerusalem, A.D. 70. (2) This division relates to the preaching of the Gospel to the Gentiles. As in the Net (ch. xiii. 47) or in the Corn-field (ch. xiii. 24), worthy and unworthy are mingled until the King separates.

2. *which made a marriage for his son*] Rather, *a marriage* **feast** *for his son.*

3. *sent forth his servants*] This was in accordance with Eastern custom. Cp. Esther v. 8, and vi. 14.

servants] Or **slaves**. In *v.* 13 a different Greek word is used for "servants."

7. *he was wroth*] For a subject to scorn the summons to the royal feast implied disloyalty and rebellion.

sent forth his armies] The soldiers of Titus literally achieved the purposes of God.

10. *So those servants went out into the highways*] Strictly, **into the places where different roads branch off.** The "servants" are the earliest Christian missionaries, Paul, Silas, Barnabas and others, who went in their journeys to such meeting-places of the nations at Rome, Antioch and Corinth.

bad and good] Who will always co-exist in the Church on earth.

11. *which had not on a wedding garment*] The festive robe which the master of the feast himself provided, so that there was no excuse. This

unto him, Friend, how camest thou in hither not having a
13 wedding garment? And he was speechless. Then said the
king to the servants, Bind him hand and foot, and take him
away, and cast *him* into outer darkness; there shall be weep-
14 ing and gnashing of teeth. For many are called, but few *are*
chosen.

15—22. *The Temptation of the Herodians. The Tribute Money.*

15 Then went the Pharisees, and took counsel how they
16 might entangle him in *his* talk. And they sent out unto
him their disciples with the Herodians, saying, Master, we
know that thou art true, and teachest the way of God in
truth, neither carest thou for any *man:* for thou regardest

man is the representative of a class—the bad (*v.* 10), who are not clothed in righteousness.

12. *was speechless*] See *v.* 34.

13. *and take him away*] Omit, on the best MS. authority.

outer darkness] The dark dungeon outside the brightness of the banqueting-hall.

15—22. THE TEMPTATION OF THE HERODIANS. THE TRIBUTE MONEY.

Mark xii. 13—17; Luke xx. 20—25.

15. *how they might entangle him*] Literally, **ensnare**, as a fowler ensnares birds. The Greek word is used here only in N.T.

All the previous attempts had been to discredit Jesus as a religious teacher; the present is an attempt to expose Him to the hostility of the Roman government. Will He follow Judas the Gaulonite, in disowning all human authority? or will He acquiesce in the Roman rule? In the one case He would incur the condemnation of Pilate, in the other the scorn of His Galilæan followers.

16. *their disciples with the Herodians*] An unnatural coalition, for the Pharisees represented the patriotic resistance to all foreign power; whereas the Herodians, as their name implies, supported the Herodian dynasty, and, as the context shews, acquiesced in the Roman rule. The Herodians are not named except in the first two Gospels; nor does Josephus include them in his account of Jewish sects. They were probably numerically insignificant, and may indeed have consisted merely of a few renegade Jews, who belonged to Herod's court. See ch. xi. 8.

we know that thou art true] Nothing could exceed the insidious hypocrisy of this attack on Jesus. His enemies approach Him as a teacher whom they trust.

regardest not the person of men] i.e. Thou art not moved by external appearance; neither wealth, power, nor prestige will influence thy decision.

not the person of men. Tell us therefore, What thinkest 17
thou? Is it lawful to give tribute unto Cesar, or not? But 18
Jesus perceived their wickedness, and said, Why tempt ye
me, *ye* hypocrites? Shew me the tribute money. And they 19
brought unto him a penny. And he saith unto them, Whose 20
is this image and superscription? They say unto him, Cesar's. 21
Then saith he unto them, Render therefore unto Cesar the
things which are Cesar's; and unto God the *things* that are
God's. When they had heard *these words*, they marvelled, 22
and left him, and went their way.

23—33. *The Sadducees tempt Jesus. The Condition of the Future Life.*

The same day came to him *the* Sadducees, which say that 23

17. *Is it lawful to give tribute unto Cesar, or not?*] The injunction, "thou mayest not set a stranger over thee" (Deut. xvii. 15), was interpreted to mean that the Jews should pay tribute to no foreign power. But their history exhibits them as tributary in turn to Assyria, Babylon, Egypt and Persia.

The question was an attempt to see whether Jesus would adopt the watchword of the Zealots. This special tribute, the poll-tax levied on each individual, was particularly offensive to the patriotic party among the Jews.

19. *they brought unto him a penny*] A *denarius*, bearing probably the image of Tiberius. The Jewish coins were not impressed with the effigy of their kings. Herod Philip, alone of his family, out of flattery to the Emperor, had caused his coins to be stamped with the likeness of Cæsar.

20. *superscription*] Rather, **inscription** or **effigy**.

21. *Render therefore unto Cesar the things which are Cesar's*] The Jewish doctors laid down the principle that "He is king whose coin passes current." St Paul expands this principle, which underlies our Lord's answer (Rom. xiii. 1 foll. Cp. also 1 Pet. ii. 13—17). *Render*= "pay back as due."

and unto God the things that are God's] The claim of the kingdom of Heaven is equally cogent. As the subjects and "husbandmen" of God, the Jews owe Him service and fruit. Neither in regard to Cæsar nor to God do the facts of the case leave any doubt as to what is due, and to whom, nor does obedience to the one of necessity clash with obedience to the other.

23—33. THE SADDUCEES TEMPT JESUS. THE CONDITION OF THE FUTURE LIFE.

Mark xii. 18—27; Luke xx. 27—38.

23. *the Sadducees*] See note ch. iii. 7. This is the only direct contact of the Sadducees with Jesus.

24 there is no resurrection, and asked him, saying, Master,
Moses said, If a man die, having no children, his brother shall marry his wife, and raise up seed unto his
25 brother. Now there were with us seven brethren: and the
first, when he had married *a wife*, deceased, and, having no
26 issue, left his wife unto his brother: likewise the second also,
27 and the third, unto the seventh. And last of all the woman
28 died also. Therefore in the resurrection whose wife shall
29 she be of the seven? for they all had her. Jesus answered
and said unto them, Ye do err, not knowing the scriptures,
30 nor the power of God. For in the resurrection they neither
marry, nor are given in marriage, but are as *the* angels of
31 God in heaven. But as touching the resurrection of the
dead, have ye not read that which was spoken unto you by
32 God, saying, I am the God of Abraham, and the God

24. *his brother shall marry his wife*] This is sometimes called the "levirate law," from Lat. *levir*, a brother-in-law; see Deut. xxv. 5. "The law on this subject is not peculiar to the Jews, but is found amongst various Oriental nations, ancient and modern." *Speaker's Comment.*, Deut. xxv. 5.

29. *not knowing*] i.e. "because ye do not know" (1) *the Scriptures*, which affirm the doctrine; nor (2) *the power of God*, which is able to effect the resurrection, and after the resurrection to create a new order of things in the new world.

30. *in the resurrection*] i.e. in that world or that phase of existence which begins with the resurrection.

The logical difficulty vanishes; for in this respect the analogy between the present world and the next does not hold good. The danger of the argument from analogy always lies in the fallacy that the things compared are alike at each point.

32. Jesus appeals to the Pentateuch when arguing with the Sadducees, with whom the books of Moses had the greatest authority.

Stated in a logical form the argument is: God is a God of the living *only*, but He is the God of Abraham, therefore Abraham is living. The same deduction from the words was made by the later Rabbinical writers.

The principle on which the proposition "God is the God of the living" rests, lies deeper. It depends upon the close relation between the life of God and the life of His children. The best illustration of the truth is the parable of the Vine (John xv. 1—8). The connection between the living God and the patriarchs, whose God He is, is as close as that between the vine and its branches. If the vine lives its branches live. If God is living and immortal the patriarchs are living and immortal. If the branches die they cease to belong to the vine; if the patriarchs were dead they would have ceased to have any relation to God, or God to them.

of Isaac, and the God of Jacob? God is not the God
of the dead, but of the living. And when the multitude 33
heard *this*, they were astonished at his doctrine.

34—40. *The Greatest Commandment.*

But when the Pharisees had heard that he had put the 34
Sadducees to silence, they were gathered together. Then 35
one of them, *which was* a lawyer, asked *him a question*,
tempting him, and saying, Master, which *is* the great com- 36
mandment in the law? Jesus said unto him, Thou shalt 37
love the Lord thy God with all thy heart, and with
all thy soul, and with all thy mind. This is the first and 38
great commandment. And the second *is* like unto it, Thou 39
shalt love thy neighbour as thyself. On these two 40
commandments hang all the law and the prophets.

So far there has been proof of immortality.

The argument for the Resurrection is inferred. For if the patriarchs are living, they are living in *Sheôl*, or Hades, and therefore they are awaiting a resurrection; cp. Heb. xi. 16. For this thought see Meyer ad loc.

33. *doctrine*] Rather, **teaching.**

34—40. The Greatest Commandment.

Mark xii. 28—34; Luke x. 25—28.

In St Luke the question is asked at an earlier period of the ministry, after the return of the Seventy; and the meaning of "neighbour" is illustrated by the parable of the "Good Samaritan."

34. *had put...to silence*] Literally, **gagged**; hence silenced completely, not only for the moment. The same Greek work is used (*v.* 12) of the guest; Mark i. 25 and Luke iv. 35, of silencing a demon; Mark iv. 39, of silencing a storm; 1 Cor. ix. 9 and 1 Tim. v. 18, of muzzling an ox.

35. *one of them, which was a lawyer*] i.e. an interpreter of the written law, as distinguished from the "traditions" or unwritten law.

37. See Deut. vi. 5.

heart...soul...mind] St Mark and St Luke add "strength." In Deut. the words are heart...soul...might. *Heart* includes the emotions, will, purpose; *soul*, the spiritual faculties; *mind*, the intellect, the thinking faculty. This greatest commandment was written on the phylactery which the "lawyer" was probably wearing. See ch. xxiii. 5.

St Mark (*vv.* 32—34) adds the lawyer's rejoinder and the commendation of Jesus, "thou art not far from the Kingdom of God."

41—46. *The Son of David.*

41 While the Pharisees were gathered together, Jesus asked
42 them, saying, What think ye of Christ? whose son is he?
43 They say unto him, *The Son* of David. He saith unto
them, How then doth David in spirit call him Lord, saying,
44 The LORD said unto my Lord, Sit thou on my right
45 hand, till I make thine enemies thy footstool? If
46 David then call him Lord, how is he his son? And no *man*
was able to answer him a word, neither durst any *man* from
that day forth ask him any moe *questions.*

1—39. *A Discourse to the Disciples respecting the Pharisees and the Jewish Nation.*

23 Then spake Jesus to the multitude, and to his disciples,
2 saying, The scribes and the Pharisees sit in Moses' seat: all
3 therefore whatsoever they bid you observe, *that* observe and
do; but do not ye after their works: for they say, and do
4 not. For they bind heavy burdens and grievous to be borne,
and lay *them* on men's shoulders; but they *themselves* will

41—46. THE SON OF DAVID.

Mark xii. 35—37; Luke xx. 41—44.

44. *The Lord said unto my Lord*] Ps. cx. 1. According to the Hebrew, "Jehovah said to Adoni," i.e. to my sovereign Lord, the Messiah, the Son of David.

said] The Hebrew word translated "said" implies divine inspiration, hence "in spirit" (*v.* 43). Canon Perowne translates, "the oracle of Jehovah unto my lord."

Sit thou on my right hand] As My co-regent, having power equal to Mine. This verse is quoted in 1 Cor. xv. 25; Heb. i. 13, and x. 12, 13. (Cp. for the expression ch. xx. 21.)

46. The Psalm was always regarded by the Jews as Messianic, hence their silence and inability to answer without acknowledging the divinity of Jesus.

CH. XXIII. 1—39. A DISCOURSE TO THE DISCIPLES RESPECTING THE PHARISEES AND THE JEWISH NATION.

The strength and weakness of the Scribes and Pharisees (*vv.* 1—12).

Only a part of this discourse appears in the other Synoptics; for this portion cp. Mark xii. 38—40; Luke xi. 43—46, xx. 46, 47.

2. *sit in Moses' seat*] i.e. succeed him as teachers. For sitting as the posture of a teacher cp. ch. v. 1.

4. *they bind heavy burdens*] Impose the grievous enactments of the Law. Cp. "My yoke is easy and my burden is light" (ch. xi. 30).

not move them with *one of* their fingers. But all their works 5
they do for to be seen of men: they make broad their
phylacteries, and enlarge the borders of their garments,
and love the uppermost rooms at feasts, and the chief 6
seats in the synagogues, and greetings in the markets, and 7
to be called of men, Rabbi, Rabbi. But be not ye called 8
Rabbi: for one is your Master, *even* Christ; and all ye are
brethren. And call no *man* your father upon the earth: for 9
one is your Father, which is in heaven. Neither be ye 10
called masters: for one is your Master, *even* Christ. But he 11
that is greatest among you shall be your servant. And who- 12
soever shall exalt himself shall be abased; and he that shall
humble himself shall be exalted.

5. *phylacteries*] Greek φυλακτήρια = "defences," and in late Greek "amulets" or "charms." The Hebrew name, *tephillin*, which is still in use, signifies "prayers." They were slips of parchment inscribed with four portions of the Law (Ex. xiii. 3—10, 11—16; Deut. vi. 5—9; xi. 13—21) enclosed in little cases or boxes made of calf-skin, and fastened by leather straps to the left arm and on the forehead, in accordance with a literal interpretation of Ex. xiii. 16 and Deut. vi. 8. To make the phylacteries, or rather the cases which contained them, broad and conspicuous was to assume a character of superior piety, for the phylacteries were symbols of devotion.

Jesus does not prohibit the practice of wearing phylacteries, but the ostentatious enlargement of them. It is thought by many that our Saviour Himself wore phylacteries.

enlarge the borders of their garments] Strictly, **the fringe of the talith,** or cloak: another instance of ostentation; the blue threads in the fringe, the colour of the sky—were a type of heavenly purity. Our Lord Himself wore the fringed talith (see ch. ix. 20); the offence of the Pharisees consisted in enlarging the symbolical fringes.

6. *the uppermost rooms*] i.e. "the most honourable seats." The Jews, like the Romans, reclined at meals on couches, called *triclinia*—each containing three seats—and each seat having its special dignity. The seats on the triclinia are here called "rooms."

7. *to be called of men, Rabbi, Rabbi*] Literally, **great [one], lord.** This title, with which the great doctors of the law were saluted, was quite modern, not having been introduced before the time of Hillel. The true teaching on this point is found in the Talmud, "Love the work but hate the title."

8. *be not ye called Rabbi*] The emphasis is on "ye," which is expressed in the Greek. Ye as Scribes of the Kingdom of Heaven must not be as the Jewish Scribes.

10. *masters*] Rather, **leaders, guides,** it is not the same word as in *v.* 8.

11. Cp. ch. xx. 26, 27.

13 But woe unto you, scribes and Pharisees, hypocrites! for
ye shut up the kingdom of heaven against men: for ye
neither go in yourselves, neither suffer ye them that are
entering to go in.
14 Woe unto you, scribes and Pharisees, hypocrites! for
ye devour widows' houses, and for a pretence make long
prayer: therefore ye shall receive the greater damnation.
15 Woe unto you, scribes and Pharisees, hypocrites! for ye
compass sea and land to make one proselyte, and when he
is made, ye make him twofold more *the* child of hell than
yourselves.
16 Woe unto you, *ye* blind guides, which say, Whosoever

Seven woes denounced against the Scribes and Pharisees. 13—36.

13. *ye shut up the kingdom of heaven against men*] In allusion to the symbolic "key of knowledge" given to the Scribe on admission to the order. They use their keys to shut rather than to open the doors of the Kingdom.

14. *ye devour widows' houses*] i.e. "consume their substance," by illegal exaction or by working upon their religious feelings; a common form of rapacity. The Vatican and Sinaitic MSS. omit this verse, which occurs Mark xii. 40, and Luke xx. 47.

15. *compass*] "go about," "traverse." The word is used of our Lord's "circuits" in Galilee, ch. iv. 23; ix. 35.

proselyte] Literally, **one who approaches**, hence, "a worshipper," (cp. Heb. x. 1), "a convert." The Pharisee, St Paul, carried with him into his new faith the same zeal, with a higher motive. He describes (2 Cor. xi. 26) "the perils by water, perils in the city, and perils in the wilderness," which this eager "compassing of land and sea" brought to him.

Judaism has been classed among the non-missionary religions. This is true at the present day, and through most of its history. Indeed, Rabbinical sayings display jealousy of proselytes. On the other hand, John Hyrcanus imposed Judaism on Edom at the point of the sword (1 Macc. v. 65, 66). The conversion is recorded of whole tribes in Arabia, and on the shores of the Caspian. Also, it appears from the Acts that the number of proselytes in Asia Minor and in Greece was considerable. And in later days Solomon Malco, a Portuguese Jew, was burnt to death under Charles V. on a charge of proselytizing. Probably the proselytism in the text is connected with the charge of rapacity; the Pharisees seeking to convert wealthy Gentiles, over whom they obtained influence.

child of hell] Rather, **son of Gehenna.**

twofold more the child of hell than yourselves] In accordance with a tendency in new converts to exaggerate the external points of the creed which they adopt, Gentile proselytes strained to the utmost the worst features of Pharisaism.

shall swear by the temple, it is nothing; but whosoever
shall swear by the gold of the temple, he is a debtor. *Ye* 17
fools and blind: for whether is greater, the gold, or the
temple that sanctifieth the gold? And, Whosoever shall 18
swear by the altar, it is nothing; but whosoever sweareth by
the gift that is upon it, he is guilty. *Ye* fools and blind: 19
for whether *is* greater, the gift, or the altar that sanctifieth
the gift? Whoso therefore shall swear by the altar, sweareth 20
by it, and by all *things* thereon. And whoso shall swear by 21
the temple, sweareth by it, and by him that dwelleth therein. And he that shall swear by heaven, sweareth by the 22
throne of God, and by him that sitteth thereon.

Woe unto you, scribes and Pharisees, hypocrites! for ye 23
pay tithe of mint and anise and cummin, and have omitted
the weightier *matters* of the law, judgment, mercy, and
faith: these ought *ye* to have done, and not to leave the
other undone. *Ye* blind guides, which strain out a gnat, and 24
swallow a camel.

16. *the gold of the temple*] i.e. the offerings made to the Temple, called "Corban," or "devoted;" the use of that word made an oath binding, see ch. xv. 5.

23. *ye pay tithe of mint and anise and cummin*] "Mint and rue and all manner of herbs," (Luke xi. 42.) Zeal in paying tithes was one of the points of reform under the Maccabees.

anise] Greek ἄνηθον, either = "anise" as in E.V., or "dill," a plant similar in appearance, and used like anise as a sedative medicine and for cooking purposes.

cummin] See Isaiah xxviii. 25, 27, where the special method of beating out cummin seeds is named. "It is used as a spice, both bruised to mix with bread, and also boiled in the various messes and stews which compose an Oriental banquet." Tristram, *Nat. Hist. of Bible.*

weightier matters of the law] The distinction between great and small precepts of the law is found in the Talmud. Schöttgen gives many instances, p. 183. One saying is: "Observance of the lesser precepts is rewarded on earth; observance of the greater precepts is rewarded in heaven."

judgment, mercy, and faith] "Judgment and the love of God" (Luke).

24. *strain out a gnat*] A correction for the reading of E. V. "strain *at* a gnat;" the reading in the text appears in the earlier editions of the English Bible from Tyndale to Bishops' Bible. See Cambridge Paragraph Bible, *Introd.*, Appendix A. The reading of the E. V. is not a misprint, as some have thought; "to strain *at*" meant, to strain the wine on the occurrence of a gnat.

25 Woe unto you, scribes and Pharisees, hypocrites! for ye
make clean the outside of the cup and of the platter, but
26 within they are full of extortion and excess. *Thou* blind
Pharisee, cleanse first that *which is* within the cup and
platter, that the outside of them may be clean also.
27 Woe unto you, scribes and Pharisees, hypocrites! for ye
are like unto whited sepulchres, which indeed appear beautiful outward, but are within full of dead *men's* bones, and of
28 all uncleanness. *Even* so ye also outwardly appear righteous
unto men, but within ye are full of hypocrisy and iniquity.
29 Woe unto you, scribes and Pharisees, hypocrites! because
ye build the tombs of the prophets, and garnish the
30 sepulchres of the righteous, and say, If we had been in the
days of our fathers, we would not have been partakers with
31 them in the blood of the prophets. Wherefore ye be
witnesses unto yourselves, that ye are the children of them
32 which killed the prophets. Fill ye up then the measure of
33 your fathers. *Ye* serpents, *ye* generation of vipers, how
can ye escape the damnation of hell?

25. *are full*] Observe how swiftly and naturally Eastern speech passes from the figurative to the literal. The outside of the cup and platter is the external behaviour and conduct of the Pharisee, the inside of the cup is his heart and real life.

extortion] The same Greek word is translated "ravening," Luke xi. 39. Instances of this sin are alluded to *vv.* 14 and 15. See notes.

excess] Opposed to sobriety and self-control. Luke in the parallel passage has "wickedness."

26. *that which is within the cup*] Rather, **the inside of the cup**. Cp. Mark vii. 4.

27. *like unto whited sepulchres*] In Luke the comparison is to "graves that appear not," by walking over which men unconsciously defile themselves. To avoid this ceremonial defilement the Jews carefully whitewashed the graves or marked them with chalk on a fixed day every year—the fifteenth of Adar. The custom still exists in the East. One of the spiteful devices of the Samaritans against the Jews was to remove the whitewash from sepulchres in order that the Jews might be contaminated by walking over them.

29. *build the tombs of the prophets*, &c.] Luke xi. 47, 48. A portion of the Temple-offerings was devoted to this purpose. See Lightfoot, *Hor. Hebr.* ad loc.

31. *witnesses unto yourselves*] You call yourselves children, and indeed you *are* children of those who slew the prophets. You inherit their wickedness in compassing the death of the Prophet of the Lord.

33. *generation of vipers*] See note ch. iii. 7.

Wherefore behold, I send unto you prophets, and wise 34
men, and scribes: and *some* of them ye shall kill and crucify;
and *some* of them shall ye scourge in your synagogues, and
persecute *them* from city to city: that upon you may come 35
all the righteous blood shed upon the earth, from the blood
of righteous Abel unto the blood of Zacharias son of
Barachias, whom ye slew between the temple and the altar.
Verily I say unto you, All these *things* shall come upon this 36
generation.

37—39. *The Fate of Jerusalem.*

O Jerusalem, Jerusalem, *thou* that killest the prophets, 37

the damnation of hell] Rather, **the judgment of Gehenna.**

34. *I send unto you prophets, and wise men, and scribes*] Marking the continuity of the Christian with the Jewish Church.

ye shall kill and crucify] Kill, directly as Stephen (Acts vii. 59), indirectly as James (Acts xii. 2), and crucify, by means of the Roman power, as Symeon, second Bishop of Jerusalem (Eus. *H. E.* III. 32).

scourge in your synagogues] See note ch. iv. 23.

from city to city] As Paul pursued Christians to Damascus; as he was himself driven from Antioch in Pisidia, from Iconium, from Philippi, and from Thessalonica.

35. *from the blood of righteous Abel unto the blood of Zacharias*] If the reading "son of Barachias" be retained (it is omitted in the Sinaitic MS.) a difficulty arises; for the Zacharias, whose death "in the court of the house of the Lord" is recorded 2 Chron. xxiv. 20—22, was the son of Jehoiada. The words, however, do not occur in Luke xi. 51, and are possibly interpolated. Zechariah the prophet was a son of Barachias: but of his death no record is preserved. Another explanation has been offered. At the commencement of the Jewish War with Vespasian a Zacharias, son of Baruch, was slain in the Temple by two zealots (Jos. *B. J.* IV. 5. 4). Accordingly many commentators have thought that Jesus spoke prophetically of that event. The coincidence is remarkable, but the explanation is hardly probable.

The space from Abel to Zacharias, son of Jehoiada, covers the whole history of the Jews; for the Jewish Canon, not being arranged in order of time, closed with the second book of Chronicles.

ye slew] The present generation shares in the guilt of that murder.

33—39. THE FATE OF JERUSALEM.

37. *Jerusalem, Jerusalem*] From Luke xiii. 34, it appears that our Lord spoke these words in a different connection at an earlier period of His ministry. For the pathetic reiteration of the name, cp. ch. xxvii. 46. The Aramaic form for Jerusalem in the text appears here only in Matthew; it is the usual form in Luke. Probably the very form—Aramaic, not Greek—employed by our Lord is retained.

killest...stonest] Recalling the precise expressions of ch. xxi. 35.

and stonest them which are sent unto thee, how often would
I have gathered thy children together, even as a hen
gathereth her chickens under *her* wings, and ye would not?
38 Behold, your house is left unto you desolate. For I say
39 unto you, Ye shall not see me henceforth, till ye shall say,
Blessed is he that cometh in the name of the Lord.

1—22. *Prediction of the Fall of Jerusalem.*

24 And Jesus went out, and departed from the temple: and

as a hen gathereth her chickens under her wings] Schöttgen *ad loc.* observes that converts to Judaism were said to come "under the wings of the Shechinah." That thought may be contained in the words of Christ. Many times by His prophets He called the children of Jerusalem to Himself—the true Shechinah—through whom the glory of the latter house was greater than that of the former.

ye would not] Note the change to the plural.

38. *your house*] i.e. Jerusalem, rather than the Temple.

desolate] Omitted in the Vatican Codex, but too strongly supported to be removed from the text.

39. *For* explains "desolate" of *v.* 38. The Temple is desolate, for Christ, who is the Lord of the Temple, leaves it for ever.

till ye shall say] Till, like the children in these Temple-courts, ye recognise Me as the Messiah. See ch. xxi. 15. The words of Jesus, and the place, and the anger of the Scribes, may have recalled to some the scene in which Jeremiah, on the same spot, denounced the sin of Israel, called them to repentance, and foretold the destruction of the Temple: "then will I make this house like Shiloh"..."and all the people took him, saying, Thou shalt surely die," Jer. xxvi. 1—8.

CH. XXIV. 1—22. PREDICTION OF THE FALL OF JERUSALEM.

Mark xiii. 1—end. Luke xxi 5—36.

This chapter opens with the great discourse of Jesus, which is continued to the end of ch. xxv. That discourse contains (1) a prediction of the fall of Jerusalem, (2) a prediction of the end of the world, (3) Parables in relation to these predictions.

It is difficult to determine the limits of the several portions. The division adopted below has the sanction of Chrysostom and Jerome, and is followed by Maldonatus.

Another arrangement of the prophecy is: (i) A general answer of the question to the end of *v.* 14; (ii) a specific reference to the fall of Jerusalem, 15—28; (iii) in *v.* 29 a resumption of the subject of (i).

The view that the two predictions are inextricably intermingled seems the least probable.

1. *went out, and departed from the temple*] Read, on the highest MS. authority, "went out from the temple, and was going on his way." On

his disciples came to *him* for to shew him the buildings of
the temple. And Jesus said unto them, See ye not all these 2
things? verily I say unto you, There shall not be left here
one stone upon another, that shall not be thrown down.
And as he sat upon the mount of Olives, the disciples came 3
unto him privately, saying, Tell us, when shall these *things*
be? and what *shall be* the sign of thy coming, and of the
end of the world? And Jesus answered and said unto them, 4
Take heed that no *man* deceive you. For many shall come 5
in my name, saying, I am Christ; and shall deceive many.
And ye shall hear of wars and rumours of wars: see that ye 6
be not troubled: for all *these things* must come to pass, but

leaving the Temple Jesus would descend into the valley of Kedron and ascend the opposite slope of the Mount of Olives. Then full in view the Temple would rise with its colonnade of dazzling white marble, surmounted with golden roof and pinnacles, and founded on a substructure of huge stones. Milman writes (*History of the Jews*, II. 322) "At a distance the whole Temple looked literally like a mount of snow, fretted with golden pinnacles."

2. *There shall not be left here one stone upon another*] Compare with the complete ruin of the Temple at Jerusalem, the still magnificent remains of temples at Karnak and Luxor, Baalbec, and Athens. The Temple was destroyed by fire, notwithstanding every effort made to save it by Titus. For a vivid description of this last awful scene in the history of the Temple, see Milman, *History of the Jews*, II. Bk. xvi.

the disciples] St Mark names the four, Peter and James and John and Andrew.

3. *when shall these things be? and what shall be the sign of thy coming*] The twofold question points to the nearer and the more distant event. See note at beginning of chapter.

thy coming] Rather, **thy presence** (*parousia*). The precise word "coming," or "advent," which the Church has adopted in reference to the second "presence" of Christ, does not occur in this prophecy.

the end of the world] See ch. xiii. 39, 40.

5. *saying, I am Christ*] Rather, **the** Christ, the Messiah. The appearance of false Messiahs shall be the first sign. St John bears witness to the fulfilment of this sign: "Even now are there many antichrists, whereby we know that it is the last time," 1 John ii. 18.

6. *wars and rumours of wars*] The second sign. Philo and Josephus describe the disturbed state of Judæa from this date to the siege of Jerusalem. Massacres of the Jews were perpetrated at Cæsarea, at Alexandria, in Babylonia and in Syria.—See Milman's *History of the Jews*, Bks. xii.—xv. Tacitus, characterising the same period, says "opus adgredior opimum casibus, atrox præliis, discors seditionibus, ipsa etiam pace sævum." *Hist.* I. 2.

7 the end is not yet. For nation shall rise against nation,
and kingdom against kingdom: and there shall be famines,
8 and pestilences, and earthquakes in divers places. All
these *are* the beginning of sorrows.
9 Then shall they deliver you up to be afflicted, and shall
kill you: and ye shall be hated of all nations for my name's
10 sake. And then shall many be offended, and shall betray
11 one another, and shall hate one another. And many false
12 prophets shall rise, and shall deceive many. And because
13 iniquity shall abound, the love of many shall wax cold. But
he that shall endure unto the end, the same shall be saved.
14 And this gospel of the kingdom shall be preached in all the

7. *famines, and pestilences, and earthquakes*] The commentators enumerate instances of all these calamities recorded by the contemporary historians.

8. *sorrows*] Literally, **pains of travail**, that preceded the birth of a new order of things, a fresh *æon*.

10. *offended*] Disappointed hopes will bring about a disruption of Christian unity and love.

11. *false prophets*] At the siege of Jerusalem "false prophets suborned by the Zealots kept the people in a state of feverish excitement, as though the appointed Deliverer would still appear." Milman's *History of the Jews*, II. 371.

12. *iniquity*] Literally, **lawlessness.**

shall abound] Translate, **hath abounded.**

the love of many] Rather, **of the many**, i.e. of "the majority." Love or *agapé* became the leading virtue and grace of the Christian life, yet this is the only instance of the word in the Synoptic Gospels, except Luke xi. 42, "the love of God." The noun itself is not classical, and therefore lent itself the more readily to Christian use. But the thought connected with the word, "family affection," was beautiful before it was spiritualised by Christianity. The E. V. has two renderings, "love" and "charity," (see especially 1 Cor. xiii.). The first seems to be too wide, the second too restricted, denoting a principal tendency or function of *agapé* rather than agapé itself. The use of the word by our Lord to express Christian unity is itself prophetic. St Paul experienced this "coldness of love:" "at my first answer no man stood with me," 2 Tim. iv. 16.

13. *he that shall endure*] Cp. "In your patience possess ye your souls," (rather, "by patience ye shall win your lives,") Luke xxi. 19.

14. *preached in all the world*] Cp. ch. x. 23 and Col. i. 5, 6, "the gospel; which is come unto you, as it is in all the world." The principle is at last established that the Gospel may be preached to Jew and Gentile alike.

world for a witness unto all nations; and then shall the end
come.
When ye therefore shall see the abomination of desolation, 15
spoken of by Daniel the prophet, stand in the holy place,
(whoso readeth, let him understand:) then let them which 16
be in Judea flee into the mountains: let him which is on 17
the housetop not come down to take any *thing* out of his
house: neither let him which is in the field return back to 18
take his clothes. And woe unto them that are with child, 19
and to them that give suck in those days. But pray ye that 20
your flight be not in the winter, neither on the sabbath day:

15. *the abomination of desolation*] i.e. "the abomination that maketh desolate," "the act of sacrilege, which is a sign and a cause of desolation." What special act of sacrilege is referred to cannot be determined for certain. The expression may refer (1) to the besieging army; cp. the parallel passage in Luke, "When ye shall see Jerusalem compassed with armies." Lightfoot, *Hor. Hebr.*, translates Dan. ix. 27 in this sense: "Until the wing (or army) of abominations shall make desolate." (2) The Roman eagles; the E.V. margin, Dan. ix. 27, reads: "Upon the battlements shall be the idols of the desolator." (3) The excesses of the Zealots. See Josephus, *B. J.* IV. 6. 3, "They (the Zealots) caused the fulfilment of the prophecies against their own country; for there was a certain ancient saying that the city would be taken at that time......for sedition would arise, and their own hands would pollute the Temple of God."

in the holy place] i.e. within the Temple area.

whoso readeth, let him understand] These words are almost beyond a doubt an insertion of the Evangelist, and not part of our Lord's discourse.

16. *let them which be in Judea flee into the mountains*] Many Christians, warned by this prediction (according to Eusebius, *H.E.* III. 5, "by a certain oracle"), took refuge at Pella in Peræa during the siege of Jerusalem.

17. *not come down to take any thing out of his house*] i.e. either (1) pass from the roof to the entrance, and thence to the street, without entering any apartments, or (2) escape along the flat roofs from house to house.

18. *return back to take his clothes*] The Greek word signifies the outer garment, which the field labourer would throw off while at work, wearing the tunic only. Cp. "Nudus ara, sere nudus." *Georg.* I. 299.

20. *not in the winter*] when swollen streams, bitter cold and long nights would increase the misery and danger of the fugitives.

on the sabbath day] when religious scruples might delay the flight. The extent of a Sabbath day's journey was 2000 cubits. Here, however, the question meets us, how far Jewish observances would affect

21 for then shall be great tribulation, such as was not since the
beginning of the world to this time, no, nor ever shall be.
22 And except those days should be shortened, there should no
flesh be saved: but for the elect's sake those days shall be
shortened.

23—31. *The Second Coming of Christ.*

23 Then if any *man* shall say unto you, Lo, here *is*
24 Christ, or there; believe *it* not. For there shall arise false

the Christians. Probably the early Christians observed both the Sabbath and the Lord's day. But in any case many impediments would arise against flight on the Sabbath day. St Matthew alone records these words of warning.

21. *great tribulation*] "Jerusalem, a city that had been liable to so many miseries during the siege, that had it enjoyed as much happiness from its first foundation, it would certainly have been the envy of the world." Josephus, *B. J.* VIII. 6. 5.

No words can describe the unequalled horrors of this siege. It was the Passover season, and Jews from all parts were crowded within the walls. Three factions, at desperate feud with each other, were posted on the heights of Sion and on the Temple Mount. These only united to fling themselves at intervals upon the Roman entrenchments, and then resumed their hate. The Temple-courts swam with the blood of civil discord, which was literally mingled with the blood of the sacrifices. Jewish prisoners were crucified by hundreds in view of their friends, while within the city the wretched inhabitants were reduced by famine to the most loathsome of food and to deeds of unspeakable cruelty. Jerusalem was taken on the 10th August, A.D. 70. 1,100,000 Jews perished in the siege, 100,000 were sold into slavery. With the fall of Jerusalem Israel ceased to exist as a nation. It was truly the end of an *æon*.

22. *those days should be shortened*] Several circumstances concurred to shorten the duration of the siege, such as the scanty supply of provisions, the crowded state of the city, the internal dissensions, and the abandonment of important defences. So strong did the place seem to Titus that he exclaimed, "We have certainly had God on our side in this war; and it was God alone who ejected the Jews from these fortifications." Josephus VI. 9. 1.

23. *Then*] The transition is marked by this word, it was possibly also marked by a pause in the Saviour's discourse.

23—31. THE SECOND COMING OF CHRIST.

Mark xiii. 21—27; Luke xxi. 24—28.

The following scheme, intended to shew a parallelism between the two Predictions, is borrowed from an interesting monograph by the

Christs, and false prophets, and shall shew great signs and
wonders; insomuch that, if *it were* possible, *they shall*
deceive the very elect. Behold, I have told you before. 25
Wherefore if they shall say unto you, Behold, he is in the 26
desert; go not forth: behold, *he is* in the secret chambers;
believe *it* not. For as the lightning cometh out of the east, 27
and shineth *even* unto the west; so shall also the coming of
the Son of man be. For wheresoever the carcase is, there 28
will the eagles be gathered together.

Immediately after the tribulation of those days shall the 29
sun be darkened, and the moon shall not give her light, and

Rev. W. Sherlock, who argues for the division of the prophecy at *v.* 22:

THE FALL OF JERUSALEM (*vv.* 5—22).	THE SECOND ADVENT (*vv.* 23—31).
1. False Christs and false prophets (*vv.* 5, 11).	1. False Christs and false prophets (*vv.* 23, 24).
2. Persecution and apostasy (*vv.* 9, 10, 12).	2. Dangers even to the elect (*v.* 24).
3. Wars, famine, pestilence (*vv.* 6, 7).	3 Distress of nations (*v.* 29).
4. Great tribulation (*v.* 21).	4. The sun and moon darkened (*v.* 29)
5. The abomination of desolation (*v.* 15).	5. The sign of the Son of man (*v.* 30).
6. The escape of the Christians (*vv.* 16—18).	6. The salvation of the elect (*v.* 31).

24. *shall deceive the very elect*] Compare this with the less dangerous influence of false prophets before the siege of Jerusalem, "shall deceive many."

26. *in the desert...in the secret chambers*] i.e. whether the false Christ shall go forth into the desert and draw men to him by an ascetic life, or shall influence by teaching in the "schools" of the synagogues, be not deceived.

secret chambers] one word in the original. The same word is translated "closet" (ch. vi. 6), that is the place for prayer on the top or in the upper part of an Eastern house.

27. *as the lightning*] All-pervading, swift, sudden and of dazzling brightness; such shall be the coming of the Son of man.

shineth] Translate, **appeareth.** The flash is instantly visible in the remotest quarter.

28. *wheresoever the carcase is*] The spiritual perception will discern when the Lord comes and where, by a subtle sense like that by which the vulture is cognisant of his distant prey.

Another interpretation fixes upon the idea of corruption in the body, and taking the "eagles" to mean the eagles of the Roman standards reads the sense thus: "where the corrupt body of sin lies there will the eagles of vengeance be gathered."

This view is excluded by the division of the prophecy adopted in these notes.

29. *Immediately after the tribulation of those days*] i.e. the tribulation which shall precede the second advent of Christ.

shall the sun be darkened, and the moon shall not give her light] Such figurative language is frequent with the Hebrew prophets; it implies (1)

the stars shall fall from heaven, and the powers of the
30 heavens shall be shaken: and then shall appear the sign of
the Son of man in heaven: and then shall all the tribes of
the earth mourn, and they shall see the Son of man coming
31 in the clouds of heaven with power and great glory. And
he shall send his angels with a great sound of a trumpet,
and they shall gather together his elect from the four winds,
from one end of heaven to the other.

32—35. *The Parable of the Fig Tree.*

32 Now learn a parable of the fig tree; When his branch is
yet tender, and putteth forth leaves, ye know that summer

the perplexity and confusion of a sudden revolution, a great change; the very sources of light become darkness. Cp. Isaiah xiii. 10, "For the stars of heaven and the constellations thereof shall not give their light: the sun shall be darkened in his going forth, and the moon shall not cause her light to shine;" and (2) the darkness of distress as Ezek. xxxii. 7, 8, "All the bright lights of heaven will I make dark over thee, and set darkness upon thy land, saith the Lord God."

30. *the sign of the Son of man in heaven*] What this shall be it is vain to conjecture, but when it appears its import will be instantly recognised by the faithful.

in the clouds] Translate, **on the clouds.**

31. *with a great sound of a trumpet*] Omit "sound" on high MS. authority, translate **with a great trumpet.** The image would be suggestive to the Jews, who were called together in the camp by silver trumpets (Numb. x. 2 foll.). Moreover, the great festivals, the commencement of the year, and other celebrations were announced by trumpets.

32—35. The Parable of the Fig Tree.

Mark xiii. 28—31; Luke xxi. 29—33.

32. *learn a parable of the fig tree*] More accurately, **learn from the fig-tree its parable**, the lesson that the fig-tree teaches. The parable relates to the siege of Jerusalem and the ruin of the Jewish nationality, illustrating *vv.* 4—22.

It was spring time, and the fig tree was putting forth its leaf-buds; no more certainly does that natural sign foretell the coming harvest than the signs of Christ shall foretell the fall of the Holy City. The sequence of historical events is as certain as the sequence of natural events. And the first, at least to some extent, is within the range of the same human intelligence that discerns the promise of summer. Thus Jesus rebuked the Pharisees for not discerning the signs of the times as they discerned the face of the sky.

is nigh: so likewise ye, when ye shall see all these *things*, 33
know that it is near, *even* at the doors. Verily I say unto 34
you, This generation shall not pass, till all these *things* be
fulfilled. Heaven and earth shall pass away, but my words 35
shall not pass away.

36—51. *The Coming of Christ; the Need of Watchfulness.*

But of that day and hour knoweth no *man*, no, not the angels 36
of heaven, but my Father only. But as the days of Noe 37
were, so shall also the coming of the Son of man be. For 38

When his branch is yet tender] Translate, **as soon as its branch becomes tender,** i.e. ready to sprout. Observe *his* for the modern *its*.

ye know] Rather, **recognise**; as also in the following verse; in *v.* 36 a different Greek word is rightly translated **knoweth.**

that summer is nigh] Or, "that **harvest time** is nigh," i.e. the corn-harvest, not the fig-harvest (Meyer). This is a probable rendering, because the sprouting of the fig-tree would coincide with the barley harvest, rather than with the summer; it gives force to our Lord's words, when it is remembered that the barley harvest was actually nigh; the omer, or first sheaf, being offered on the day following the Passover. Again, the siege of Jerusalem prefigured by this "parable" took place at the time of harvest (see note, *v.* 21).

33. *know that it is near*] *it* = the harvest time of God—the end of this *æon* or period at the fall of Jerusalem.

34. *This generation*] See note, ch. xvi. 28.

35. This verse was originally omitted in the Sinaitic MS., but is inserted by a later hand.

36—End of Ch. XXV. Parables and Teachings concerning the Second Advent.

36—51. The Coming of Christ; the Need of Watchfulness.

More briefly reported in Mark xiii. 32—37; Luke xxi. 34—36.

36. *But of that day and hour*] the Day of Judgment. The discourse turns from the type—the fall of Jerusalem—to the antitype—the Day of Judgment, and continues on this subject to the end of the following chapter.

37. *Noe*] This, the Greek form of the name, appears in E. V., Luke xvii. 26; "Noah" is read in the other passages where the name occurs, 1 Pet. iii. 20; 2 Pet. ii. 5; Heb. xi. 7.

The Last Day will surprise men occupied in their pleasures and their business, as the Flood or the destruction of Sodom and Gomorrah (Luke xvii. 27—29) surprised all except those who "watched." All such great and critical events are typical of the End of the World.

coming] See *v.* 3.

as in the days that were before the flood they were eating
and drinking, marrying and giving in marriage, until the day
39 that Noe entered into the ark, and knew not until the flood
came, and took *them* all away; so shall also the coming of
40 the Son of man be. Then shall two be in the field; the one
41 shall be taken, and the other left. Two *women shall be*
grinding at the mill; *the* one shall be taken, and *the* other
42 left. Watch therefore: for ye know not what hour your
Lord doth come.

43—45. *The Lord cometh as a Thief in the Night.*

43 But know this, that if the goodman of the house had
known in what watch the thief would come, he would have
watched, and would not have suffered his house to be
44 broken up. Therefore be ye also ready: for in such an
hour as you think not the Son of man cometh.

40, 41. Instances like these serve to bring out the reflection that the world's work will be going on then as now; there is also the thought of a real separation in this life beneath an external sameness.

40. *shall be taken*] Properly, **is taken** or withdrawn. For this present for future of certainty see ch. xxvii. 63.

41. *Two women shall be grinding at the mill*] In southern Palestine, where there are no mill-streams, hand-mills are to be seen and heard in every village. "Two women sit at the mill facing each other; both having hold of the handle by which the upper is turned round on the nether mill-stone." *Land and Book*, p. 526.

shall be taken] See preceding verse.

43—45. The Lord cometh as a Thief in the Night.

Luke xii. 39, 40.

43. *know this*] The same word as in *v.* 33, see note. The word is probably indicative, "ye know this," not imperative.

the goodman of the house] "The master of the house." "Goodman" is probably a corruption for *gummann* or A. S. *guma*, a man (*Bible Word Book*).

in what watch] See ch. xiv. 25.

the thief would come] Cp. "For yourselves know perfectly that the day of the Lord so cometh as a thief in the night," 1 Thess. v. 2; see also 2 Pet. iii. 10.

would come] Rather, **doth come**, as in the preceding verse.

to be broken up] Rather, **dug through**; see ch. vi. 19, 20.

45—51. *The Stewards of God.*

Who then is a faithful and wise servant, whom his lord hath 45
made ruler over his household, to give them meat in due
season? Blessed *is* that servant, whom his lord when he 46
cometh shall find so doing. Verily I say unto you, That he 47
shall make him ruler over all his goods. But *and* if that evil 48
servant shall say in his heart, My lord delayeth his coming;
and shall begin to smite *his* fellowservants, and to eat and 49
drink with the drunken; the lord of that servant shall come 50
in a day when he looketh not for *him*, and in an hour that
he is not ware of, and shall cut him asunder, and appoint 51
him his portion with the hypocrites: there shall be weeping
and gnashing of teeth.

45—51. The Stewards of God.

Luke xii. 41—48, where this parable is joined on to the preceding one by a question of St Peter, "Lord, speakest thou this parable unto us, or even to all?" Mark xiii. 37 has "what I say unto you I say unto all, Watch." Here, and throughout the discourse, the disciples are specially addressed.

45. *Who then is a faithful and wise servant*] The steward was generally a slave whom his master had chosen on account of his trustworthiness and intelligence to be the steward of his estate, his *villicus* or *dispensator*. The word "*dispensation*," in such expressions as "the present dispensation," "the Christian dispensation," has passed into religious language from this and the parallel passages.

his household] all his other slaves, Lat. *familia*.

to give them meat in due season] The daily (diarium) or monthly (menstruum) allowance; cp. "Cum servis urbana diaria rodere mavis?" Hor. *Ep.* I. 14. 41. This imagery, drawn from a large Roman estate (latifundium), has given rise to the often-recurring thought of the Stewardship of the Apostles and Ministers of Christ. "Stewards of the mysteries of God," 1 Cor. iv. 1; "blameless, as the steward of God," Tit. i. 7.

51. *shall cut him asunder*] See Dan. ii. 5 and iii. 29. "The angel of God waiteth with the sword to cut thee in two," (Susanna, 59.) Comp. also "Multos honesti ordinis aut ad bestias condemnavit, aut serra dissecuit." Sueton. *Calig.* 17, quoted by Wetstein, who gives other instances.

his portion with the hypocrites] St Luke has "with the unbelievers." Such adaptations of the Gentile Evangelist to his readers are always interesting. Hypocrisy was especially a Jewish sin. St Luke adds our Lord's words on the degrees of punishment, varying with the degrees of responsibility.

XXV. 1—13. *The Parable of the Ten Virgins.*

25 Then shall the kingdom of heaven be likened unto ten
virgins, which took their lamps, and went forth to meet the
2 bridegroom. And five of them were wise, and five *were*
3 foolish. They that *were* foolish took their lamps, and took
4 no oil with them: but the wise took oil in their vessels with
5 their lamps. While the bridegroom tarried, they all slum-

CH. XXV. 1—13. THE PARABLE OF THE TEN VIRGINS.

In St Matthew only.

1. *Then*] In the Last Day—the time just spoken of.

the kingdom of heaven be likened unto ten virgins] The condition of the Church at the End of the World shall be like the condition of the ten virgins described in the parable.

This parable is another warning for the disciples of Christ "to watch." Like the rest of the discourse it is primarily addressed to the Apostles, and after them to the pastors of the Church, who are posted as sentinels for the coming of Christ; lastly, to all Christians. Whatever interpretation may be put on the lesser incidents they must be subordinated to the lesson of the parable—vigilance, and the reason for vigilance—the certainty of the event, and the uncertainty as to the time of its occurrence.

their lamps] Either like the familiar Roman lamps carried in the hand or attached to staves, or else torches which were sometimes fed with oil.

to meet the bridegroom] The usual Jewish custom was for the "friends of the bridegroom" to conduct the bride to her husband's home; and when the procession arrived, the bridegroom went forth to lead the bride across the threshold (Lightfoot, *Hor. Hebr.* ad loc., and Dr Ginsburg in Kitto's *Cycl. of Bib. Lit.*). The imagery of the parable, however, implies that the bridegroom himself went to fetch his bride perhaps from a great distance, while a group of maidens await his return ready to welcome him in Oriental fashion with lamps and flambeaux.

2. *wise*] The word is used of prudence or practical intelligence, a characteristic of the steward, ch. xxiv. 45, and Luke xvi. 8.

3. *They that were foolish took their lamps*] All watch for their Lord, but some only—"the wise"—with true intensity and with due provision for the watch. The foolish virgins have sufficient oil if the Lord come quickly; not sufficient for long and patient expectation. It is a rebuke to shallow religion that dies away when the excitement passes.

The oil seems to mean generally the perfection of the Christian life or preparedness for the Lord's coming.

5. *the bridegroom*] The thought of Christ as the Bridegroom of the Church is hardly appropriate here, for in the parable the maidens, and

bered and slept. And at midnight there was a cry made, 6
Behold, the bridegroom cometh; go ye out to meet him.
Then all those virgins arose, and trimmed their lamps. 7
And the foolish said unto the wise, Give us of your oil; for 8
our lamps are gone out. But the wise answered, saying, 9
Not so; lest there be not enough for us and you: but go ye
rather to them that sell, and buy for yourselves. And while 10
they went to buy, the bridegroom came; and they *that were*
ready went in with him to the marriage: and the door was
shut. Afterward came also the other virgins, saying, Lord, 11
Lord, open to us. But he answered and said, Verily I say 12
unto you, I know you not. Watch therefore, for ye know 13
neither the day nor the hour wherein the Son of man
cometh.

not the bride, are the expectant Church. The thought of the "children of the bridechamber," ch. ix. 15, is a nearer parallel.

they all slumbered and slept] Sleep represents the ignorance as to the time of Christ's coming; it is not to be interpreted of unwatchfulness, it is not a guilty or imprudent sleep, as in the parable of the thief coming by night (ch. xxiv. 43).

slumbered and slept] Rather, "**nodded**" from drowsiness, and fell asleep.

6. *there was a cry made*] Literally, "*there* **is** *a cry made.*"

7. *trimmed their lamps*] By addition of oil, and by clearing the fibres with a needle.

8. *are gone out*] Rather, "*are* **going** *out.*" Even the foolish virgins had not been quite unwatchful, they were nearly ready for the Lord's appearing.

9. *lest there be not enough for us and you*] The bridal procession was still to be made in which there would be need of burning lamps. The wise cannot impart their oil:—an incident necessary to the leading idea of the parable;—nothing can make up for unreadiness at the last moment. This point has been adduced as an argument against works of supererogation.

Not so; lest there be not] Accepting a variation in the text adopted by Lachmann and Tregelles and Meyer, translate "Not so;" (which now comes into the text,) "there will surely not be enough," &c.

10. *went in with him to the marriage*] Rather, **to the marriage feast.** The happiness of the blest is often described by the image of a great supper, cp. ch. xxvi. 29.

11. *Lord, Lord, open to us*] Cp. ch. vii. 22, 23.

13. *Watch therefore*] Our Lord's explanation of the parable, shewing the true purport of it.

14—30. *The Parable of the Talents.*

14 For *the kingdom of heaven is* as a man travelling into a far
country, *who* called his own servants, and delivered unto
15 them his goods. And unto one he gave five talents, to another two, and to another one; to every man according to
16 his several ability; and straightway took his journey. Then
he that had received the five talents went and traded with
17 the same, and made *them* other five talents. And likewise
18 he that *had received* two, he also gained other two. But he
that had received one went and digged in the earth, and
19 hid his lord's money. After a long time the lord of those

14—30. The Parable of the Talents, in this Gospel only.

The parable of the Pounds, Luke xix. 12—27, is similar, but there are important points of distinction; (1) in regard to the occasions on which the two parables are given; (2) in the special incidents of each.

The lesson is still partly of watchfulness, it is still in the first instance for the apostles. But fresh thoughts enter into this parable: (1) There is work to be done in the time of waiting; the watching must not be idle or unemployed; (2) Even the least talented is responsible.

14. *into a far country*] These words do not occur in the original, the word translated "travelling into a far country," is rendered in the next verse "took his journey."

delivered unto them his goods] Cp. Mark xiii. 34. "A man taking a far journey, who left his house and gave authority (rather, his authority) to his servants, and to every man his work." Christ in His absence gives to each a portion of His own authority and of His own work on earth.

A great deal of the commerce of antiquity was managed by slaves, who were thus often entrusted with responsible functions (cp. ch. xxiv. 45). In this case they are expected to use their Master's money in trade or in cultivation of the soil, and to make as large an increase as possible.

15. *unto one he gave five talents*] In the parable of the Pounds or "minæ," (Luke xix.) each subject receives one pound. Here the truth is indicated that there is variety in the services wrought for God in respect of dignity and of difficulty. More will be required of the influential and enlightened than of the ignorant and poor. "Nemo urgetur ultra quam potest" (Bengel).

talents] See ch. xviii. 24. It is from this parable that the word "talents" has passed into modern languages in the sense of "abilities," or "mental gifts."

16. *went and traded*] i.e. went on a journey. The ideas of trade and travelling were very nearly connected in ancient times, as the Greek words for traffic shew. In *v.* 18 *went*=departed.

19. *After a long time*] Another hint that the second coming of Christ would be long deferred.

servants cometh, and reckoneth with them. And *so* he that 20
had received five talents came and brought other five talents,
saying, Lord, thou deliveredst unto me five talents: behold,
I have gained besides them five talents moe. His lord said 21
unto him, Well *done*, *thou* good and faithful servant: thou
hast been faithful over a few *things*, I will make thee ruler
over many *things:* enter thou into the joy of thy lord. He 22
also that had received two talents came and said, Lord,
thou deliveredst unto me two talents: behold, I have gained
two other talents besides them. His lord said unto him, 23
Well *done*, good and faithful servant; thou hast been faithful
over a few *things*, I will make thee ruler over many *things:*
enter thou into the joy of thy lord. Then he which had re- 24
ceived the one talent came and said, Lord, I knew thee that
thou art a hard man, reaping where thou hast not sown, and
gathering where thou hast not strawed: and I was afraid, 25
and went and hid thy talent in the earth: lo, *there* thou hast
that is thine. His lord answered and said unto him, *Thou* 26
wicked and slothful servant, thou knewest that I reap where
I sowed not, and gather where I have not strawed: thou 27
oughtest therefore to have put my money to the exchangers,

reckoneth with them] In order to have his stipulated share of the profits.

20. *moe*] for more, the reading of the Authorised Version (1611), altered in later editions. Cp. Shaks. *Jul. Cæs.* II. 1:

"*Bru.* Is he alone?
Luc. No, sir, there are moe with him."
(*Bible Word-Book*, p. 321).

21. *ruler over many things*] The privileges of heaven shall be in proportion to the services wrought on earth.

enter thou into the joy of thy lord] Either (1) share the life of happiness which thy lord enjoys, and which shall be the reward of thy zeal; or (2) the joyous feast; as in the last parable; cp. also Esther ix. 18, 19. (See especially the LXX. version).

24. *came and said*] This slave anticipates his lord's condemnation; "qui s'excuse s'accuse."

gathering where thou hast not strawed] i.e. "gathering into the garner from another's threshing-floor where thou hast not winnowed" (Meyer); so, "exacting interest where thou hast invested no money." The accusation was false, but the lord takes his slave at his word, "thou oughtest *therefore*," for that very reason.

27. *put my money*] It was not thine own.

to the exchangers] i.e. "to the bankers," literally, **to those who stand at tables**, (Lat. *mensarii*), because the bankers had tables before

and *then* at my coming I should have received mine own
28 with usury. Take therefore the talent from him, and give
29 *it* unto him which hath ten talents. For unto every one
that hath shall be given, and he shall have abundance: but
from him that hath not shall be taken away even *that* which
30 he hath. And cast ye the unprofitable servant into outer
darkness: there shall be weeping and gnashing of teeth.

31—46. *The Day of Judgment.*

31 When the Son of man shall come in his glory, and all the
holy angels with him, then shall he sit upon the throne of
32 his glory: and before him shall be gathered all nations: and
he shall separate them one from another, as a shepherd
33 divideth *his* sheep from the goats: and he shall set the
sheep on his right hand, but the goats on the left.

them. This was the very least the slave could have done, to make money in this way required no personal exertion or intelligence.

with usury] In modern language "with interest."

29. The thought conveyed by this verse is true, even in worldly matters: talents not used pass away from their possessor: and the strenuous worker seems to gather to himself what is lost by the idle. Demosthenes says (*Phil.* I. 5) "the possessions of the negligent belong of right to those who will endure toil and danger."

31—46. The Day of Judgment.

32. *all nations*] Either (1) all the nations of the world, including the Jews; or (2) all the Gentiles. The almost invariable use of τὰ ἔθνη to signify the Gentiles; the unconsciousness of service to Christ shewn by just and unjust alike; the simplicity of the standard proposed by the Judge, favour the second interpretation. On the other hand the special warning to the Apostles, and to the Jewish race, in the previous parts of the discourse render it probable that Jews and Christians are not excluded from this picture of the judgment. The unconsciousness of the judged may be referred not to ignorance of Christ, but to unconsciousness that in relieving the distressed they were actually relieving Christ. The simplicity of the standard may be intended to include what is called "natural" religion, as well as revealed religion. The nations are judged by a standard of justice which *all* recognise. (Read Rom. i. 18—20; ii. 9—16.)

as a shepherd divideth his sheep from the goats] "The sheep and goats are always seen together under the same shepherd and in company; yet they never trespass on the domain of each other....When folded together at night they may always be seen gathered in distinct groups; and so, round the wells they appear instinctively to classify themselves apart, as they wait for the troughs to be filled."—Tristram,

Then shall the King say unto them on his right hand, 34
Come, ye blessed of my Father, inherit the kingdom prepared for you from the foundation of the world: for I was a 35
hungred, and ye gave me meat: I was thirsty, and ye gave
me drink: I was a stranger, and ye took me in: naked, and 36
ye clothed me: I was sick, and ye visited me: I was in
prison, and ye came unto me. Then shall the righteous 37
answer him, saying, Lord, when saw we thee a hungred, and
fed *thee?* or thirsty, and gave *thee* drink? When saw we thee 38
a stranger, and took *thee* in? or naked, and clothed *thee?*
Or when saw we thee sick, or in prison, and came unto 39
thee? And the King shall answer and say unto them, Verily 40
I say unto you, Inasmuch as ye have done *it* unto one of
the least of these my brethren, ye have done *it* unto me.

Natural History of the Bible, pp. 89, 90. The goat was not in evil repute in the East, as contrasted with the sheep; on the contrary, the he-goat was a symbol of dignity, so that the point of analogy is merely the separation between the sheep and the goats.

34. *the King*] "Appellatio majestatis plena solisque piis læta," Bengel, who also points out the correspondence between the sentence passed on the just, and that passed on the unjust, *v.* 41.

Come,	Depart from me,
ye blessed of my Father,	ye cursed,
inherit the kingdom	into fire,
prepared for you	prepared for the devil and his angels
from the foundation of the world.	everlasting.

ye blessed of my Father] Observe that the words, "of my Father," do not follow "ye cursed," *v.* 41. The blessing comes from God, the curse is brought by the sinner on himself.

35, 36. There is a climax in this enumeration. The first three are recognised duties, the last three are voluntary acts of self-forgetting love. Common humanity would move a man to relieve his bitterest foe when perishing by hunger or by thirst (see Rom. xii. 20). Oriental custom required at least a bare hospitality. But to clothe the naked implies a liberal and loving spirit, to visit the sick is an act of spontaneous self-sacrifice, to go to the wretched outcasts in prison was perhaps an unheard of act of charity in those days; it was to enter places horrible and foul beyond description; Sallust, speaking of the Tullianum (the state prison at Rome), says "incultu, tenebris, odore fæda atque terribilis ejus facies est."

40. *ye have done it unto me*] This unconscious personal service of Christ may be contrasted with the conscious but unreal knowledge of Christ assumed by false prophets; see Luke xiii. 26.

Christ identifies Himself with His Church, as in His words to Saul, "Why persecutest thou *me?*" (Acts ix. 4).

41 Then shall he say also unto them on the left hand,
Depart from me, ye cursed, into everlasting fire, prepared
42 for the devil and his angels: for I was a hungred, and ye
gave me no meat: I was thirsty, and ye gave me no drink:
43 I was a stranger, and ye took me not in: naked, and ye
clothed me not: sick, and in prison, and ye visited me not.
44 Then shall they also answer him, saying, Lord, when saw we
thee a hungred, or athirst, or a stranger, or naked, or sick,
45 or in prison, and did not minister unto thee? Then shall he
answer them, saying, Verily I say unto you, Inasmuch as ye
did *it* not to one of the least of these, ye did *it* not to me.
46 And these shall go away into everlasting punishment: but
the righteous into life eternal.

1—5. *Wednesday, Nisan 12. The Approach of the Passover. Jesus again foretells His Death. The Sanhedrin meet.*

26 And it came to pass, when Jesus had finished all these
2 sayings, he said unto his disciples, Ye know that after two

45. *Inasmuch as ye did it not*] Men will be judged not only for evil done, but for good left undone.

46. The same Greek word (*aiônios*) is translated *everlasting* (punishment) and (life) *eternal;* also in each case the adjective in the Greek text follows the noun—the place of emphasis. The adjective *aiônios* (eternal) = of or belonging to (1) an *aiôn* or period, (*a*) past, (*b*) present, (*c*) future, or (2) to a succession of *aiôns* or periods. It does not, therefore, in itself = "unending." But life eternal, which is "to know the true God and Jesus Christ" (John xvii. 3), can only be conceived of as unending and infinite; cp. "Art thou not from everlasting, O Lord my God, mine Holy One? we shall not die" (Hab. i. 12).

punishment] (Greek, *kolasis*), not "vengeance," but punishment that checks or reforms.

CH. XXVI. **1—5.** WEDNESDAY, NISAN 12. THE APPROACH OF THE PASSOVER. JESUS AGAIN FORETELLS HIS DEATH. THE SANHEDRIN MEET.

Mark xiv. 1, 2; Luke xxii. 1, 2.

Cp. John xi. 55—57, where we read that "the chief priests and Pharisees had given a commandment, that, if any man knew where he were, he should shew it, that they might take him."

That Jesus should be able for so many days to "speak openly in the Temple" and shew Himself to the people without fear of capture is a proof of the deep hold He had taken on the enthusiasm and affection of

days is *the feast of* the passover, and the Son of man is
betrayed to be crucified. Then assembled together the 3
chief priests, and the scribes, and the elders of the people,

His fellow-countrymen. The words of St John (quoted above) imply a combination of the priestly and aristocratic party—the Sadducees—with the democratic Pharisees, against the despised Galilæan, and yet it requires treachery of the deepest dye and a deed of darkness to secure Him.

2. *the passover*] (1) The *word* is interesting in its (*a*) Hebrew, (*b*) Greek, and (*c*) English form. (*a*) The Hebrew *pesach* is from a root meaning "to leap over," and, figuratively, to "save," "shew mercy." (*b*) The Greek *pascha* represents the Aramaic or later Hebrew form of the same word, but the affinity in sound and letters to the Greek word *paschein*, "to suffer," led to a connection in thought between the Passover and the Passion of our Lord: indeed, some of the early Christian writers state the connection as if it were the true etymology. (*c*) Tyndale has the merit of introducing into English the word "passover," which keeps up the play on the words in the original Hebrew (Exod. xii. 11 and 13). Before Tyndale the word "*phase*" (for *pascha*) was transferred from the Vulgate, with an explanation: "For it is phase, that is, the passyng of the Lord" (Wyclif).

the feast of the passover commemorated the deliverance of Israel from the Egyptian bondage. The ordinances of the first Passover are narrated Exod. xii. 1—14, but some of those were modified in later times. It was no longer necessary to choose the lamb on the 10th of Nisan. The blood was sprinkled on the altar, not on the door-post, those who partook of the paschal meal no longer "stood with loins girded, with shoes on their feet, with staff in hand," but reclined on couches, as at an ordinary meal; it was no longer unlawful to leave the house before morning (Exod. xii. 22). The regular celebration of the Passover was part of the religious revival after the return from Captivity. During the kingly period only three celebrations of the Passover are recorded; in the reigns of Solomon, of Hezekiah and of Josiah. For the relation of the Last Supper to the Passover and for further notes on the paschal observance, see below.

The date of this Passover was probably April 3 (old style), A.D. 33 (Mr J. W. Bosanquet in *Trans. Soc. Bib. Arch.* vol. IV. 2). See note, ch. ii. 1.

is betrayed] either (1) the present for the future, denoting greater certainty or (2) the full relative present "is now being betrayed;" the treacherous scheme of Judas is already afoot.

3. *the chief priests, and the scribes, and the elders*] i.e. the Sanhedrim or *Synedrion* (Greek), or *Sanhedrin* (the later Hebrew form of the word), the supreme council, legislative and administrative, of the Jewish people.

A. The history of the Sanhedrin. Many learned Rabbis endeavoured to trace the origin of the Sanhedrin to the council of 70 elders whom Moses, by the advice of Jethro, appointed to assist him. But it is

unto the palace of the high priest, who was called Caia-
4 phas, and consulted that they might take Jesus by subtilty,
5 and kill *him*. But they said, Not on the feast *day*, lest there
be an uproar among the people.

improbable that this council existed before the Macedonian conquest. (1) The name is Greek, not Hebrew. (2) It finds its equivalent among the political institutions of Macedonia. Finally, (3) no allusion to the Sanhedrin is to be found in the Historical Books or in the Prophets.

B. Constitution. The President or *Nasi* (prince) was generally, but not always, the high priest; next in authority was the vice-president or *Ab Beth Dîn* (father of the house of judgment); the third in rank was the *Chacham* (sage or interpreter). The members were 71 in number, and consisted (1) of the chief priests or heads of the priestly "courses" (see Luke i. 5); (2) the scribes or lawyers; (3) the elders of the people or heads of families, who were the representatives of the laity.

C. Authority and functions. The Sanhedrin formed the highest court of the Jewish commonwealth. It originally possessed the power of life and death, but this power no longer belonged to it; John xviii. 31, "It is not lawful for us to put any man to death," a statement which agrees with a tradition in the Talmud, "forty years before the temple was destroyed judgment in capital causes was taken away from Israel."

All questions of the Jewish law, and such as concerned the ecclesiastical polity, religious life of the nation and discipline of the priests fell under the jurisdiction of the Sanhedrin.

D. Place of meeting. In the present instance the Sanhedrin met at the high priest's house; from ch. xxvii. 6 we may conjecture that the Temple was sometimes the place of meeting, but their usual house of assembly at this particular epoch was called the "Halls of Purchase," on the east of the Temple Mount (Dr Ginsburg in Kitto's *Encyc. Bib. Lit.* and Lightfoot's *Hor. Hebr.*).

Caiaphas] Joseph Caiaphas, the son-in-law of Annas, was appointed high priest by the Procurator Valerius Gratus A.D. 26, and was deposed A.D. 38. The high priesthood had long ceased to be held for life and to descend from father to son; appointments were made at the caprice of the Roman government. Annas who had been high priest was still regarded as such by popular opinion, which did not recognise his deposition. St Luke says, "Annas and Caiaphas being the high priests."

4. *consulted that they might take Jesus by subtilty*] It was no longer possible (1) to entrap Him by argument (xxii. 46); (2) to discredit Him with the Roman government (xxii. 22); or (3) to take Him by force.

5. *on the feast day*] Better, **during the feast**, including the Passover and the seven days of unleavened bread.

lest there be an uproar among the people] The great danger at the time of the Passover, when the people, numbering hundreds of thousands, filled the city and encamped in tents outside the walls like a vast army.

6—13. *The Feast in the house of Simon the Leper.*

Now when Jesus was in Bethany, in the house of Simon 6
the leper, there came unto him a woman having an alabaster 7
box of very precious ointment, and poured *it* on his head,
as he sat at meat. But when his disciples saw *it*, they had 8
indignation, saying, To what purpose *is* this waste? For this 9

At a Passover, less than 30 years before, the people, partly to avenge the death of two Rabbis, rose against Archelaus, and were cruelly repressed with a slaughter of 3000 men (Joseph. *Ant.* XVII. 9. 3); see also XVII. 10. 2, where a similar rising against Sabinus, during the feast of Pentecost, is described.

6—13. THE FEAST IN THE HOUSE OF SIMON THE LEPER.

Mark xiv. 3—9; John xii. 1—8.

St John's narrative places this incident on the evening of the Sabbath—the last Sabbath spent by Jesus on earth—before the triumphal entry. St Matthew has here disregarded the strictly chronological order.

Compare a similar act of devotion on the part of a "woman that was a sinner" (Luke vii. 36—39).

6. *Simon the leper*] i.e. he had been a leper. St John, in the parallel passage, says "they made him a supper, and Martha served; but Lazarus was one of them that sat at the table with him." Nothing further is known of Simon. He was evidently a disciple of Jesus and probably a near friend of Lazarus and his sisters.

7. *a woman having an alabaster box of very precious ointment*] "Then took Mary a pound of ointment, very costly" (John). "Ointment of spikenard, very precious" (Mark). The "alabaster box" was "a flask of fragrant oil;" the special kind of ointment named by the Evangelists—nard or spikenard—was extracted from the blossoms of the Indian and Arabian nard-grass (Becker's *Gallus*).

These *alabastra* or unguent-flasks were usually made of the Oriental or onyx alabaster, with long narrow necks, which let the oil escape drop by drop, and could easily be broken (Mark xiv. 3). But the shape and material varied. Herodotus (III. 20) mentions an "*alabastron* of fragrant oil"—the precise expression in the text—sent among other royal gifts of gold and purple by Cambyses to the king of Æthiopia.

The costliness of Mary's offering may be judged from this. The other Evangelists name three hundred pence or *denarii* as the price; (St Mark says, "more than three hundred pence"). Now a denarius was a day's wages for a labourer (see ch. xx. 2); equivalent, therefore, to two shillings at least of English money; hence, relatively to English ideas, Mary's offering would amount to £30. It was probably the whole of her wealth.

8. *when his disciples saw it, they had indignation*] "There were some that had indignation" (Mark); "Then said one of his disciples, Judas Iscariot" (John).

ointment might have been sold for much, and given to the
10 poor. When Jesus understood *it*, he said unto them, Why
trouble ye the woman? for she hath wrought a good work
11 upon me. For ye have the poor always with you; but me
12 ye have not always. For in that she hath poured this oint-
13 ment on my body, she did *it* for my burial. Verily I say
unto you, Wheresoever this gospel shall be preached in the
whole world, *there* shall also *this*, that this *woman* hath done,
be told for a memorial of her.

14—16. *The Treachery of Judas.*

14 Then one of the twelve, called Judas Iscariot, went unto
15 the chief priests, and said *unto them*, What will ye give me,

10. *When Jesus understood it*] The murmurings had been whispered at first. St Mark says, "had indignation *within themselves*, and said, &c."

a good work] Rather, **a noble and beautiful work**, denoting a delicate and refined, almost artistic, sense of the fitness of things, which was lacking to the blunter perception of the rest.

The Lord passes a higher commendation on this than on any other act recorded in the N.T.; it implied a faith that enabled Mary to see, as no else then did, the truth of the Kingdom. She saw that Jesus was still a King, though destined to die. The same thought—the certainty of the death of Jesus—that estranged Judas made her devotion more intense.

12. *for my burial*] For this use of perfumes cp. 2 Chron. xvi. 14, "They laid him (Asa) in the bed which was filled with sweet odours and divers kinds of spices prepared by the apothecaries' art."

14—16. The Treachery of Judas.

Mark xiv. 10, 11; Luke xxii. 3—6.

St Mark, like St Matthew, connects the treachery of Judas with the scene in Simon's house. His worldly hopes fell altogether at the thought of "burial." It is a striking juxtaposition: as Mary's is the highest deed of loving and clear-sighted faith, Judas' is the darkest act of treacherous and misguided hate.

The motive that impelled Judas was probably not so much avarice as disappointed worldly ambition. Jesus said of him that he was a "devil" (*diabolus* or *Satan*), the term that was on a special occasion applied to St Peter, and for the same reason. Peter for a moment allowed the thought of the earthly kingdom to prevail; with Judas it was the predominant idea which gained a stronger and stronger hold on his mind until it forced out whatever element of good he once possessed. "When the manifestation of Christ ceased to be attractive it became *repulsive;* and more so every day" (Neander, *Life of Christ*, Bohn's trans., p. 424).

and I will deliver him unto you? And they covenanted with
him for thirty pieces of silver. And from that time he sought 16
opportunity to betray him.

17—19. *Preparations for the Last Supper.*

Now the first *day* of the *feast of* unleavened bread the dis- 17
ciples came to Jesus, saying unto him, Where wilt thou *that*

15. *covenanted with him*] Rather, **weighed out for him**; either literally or = "paid him."

thirty pieces of silver] i.e. thirty silver shekels. St Matthew alone names the sum, which = 120 denarii. The shekel is sometimes reckoned at three shillings, but for the real equivalent in English money see note on *v.* 7. Thirty shekels was the price of a slave (Ex. xxi. 32); a fact which gives force to our Lord's words, xx. 28, "The Son of man came ...to minister (to be a slave), and to give his life a ransom for many."

17—19. PREPARATIONS FOR THE LAST SUPPER.
Mark xiv. 12—16; Luke xxii. 7—13.

Nisan 13—from the sunset of Wednesday to the sunset of Thursday —Jesus seems to have passed in retirement; no events are recorded.

17. *the first day of the feast of unleavened bread*] This was the 14th of Nisan, which commenced after sunset on the 13th; it was also called the preparation (paraskeuê) of the passover. The feast of unleavened bread followed the passover, and lasted seven days, from the 15th to the 21st of Nisan. Hence the two feasts are somtimes included in the term "passover," sometimes in that of "unleavened bread." On the evening of 13th of Nisan every head of the family carefully searched for and collected by the light of a candle all the leaven, which was kept and destroyed before midday on the 14th. The offering of the lamb took place on the 14th at the evening sacrifice, which on this day commenced at 1.30; or if the *preparation* fell on a Friday, at 12.30. The paschal meal was celebrated after sunset on the 14th, i.e. strictly on the 15th of Nisan.

The events of the Passover are full of difficulty for the harmonist. It is however almost certain that the "Last Supper" was not the paschal meal, but was partaken of on the 14th, that is after sunset on the 13th of Nisan. It is quite certain, from John xviii. 28, that Jesus was crucified on the *preparation*, and although the synoptic narratives seem at first sight to disagree with this, it is probably only the want of a complete knowledge of the facts that creates the apparent discrepancy.

The order of events in the "Passion" was as follows: when the 14th commenced, at sunset, Jesus sent two disciples to prepare the feast for that evening, instead of for the following evening. A sign of hastening on the meal may be detected in the words "my time is at hand," *v.* 18, cp. Luke xxii. 15, "with desire I have desired to eat this passover with you *before I suffer*." The supper follows, which bears a paschal character, and follows the paschal ceremonial. Early in the

18 we prepare for thee to eat the passover? And he said, Go
into the city to such a man, and say unto him, The Master
saith, My time is at hand; I will keep the passover at thy
19 house with my disciples. And the disciples did as Jesus
had appointed them; and they made ready the passover.

20—30. *The Last Supper.*

20 Now when the even was come, he sat down with the
21 twelve. And as they did eat, he said, Verily I say unto

morning of the 14th of Nisan the irregular sitting of the Sanhedrin took place. Then followed the formal sitting of the Sanhedrin, and the trial before Pilate, the "remission" to Herod, and, finally, the Crucifixion. This view meets the typical requirements of our Lord's death completely. During the very hours when our Great High Priest was offering Himself as a sacrifice for our sins upon the cross, the Jewish people were engaged in slaying thousands of lambs in view of the paschal feast about to commence.

18. *to such a man*] "To a certain man" (one who is known, but not named), with whom the arrangements had been previously made. He was doubtless a follower of Jesus. It was usual for the inhabitants of Jerusalem to lend guestchambers to the strangers who came to the feast.

20—30. The Last Supper.

Mark xiv. 17—26; Luke xxii. 14—38, where the dispute as to who should be the greatest is recorded, and the warning to Peter related as happening before Jesus departed for the Mount of Olives. St John omits the institution of the Eucharist, but relates the washing of the disciples' feet by our Lord, and has preserved the discourses of Jesus, chs. xiii.—xvii. end. 1 Cor. xi. 23—26; where the institution of the Eucharist is narrated nearly in St Luke's words.

20. *he sat down with the twelve*] Rather, **reclined with.** This posture had not only become customary at ordinary meals, but was especially enjoined in the passover ritual. The Paschal ceremonial, so far as it bears on the Gospel narrative, may be described as follows:

(*a*) The meal began with a cup of red wine mixed with water: this is the *first* cup mentioned, Luke xxii. 17. After this the guests washed their hands. Here probably must be placed the washing of the disciples' feet, John xiii.

(*b*) The bitter herbs, symbolic of the bitter bondage in Egypt, were then brought in together with unleavened cakes, and a sauce called *charoseth*, made of fruits and vinegar, into which the unleavened bread and bitter herbs were dipped. This explains "He it is, to whom I shall give a *sop*," John xiii. 26.

(*c*) The *second* cup was then mixed and blessed like the first. The father then explained the meaning of the rite (Exod. xiii. 8). This was

you, that one of you shall betray me. And they were ex- 22
ceeding sorrowful, and began every one of them to say unto
him, Lord, is it I? And he answered and said. He that dip- 23
peth *his* hand with me in the dish, the same shall betray me.
The Son of man goeth as it is written of him: but woe unto 24
that man by whom the Son of man is betrayed: it had been
good for that man if he had not been born. Then Judas, 25
which betrayed him, answered and said, Master, is it I? He
said unto him, Thou hast said.

the *haggadah* or "shewing forth," a term transferred by St Paul to the Christian meaning of the rite (1 Cor. xi. 26). The first part of the "*hallel*" (Psalms cxiii. and cxiv.) was then chanted by the company.

(*d*) After this the paschal lamb was placed before the guests. This is called in a special sense "the supper." But at the Last Supper there was no paschal lamb. There was no need now of the typical lamb without blemish, for the antitype was there. Christ Himself was our Passover "sacrificed for us" (1 Cor. v. 7). He was there being slain for us—His body was being given, His blood being shed. At this point, when according to the ordinary ritual the company partook of the paschal lamb, Jesus "took bread and blessed it, and gave it to his disciples" (*v.* 26).

(*e*) The *third* cup, or "cup of blessing," so called because a special blessing was pronounced upon it, followed: "after *supper* he took the cup" (Luke). "He took the cup *when he had supped*" (Paul). This is the "cup" named in *v.* 27.

(*f*) After a *fourth* cup the company chanted (see *v.* 30) the second part of the "*hallel*" (Psalms cxv.—cxviii.). (Lightfoot *Hor. Hebr.* Dr Ginsburg in *Kitto's Encycl.*, Dr Edersheim *Temple Services.*)

22. *they were exceeding sorrowful*] St John (xiii. 22) has the graphic words "then the disciples looked on one another, doubting of whom he spake." It is this moment of intense and painful emotion which Leonardo da Vinci has interpreted by his immortal picture, so true to the spirit of this scene, so unlike the external reality of it.

23. *He that dippeth his hand with me in the dish*] "He it is to whom I shall give a sop when I have dipped it," John xiii. 26; here we have the words of the disciple who heard the reply of Jesus, which was probably whispered and not heard by the rest.

dippeth his hand...in the dish] i.e. in the *charoseth*, see above, *v.* 20 (*b*).

24. *good for that man if he had not been born*] A familiar phrase in the Rabbinical Schools, used here with awful depth of certainty.

25. *Thou hast said*] This is a formula of assent both in Hebrew and Greek, and is still used in Palestine in that sense. These words seem also to have been spoken in a low voice inaudible to the rest.

The special mention of Judas is omitted by St Mark and St Luke.

26 And as they were eating, Jesus took bread, and blessed *it*,
and brake *it*, and gave *it* to the disciples, and said, Take,
27 eat; this is my body. And he took the cup, and gave
28 thanks, and gave *it* to them, saying, Drink ye all of it; for
this is my blood of the new testament, which is shed for
29 many for the remission of sins. But I say unto you, I will
not drink henceforth of this fruit of the vine, until that day
when I drink it new with you in my Father's kingdom.

26. *this is my body*] The exact Greek is "this is the body of me;" St Luke adds, "which is being given for you;" St Paul, "which is being broken for you;" the sacrifice had begun, the body of Christ was already being offered. The expression may be paraphrased: "This—the bread—and not the paschal lamb, represents—*is* to the faithful—the body of Me, who am even now being offered a sacrifice for you." Without entering on the great controversy of which these four words have been the centre, we may note that; (1) the thought is not presented now for the first time to the disciples. It was the "hard saying" which had turned many from Christ, see John vi. 51—57, 66. (2) The special form of the controversy is due to a mediæval philosophy which has passed away leaving "the dispute of the sacraments" as a legacy. St Luke and St Paul have the addition, "this do in remembrance of me"—now, as a memorial of *Me*, not of the Passover deliverance.

27. *he took the cup*] Accurately, according to the highest MS. authority, "*a* cup," see note *v.* 20 (*e*).

28. *this is my blood*] The blood of the sacrifice was the seal and assurance of the old covenant, so wine is the seal of the new covenant, under which there is no shedding of blood.

new testament] The word "new" is omitted in the most ancient MSS. here and in Mark.

testament] The Greek word means either (1) a "covenant," "contract," or (2) "a will." The first is the preferable sense here, as in most passages where the word occurs in N. T. the new covenant is contrasted with "the covenant which God made with our fathers," Acts iii. 25. It need hardly be remarked that the title of the New Testament is derived from this passage.

for many] i.e. to save many; "for" is used in the sense of dying *for* one's country.

many] See note ch. xx. 28.

for the remission of sins] "For" here marks the intention, "in order that there may be remission of sins." These words are in Matthew only.

29. *when I drink it new with you*] The reference is to the feast, which is a symbol of the glorified life, cp. Luke xxii. 30. The new wine signifies the new higher existence (ch. ix. 17), which Christ would share with His Saints. The expression may also symbolize the Christian as distinguished from the Jewish dispensation, and be referred specially

And when they had sung a hymn, they went out into the 30
mount of Olives.

31—35. *All shall be offended.*

Then saith Jesus unto them, All ye shall be offended 31
because of me this night: for it is written, I will smite
the shepherd, and the sheep of the flock shall be
scattered abroad. But after I am risen *again*, I will 32
go before you into Galilee. Peter answered and said unto 33
him, Though all *men* shall be offended because of thee,
yet will I never be offended. Jesus said unto him, Verily I 34
say unto thee, That this night, before *the* cock crow, thou
shalt deny me thrice. Peter said unto him, Though I 35

to the celebration of the Eucharist, in which Christ joins with the faithful in the feast of the Kingdom of God on earth.

30. *when they had sung a hymn*] Properly, "*the* hymn," the second part of the hallel. See note on *v.* 20 (*f*).

31—35. ALL SHALL BE OFFENDED.

Mark xiv. 26—31; Luke xxii. 32—34. Cp. John xvi. 32.

31. *I will smite the shepherd*] Zech. xiii. 7. The words do not literally follow the Hebrew. The context describes the purification of Jerusalem in the last days—"in that day there shall be a fountain opened to the house of David and to the inhabitants of Jerusalem"—the discomfiture of the false prophets, and the victory of Jehovah on the Mount of Olives.

It may be fitly remembered that the Valley of Jehoshaphat (in N.T. the Valley of Kedron) according to the most probable view derived its name—the Valley of the Judgment of Jehovah—not from the king of Judah, but from the vision of Joel (iii. 2 and 9—17), of which the prophecy of Zechariah is the repetition in a later age. If so, there is deep significance in the words recurring to the mind of Christ, as He trod the very field of Jehovah's destined victory. Nor is it irreverent to believe that the thought of this vision brought consolation to the human heart of Jesus as He passed to His Supreme self-surrender with the knowledge that He would be left alone, deserted even by His chosen followers.

32. The expression, *I will go before you*, lit., **I will lead you as a shepherd**, falls in with the thought of the quotation.

34. *before the cock crow, thou shalt deny me thrice*] "This day, even in this night, before the cock crow twice, thou shalt deny me thrice" (Mark). A curious difficulty has been raised here from the fact that it was unlawful for Jews to keep fowls in the Holy City. Such rules, however, could not be applied to the Romans.

35. *Though I should die with thee*] Accurately, **Even if I shall be obliged to die with thee.**

should die with thee, *yet* will I not deny thee. Likewise also said all the disciples.

36—46. *The Agony in the Garden of Gethsemane.*

36 Then cometh Jesus with them unto a place called Gethsemane, and saith unto the disciples, Sit ye here, while I
37 go and pray yonder. And he took with *him* Peter and the
two sons of Zebedee, and began to be sorrowful and very
38 heavy. Then saith he unto them, My soul is exceeding
sorrowful, *even* unto death: tarry ye here, and watch with
39 me. And he went a little further, and fell on his face, and
prayed, saying, O my Father, if it be possible, let this cup
pass from me: nevertheless not as I will, but as thou *wilt.*
40 And he cometh unto the disciples, and findeth them asleep,

36—46. The Agony in the Garden of Gethsemane.

Mark xiv. 32—42; Luke xxii. 39—46; John xviii. 1.

In St Luke's account verses 43, 44 are peculiar to his Gospel. The use of the rare word "agony" by the same evangelist has given the title to this passage.

St Luke also relates that "there appeared an angel unto him from heaven, strengthening him." There is, however, some reason for doubting the genuineness of these verses.

36. *Gethsemane*] = the oil press; "over the brook Cedron, where was a garden" (John).

37. *Peter and the two sons of Zebedee*] See ch. xvii. 1 and Mark v. 37. The Evangelist, St John, was thus a witness of this scene; hence, as we should expect, his narrative of the arrest of Jesus is very full of particulars.

very heavy] The Greek word conveys the impression of the deepest sorrow; it is used of "maddening grief."

38. *My soul*] This is important as the one passage in which Jesus ascribes to Himself a human soul.

watch with me] The Son of man in this dark hour asks for human sympathy.

with me] Only in Matthew.

39. *went a little further*] The paschal full moon would make deep shadow for the retirement of Jesus.

O my Father] St Mark has the Aramaic *Abba* as well as the Greek word for Father.

this cup] See note, ch. xx. 22. Were these words overheard by the sons of Zebedee? If so, the thought of their ambition and of their Master's answer would surely recur to them (ch. xx. 20—23).

not as I will] In the "Agony," as in the Temptation, the Son submits Himself to His Father's will.

and saith unto Peter, What, could ye not watch with me
one hour? Watch and pray, that ye enter not into tempta- 41
tion: the spirit indeed *is* willing, but the flesh *is* weak. He 42
went away again the second time, and prayed, saying, O
my Father, if this cup may not pass away from me, except
I drink it, thy will be done. And he came and found them 43
asleep again: for their eyes were heavy. And he left them, 44
and went away again, and prayed the third time, saying
the same words. Then cometh he to his disciples, and 45
saith unto them, Sleep on now, and take your rest: behold,
the hour is at hand, and the Son of man is betrayed into
the hands of sinners. Rise, let us be going: behold, he is 46
at hand that doth betray me.

47—56. *The Arrest of Jesus.*

And while he yet spake, lo, Judas, one of the twelve, 47
came, and with him a great multitude with swords and

40. *saith unto Peter, What, could ye not watch*] Note that the verb is in the plural. As Peter took the lead in the promise of devotion, Jesus singles him out for rebuke. St Mark has "Simon (the name of the old life), sleepest thou? Couldest not thou watch one hour?"

41. *the spirit indeed is willing, but the flesh is weak*] The touch of clemency mingled with the rebuke is characteristic of the gentleness of Jesus.

44. *saying the same words*] This repetition of earnestness must be distinguished from the vain repetitions of ch. vi. 7.

45, 46. *Sleep on now...Rise, let us be going*] The sudden transition may be explained either (1) by regarding the first words as intended for a rebuke, or else (2) at that very moment Judas appeared, and the time for action had come. The short, quick sentences, especially as reported by St Mark, favour the second suggestion.

47—56. The Arrest of Jesus.

St Mark xiv. 43—50; St Luke xxii. 47—53; St John xviii. 3—11.

47. *a great multitude with swords and staves*] St John more definitely, "having received a (strictly, *the*) band (of men) and officers from the chief priests and Pharisees" (xviii. 3). The band of men here = the company of Roman soldiers, placed at the service of the Sanhedrin by the Procurator. The same word is used Acts x. 1, xxi. 32, xxvii. 1. St Luke names the "captains of the temple" (xxii. 52). Hence the body, guided by Judas, consisted of (1) a company (*speira*) of Roman soldiers; (2) a detachment of the Levitical temple-guard (Luke); (3) certain members of the Sanhedrin and Pharisees.

48 staves, from the chief priests and elders of the people. Now
he that betrayed him gave them a sign, saying, Whomsoever
49 I shall kiss, that *same* is he: hold him fast. And forthwith
he came to Jesus, and said, Hail, master; and kissed him.
50 And Jesus said unto him, Friend, wherefore art thou come?
Then came they, and laid hands on Jesus, and took him.
51 And behold, one of them which were with Jesus stretched
out *his* hand, and drew his sword, and stroke a servant of
52 the high priest's, and smote off his ear. Then said Jesus
unto him, Put up again thy sword into his place: for all
they that take the sword shall perish with the sword.
53 Thinkest thou that I cannot now pray to my Father, and
he shall presently give me more than twelve legions of

with swords and staves] St John has "with lanterns and torches and weapons." *Staves*, rather, **clubs**; different from the travellers' "staves" of ch. x. 10, where another Greek word is used.

49. *Hail, master*] Rather, **Rabbi**.

kissed him] The Greek verb is forcible, **kissed him with fervour or repeatedly**.

50. *Friend, wherefore art thou come?*] The Greek word denotes, not friendship, but companionship. It is used in rebuke, ch. xx. 13 and xxii. 12. Here the word is relative to the Rabbi, *v.* 49, "thou, my disciple."

St Luke preserves a further answer to Judas, "betrayest thou the Son of man with a kiss?"

Then came they, and laid hands on Jesus] St John, who does not mention the kiss of Judas, sets the self-surrender of Jesus in a clear light: "I have told you that I am he: if therefore ye seek me, let these go their way."

51. *one of them*] This was St Peter, named by St John, but not by the earlier Evangelists, probably from motives of prudence.

his sword] Probably a short sword or dirk, worn in the belt.

a servant] Rather, **the servant**, or rather **slave**; St John gives his name, Malchus. St Luke alone records the cure of Malchus.

52—54. These verses are peculiar to Matthew; each Evangelist has recorded sayings unnoticed by the others. It is easy to understand that in these exciting moments each bystander should perceive a part only of what was said or done.

52. *all they that take the sword shall perish with the sword*] To this reason for non-resistance Christ added another, "The cup which my Father has given me shall I not drink it?" (John).

take the sword] i.e. against rightful authority. The truth of this saying was exemplified by the slaughter of nearly a million and a half of Jews, who "took the sword" against Rome A.D. 67—70.

53. *presently*] = "immediately"; see ch. xxi. 19.

angels? *But* how then shall the scriptures be fulfilled, that 54
thus it must be? In that *same* hour said Jesus to the multi- 55
tudes, Are ye come out as against a thief with swords and
staves for to take me? I sat daily with you teaching in the
temple, and ye laid no hold on me. But all this was done, 56
that the scriptures of the prophets might be fulfilled. Then
all the disciples forsook him, and fled.

57—68. *Jesus is brought before Caiaphas. The first and informal Meeting of the Sanhedrin.*

And they that had laid hold on Jesus led *him* away to 57
Caiaphas the high priest, where the scribes and the elders

twelve legions of angels] It is characteristic of this gospel that the authority and kingly majesty of Jesus should be suggested at a moment when every hope seemed to have perished.

legions] In contrast to the small company of Roman soldiers.

54. *But how then*] Rather, **how then**, omit "but."

55. *a thief*] Rather, **a robber**; see St John x. 1, whence the two words are distinguished. See note, ch. xxi. 13.

According to St Luke these words were addressed to "the chief priests, and captains of the temple, and elders," where it appears that some members of the Sanhedrin had in their evil zeal joined in the capture. The same Evangelist adds, "this is your hour, and the power of darkness" (xxii. 53).

56. *all this was done*, &c.] These are probably the words of Christ, and not a reflection by the Evangelist (cp. Mark xiv. 49); if so, they were, for most of the disciples, their Master's last words.

57—68. JESUS IS BROUGHT BEFORE CAIAPHAS. THE FIRST AND INFORMAL MEETING OF THE SANHEDRIN.

St Mark xiv. 53—65; St Luke xxii. 54 and 63—65.

St Luke reports this first irregular trial with less detail than the other synoptists, but gives the account of the second *formal* sitting at greater length.

It is not clear whether the private examination, related by St John xviii. 19—23, was conducted by Annas or Caiaphas. Probably Jesus was first taken to Annas, whose great influence (he was still high priest in the eyes of the people) would make it necessary to have his sanction for the subsequent measures. The examination, narrated John xviii. 19—23, according to this view, was by Annas; "had sent," *v.* 24, should be translated "sent."

The subjoined order of events is certainly not free from difficulties, but is the most probable solution of the question:

(1) From the garden Gethsemane Jesus was taken to Annas; thence, after brief questioning (St John xviii. 19—23),

58 were assembled. But Peter followed him afar off unto the
high priest's palace, and went in, and sat with the servants,
59 to see the end. Now the chief priests, and elders, and all
the council, sought false witness against Jesus, to put him
60 to death; but found none: yea, though many false witnesses came, *yet* found they none. At the last came two
61 false witnesses, and said, This *fellow* said, I am able to
destroy the temple of God, and to build it in three days.

(2) To Caiaphas, in another part of the Sacerdotal palace, where some members of the Sanhedrin had hastily met, and the *first* irregular trial of Jesus took place at night; Matt. xxvi. 57—68; Mark xiv. 52—65; Luke xxii. 54 and 63—65.

(3) Early in the morning a *second* and formal trial was held by the Sanhedrin. This is related by St Luke ch. xxii. 66—71; and is mentioned by St Matthew ch. xxvii. 1; and in St Mark xv. 1.

(4) The trial before Pontius Pilate, consisting of two parts: (*a*) a preliminary examination (for which there is a technical legal phrase in St Luke xxiii. 14); (*b*) a final trial and sentence to death.

(5) The *remission* to Herod, recorded by St Luke only, xxiii. 7—11; between the two Roman trials, (*a*) and (*b*).

The question is sometimes asked, Was the trial of Jesus fair and legal according to the rules of Jewish law? The answer must be that the proceedings against Jesus violated both (1) the spirit, and (2) the express rules of Hebrew jurisdiction, the general tendency of which was to extreme clemency.

(1) The Talmud states: "the Sanhedrin is to save, not to destroy life." No man could be condemned in his absence, or without a majority of two to one; the penalty for procuring false witnesses was death; the condemned was not to be executed on the day of his trial. This clemency was violated in the trial of Jesus Christ.

(2) But even the ordinary legal rules were disregarded in the following particulars: (*a*) The examination by Annas without witnesses. (*b*) The trial by night. (*c*) The sentence on the first day of trial. (*d*) The trial of a capital charge on the day before the Sabbath. (*e*) The suborning of witnesses. (*f*) The direct interrogation by the High Priest.

58. *servants*] "Attendants," "retinue."

59. *sought false witness*] See above (1): to *seek* witnesses at all was against the spirit of the law.

61. *I am able to destroy the temple of God, and to build it in three days*] The actual words of Jesus spoken (John ii. 19) in the first year of his ministry were, "Destroy" (a weaker Greek verb, and not "I am able to destroy") "this temple, and in three days I will raise it up," (the word is appropriate to raising from the dead, and is quite different from the verb "to build"). The attempt was to convict Jesus of blasphemy in asserting a superhuman power.

And the high priest arose, and said unto him, Answerest 62
thou nothing? what *is it which* these witness against thee?
But Jesus held his peace. And the high priest answered 63
and said unto him, I adjure thee by the living God, that
thou tell us whether thou be the Christ, the Son of God.
Jesus saith unto him, Thou hast said: nevertheless I say 64
unto you, Hereafter shall ye see the Son of man sitting on
the right hand of power, and coming in the clouds of heaven.
Then the high priest rent his clothes, saying, He hath spoken 65
blasphemy; what further need have we of witnesses? behold, now ye have heard his blasphemy. What think ye? 66
They answered and said, He is guilty of death. Then did 67
they spit in his face, and buffeted him; and others smote
him with the palms of their hands, saying, Prophesy unto 68
us, *thou* Christ, Who is he that smote thee?

69—75. *The Denial of Peter.*

Now Peter sat without in the palace: and a damsel came 69

64. *Thou hast said*] See note *v.* 25.

Hereafter shall ye see] Cp. Dan. vii. 13; ch. xvi. 27, xxiv. 30, xxv. 31.

65. *rent his clothes*] This act was enjoined by the Rabbinical rules. When the charge of blasphemy was proved "the judges standing on their feet rend their garments, and do not sew them up again." *Clothes* in the plural, because according to Rabbinical directions all the *under*-garments were to be rent, "even if there were ten of them."

66. *He is guilty of death*] i.e. "has incurred the penalty of death." The Sanhedrin do not pass sentence, but merely re-affirm their foregone conclusion, and endeavour to have sentence passed and judgment executed by the Procurator.

67. *buffeted him*] Struck Him with clenched fist.

68. *Prophesy unto us*] Observe the coarse popular idea of prophecy breaking out, according to which prophecy is a meaningless exhibition of miraculous power. A similar vein of thought shews itself in the second temptation (ch. iv. 6).

69—75. The Denial of Peter.

St Mark xiv. 66—72; Luke xxii. 55—62; John xviii. 15—18, and 25—27.

The accounts differ slightly, and exactly in such a way as the evidence of honest witnesses might be expected to differ in describing the minor details (which at the time would appear unimportant) in a scene full of stir and momentous incidents. Discrepancies of this kind form the strongest argument for the independence of the different gospels. St

70 unto him, saying, Thou also wast with Jesus of Galilee. But
he denied before *them* all, saying, I know not what thou
71 sayest. And when he was gone out into the porch, another
maid saw him, and said unto them that were there, This
72 *fellow* was also with Jesus of Nazareth. And again he denied
73 with an oath, I do not know the man. And after a while
came unto *him* they that stood *by*, and said to Peter, Surely
thou also art *one* of them; for thy speech bewrayeth thee.
74 Then began he to curse and to swear, *saying*, I know not
75 the man. And immediately *the* cock crew. And Peter
remembered the word of Jesus, which said unto him, Before
the cock crow, thou shalt deny me thrice. And he went
out, and wept bitterly.

1. *The Second and formal Meeting of the Sanhedrin.*

2. *The Delivery to Pontius Pilate.*

27 When the morning was come, all the chief priests and

Luke mentions that "the Lord turned and looked upon Peter." St John states that the third question was put by a kinsman of Malchus.

69. *in the palace*] Rather, **in the court**. In Oriental houses the street door opens into an entrance hall or passage: this is the "porch" of *v.* 71; beyond this is a central court open to the sky and surrounded by pillars. The reception rooms are usually on the ground floor, and are built round the central court. Probably the hall or room in which Jesus was being tried opened upon the court. Thus Jesus was able to look upon Peter.

73. *thy speech bewrayeth thee*] Peter was discovered by his use of the Galilæan dialect. The Galilæans were unable to pronounce the gutturals distinctly, and they lisped, pronouncing *sh* like *th*. Perhaps Peter said, "I know not the *ith*," instead of, "I know not the *ish*" (man).

To bewray, from the Anglo-Saxon *wreian*, to accuse, then, to point out, make evident,—the literal meaning of the Greek words.

"Here comes the queen, whose looks bewray her anger."
Shaks. 3 *Henry VI.* I. I. (*Bible Word-Book.*)

CH. XXVII. 1. THE SECOND AND FORMAL MEETING OF THE SANHEDRIN.

St Mark xv. 1; St Luke xxii. 66—71; not mentioned by St John.

2. THE DELIVERY TO PONTIUS PILATE.

St Mark xv. 1; St Luke xxiii. 1; St John xviii. 28; "then led they Jesus from Caiaphas unto the hall of Judgment (or *Prætorium*), and it was early."

elders of the people took counsel against Jesus to put him
to death: and when they had bound him, they led *him* away, 2
and delivered him to Pontius Pilate the governor.

3—10. *The remorse of Judas. He returns the silver Shekels. The use made of them.*

Then Judas, which had betrayed him, when he saw that 3
he was condemned, repented himself, and brought again

2. *Pontius Pilate the governor*] Pontius Pilate was the governor, or more accurately, the Procurator of Judæa, which after the banishment of Archelaus (see ch. ii. 22) had been placed under the direct government of Rome, and attached as a dependency to Syria. Pilate filled this office during the last ten years of the reign of Tiberius, to whom as Procurator in an imperial province he was directly responsible. In the year A. D. 35 or 36, he was sent to Rome on a charge of cruelty to the Samaritans. The death of Tiberius probably deferred his trial, and according to Eusebius, "wearied with his misfortunes," he put himself to death. In character Pilate appears to have been impolitic, cruel and weak. On three signal occasions he had trampled on the religious feelings of the Jews, and repressed their resistance with merciless severity. A further instance of cruelty, combined with profanation, is alluded to, St Luke xiii. 1: "the Galilæans, whose blood Pilate had mingled with their sacrifices." The name Pontius connects Pilate with the *gens* of the Pontii, to which the great Samnite General, C. Pontius Telesinus, belonged. (Read history of second and third Samnite wars, B. C. 327—290.) The *cognomen* Pilatus probably signifies "armed with a *pilum*" (javelin). Tacitus mentions Pontius Pilate in a well-known passage (*Ann.* xv. 44), Auctor nominis ejus Christus Tiberio imperitante per procuratorem Pontium Pilatum supplicio affectus erat. "Christus, from whom the Christians are called, suffered death in the reign of Tiberius, under the procurator, P. Pilate." Many traditions have gathered round the name of Pontius Pilate. According to one, he was banished to Vienne in the south of France; according to another, he ended a restless life by plunging into a deep and gloomy lake on Mount Pilatus, near Lucerne. The shallow pool, often dry in the summer months, sufficiently disproves this story. The usual residence of the Roman Procurator in Judæa was Cæsarea Stratonis (see map).

The wish of the Sanhedrin in delivering Jesus to Pilate was to have their sentence confirmed without enquiry, see ch. xxvi. 66.

3—10. The remorse of Judas. He returns the silver Shekels. The use made of them. Peculiar to St Matthew.

3. *when he saw that he was condemned*] It has been argued from these words that Judas had not expected this result of his treachery. He had hoped that Jesus would by a mighty manifestation of His divine power usher in at once the Kingdom whose coming was too long de-

the thirty pieces of silver to the chief priests and elders,
4 saying, I have sinned in that I have betrayed *the* innocent
blood. And they said, What *is that* to us? see thou *to that.*
5 And he cast down the pieces of silver in the temple, and
6 departed, and went and hanged himself. And the chief
priests took the silver pieces, and said, It is not lawful for to
put them into the treasury, because it is the price of blood.
7 And they took counsel, and bought with them the potter's
8 field, to bury strangers in. Wherefore that field was called,
9 The field of blood, unto this day. Then was fulfilled that
which was spoken by Jeremie the prophet, saying, And

layed. The whole tenour of the narrative, however, contradicts such an inference.

repented himself] A different Greek word from that used, ch. iii. 2; it implies no change of heart or life, but merely remorse or regret. See note ch. xxi. 29, 32.

4. *I have sinned in that I have betrayed*] Rather, **I sinned in betraying.**

the innocent blood] "the" should be omitted.

see thou (*to that*)] Lit., **thou shalt see**, it shall be thy **concern.** "Impii in facto consortes, post factum deserunt." (Bengel.)

5. *in the temple*] Properly, "in the holy place," which only the priests could enter.

went and hanged himself] A different account of the end of Judas is given Acts i. 18; either by St Peter, or by St Luke in a parenthetical insertion. It is there stated (1) that Judas, not the Priests, bought the field: (2) that "falling headlong he burst asunder in the midst, and all his bowels gushed out;" (3) that the field was called Aceldama for that reason, not for the reason stated in this passage. The two accounts are not actually inconsistent, but the key to their concordance is lost. No entirely satisfactory solution of the discrepancy has been given.

6. *into the treasury*] "Into the Corban" in the original. For the prohibition cp. Deut. xxiii. 18.

7. *the potter's field*] Tradition places *Aceldama* in the valley of Hinnom, south of Jerusalem.

strangers] i. e. Jews of the dispersion, Hellenists and proselytes.

9. *that which was spoken by Jeremie the prophet*] The citation is from Zech. xi. 13, but neither the Hebrew nor the LXX. version is followed exactly. The Hebrew literally translated is: "And Jehovah said to me, 'Cast it unto the potter,' a goodly price that I was prized at by them. And I took the thirty pieces of silver, and cast them unto the potter in the house of Jehovah." Zechariah, under the image of a shepherd, refuses any longer to lead the disobedient and divided flock, and asks for the price of his hire, which he then casts into the treasury. The discrepancy is probably due to the citation being made from memory. The ascription of the words to Jeremiah instead of to Zechariah

they took the thirty pieces of silver, the price of him
that was valued, whom they of the children of Israel
did value; and gave them for the potter's field, as 10
the Lord appointed me.

11—26. *The Trial before Pontius Pilate.*

And Jesus stood before the governor, and the governor 11
asked him, saying, Art thou the King of the Jews? And
Jesus said unto him, Thou sayest. And when he was ac- 12
cused of the chief priests and elders, he answered nothing.
Then said Pilate unto him, Hearest thou not how many 13
things they witness against thee? And he answered him 14

may be assigned to the same cause, or explained, with Lightfoot (*Hor. Hebr. ad loc.*), by supposing that Jeremiah, who begins the Book of the Prophets in the Hebrew Canon, is intended to indicate the whole of that division of the Scriptures.

11—26. THE TRIAL BEFORE PONTIUS PILATE.

St Mark xv. 2—15; St Luke xxiii. 2—7 and 13—24; St John xviii. 29—xix. 16.

St Luke states the threefold charge most clearly: "We found this [fellow] (1) perverting the nation; (2) and forbidding to give tribute to Cæsar; (3) saying that he himself is Christ a King."

Pilate, true to the Roman sense of justice, refused merely to confirm the sentence of the Sanhedrin. "He asked, what accusation bring ye against this man?" (John xviii. 29), being determined to try the case. This accusation amounted to a charge of treason—the greatest crime known to Roman law. Of the three points of accusation, (2) was utterly false; (1) and (3) though *in a sense* true, were not true in the sense intended. The answer or defence of Jesus is that He is a King, but that His "kingdom is not of this world," therefore (it is inferred) the "perversion of the people" was not a rebellion that threatened the Roman government; see note *v.* 11. The defence was complete, as Pilate admits: "I find no fault in him."

11. *the governor*] The Evangelist uses a general word instead of the more exact term "Procurator."

Art thou the King of the Jews?] The answer of Jesus to this question, and His explanation to Pilate of the Kingdom of God are given at length, John xviii. 33—37; observe especially that the servants of the kingdom would fight, if they fought at all, not against Rome but against Israel who had rejected the Messiah: "If my Kingdom were of this world, then would my servants fight that I should not be delivered to the *Jews*."

Thou sayest] See note ch. xxvi. 25.

to never a word; insomuch that the governor marvelled
greatly.
15 Now at *that* feast the governor was wont to release unto
16 the people a prisoner, whom they would. And they had
17 then a notable prisoner, called Barabbas. Therefore when
they were gathered together, Pilate said unto them, Whom
will ye *that* I release unto you? Barabbas, or Jesus which
18 is called Christ? For he knew that for envy they had deli-
19 vered him. When he was set down on the judgment seat,
his wife sent unto him, saying, Have thou nothing to do

15. *the governor was wont to release unto the people a prisoner*] The origin of this custom is quite unknown; St Mark says, "as he had ever done unto them," as if the custom originated with Pilate; St Luke has, "of necessity he must release;" St John, "Ye have a custom."

No trace of this custom is found in the Talmud. But the release of prisoners was usual at certain festivals at Rome, and at Athens during the Panathenaic festival prisoners enjoyed temporary liberty. It is not, therefore, improbable that Herod the Great, who certainly familiarised the Jews with other usages of Greece and Rome, introduced this custom, and that the Roman governor, finding the custom established and gratifying to the Jews, in accordance with Roman practice (see Introd. p. 22 (3)) retained the observance of it.

16. *Barabbas*]="Son of a father," or perhaps, "Son of a Rabbi." The reading, "Jesus Barabbas" (v. 17), which appears in some copies, is rightly rejected by the best editors. As Alford remarks, *v.* 20 is fatal to the insertion. St Mark and St Luke add that Barabbas had committed murder in the insurrection.

17. *Therefore when they were gathered together*] In accordance, probably, with the custom named, *v.* 15, an appeal was made to the *people*, not to the Sanhedrin. Pilate was sitting on the tribunal to ascertain the popular decision; at this point he was interrupted by his wife's messengers, and while he was engaged with them, the chief priests employed themselves in persuading the people to demand Barabbas rather than Christ.

19. *the judgment seat*]="the tribunal," generally a raised platform in the Basilica or court where the judges sat; here a portable tribunal, from which the sentence was pronounced; it was placed on a tesselated pavement called Gabbatha (John xix. 13).

his wife] Claudia Procula or Procla: traditions state that she was a proselyte of the gate, which is by no means unlikely, as many of the Jewish proselytes were women. By an imperial regulation provincial governors had been prohibited from taking their wives with them. But the rule gradually fell into disuse, and an attempt made in the Senate (A.D. 21) to revive it completely failed. Tac. *Ann.* III. 33, 34. The dream of Pilate's wife is recorded by St Matthew only.

with that just *man:* for I have suffered many *things* this day
in a dream because of him. But the chief priests and elders 20
persuaded the multitude that they should ask Barabbas, and
destroy Jesus. The governor answered and said unto them, 21
Whether of the twain will ye *that* I release unto you? They
said, Barabbas. Pilate saith unto them, What shall I do then 22
with Jesus which is called Christ? *They* all say unto him,
Let him be crucified. And the governor said, Why, what 23
evil hath he done? But they cried out the more, saying, Let
him be crucified. When Pilate saw that he could prevail 24
nothing, but *that* rather a tumult was made, he took water,
and washed *his* hands before the multitude, saying, I am

20. *ask Barabbas, and destroy Jesus*] St Peter brings out the full meaning of this choice: "ye denied the Holy One and the Just, and desired a murderer to be granted unto you; and killed the Prince of life" (Acts iii. 14, 15). They saved the murderer, and slew the Saviour.

21. *Whether of the twain will ye that I release unto you?*] Once more the question is put to the people (see *v.* 17). His wife's message had made Pilate anxious to acquit Jesus. But the very form of the question implied condemnation. Jesus was classed with Barabbas in the category of condemned prisoners.

22. *all say unto him, Let him be crucified*] There is no further question even of a show of legality or justice: the traditional clemency is quite forgotten; the fanatical crowd, pressing round the doors of the Prætorium, which they cannot enter, join with excited gesticulation in one loud and furious cry for the blood of Jesus.

24. *When Pilate saw that he could prevail nothing*] St Luke relates a further attempt on Pilate's part to release Jesus, "I will chastise Him and let Him go" (Luke xxiii. 22). Will not the cruel torture of a Roman scourging melt their hearts?

St John, at still greater length, narrates the struggle in Pilate's mind between his sense of justice and his respect for Jesus on the one hand, and on the other his double fear of the Jews and of Cæsar. (1) He tried to stir their compassion by shewing Jesus to them crowned with thorns and mangled with the scourging; (2) hearing that Jesus called Himself the "Son of God," he "was the more afraid;" (3) at length he even "sought to release Him," but the chief priests conquered his scruples by a threat that moved his fears, "If thou let this man go thou art not Cæsar's friend." This was the charge of treason which Tacitus says (*Ann.* III. 39) was "omnium accusationum complementum." The vision of the implacable Tiberius in the background clenched the argument for Pilate. It is the curse of despotism that it makes fear stronger than justice.

took water, and washed his hands] Recorded by St Matthew only.

25 innocent of the blood of this just *person:* see ye *to it.* Then
answered all the people, and said, His blood *be* on us, and
26 on our children. Then released he Barabbas unto them:
and when he had scourged Jesus, he delivered *him* to be
crucified.

27—30. *Jesus is mocked by the Roman Soldiers.*

27 Then the soldiers of the governor took Jesus into the
common hall, and gathered unto him the whole band *of*
28 *soldiers.* And they stripped him, and put on him a scarlet
29 robe. And when they had platted a crown of thorns, they

In so doing Pilate followed a Jewish custom which all would understand. Deut. xxi. 6; Ps. xxvi. 6.

see ye (to it)] See note *v.* 4.

25. *His blood be on us, and on our children*] Also peculiar to Matthew. St Peter finds as the sole excuse for his fellow countrymen, "I wot that through ignorance ye did it, as did also your rulers" (Acts iii. 17). The prayer of Jesus on the cross for His murderers was meant for these as well as for the Roman soldiers.

26. *when he had scourged Jesus*] Scourging usually preceded crucifixion. It was in itself a cruel and barbarous torture, under which the victim often perished.

27—30. Jesus is mocked by the Roman Soldiers.
Mark xv. 16—19.

St Luke, who records the mockery of Herod's soldiers, perhaps as St Paul's companion in the Prætorium at Rome makes no mention of this stain on the Roman soldiery.

27. *the common hall*] i.e. "the Prætorium" (Mark), which meant originally (1) the general's tent; (2) it was then used for the residence of the governor or prince, cp. Acts xxiii. 35; (3) then for an official Roman villa or country house; (4) barracks especially for the Prætorian guard; (5) the Prætorian guard itself (Phil. i. 13). The second meaning (2) is to be preferred here.

band] Greek *speira*, the thirtieth part of a Roman legion consisting of two centuries.

28. *a scarlet robe*] A soldier's scarf, Lat. *chlamys:* it was generally worn by superior officers, but its use was not confined to them. This may have been a worn-out scarf belonging to Pilate; it is different from "the gorgeous robe" (Luke xxiii. 11), which Herod's soldiers put on Jesus. Scarlet was the proper colour for the military chlamys. (See *Dict. of Ant.*) St Mark has the less definite "purple;" St John "a purple robe." Purple, however, is used by Latin writers to denote any bright colour.

29. *a crown of thorns*] It cannot be ascertained what especial kind of thorn was used. The soldiers, as Bp Ellicott remarks, would take

put *it* upon his head, and a reed in his right hand: and they
bowed the knee before him, and mocked him, saying, Hail,
King of the Jews! And they spit upon him, and took the 30
reed, and smote him on the head.

31, 32. *Jesus is led to Crucifixion.*

And after that they had mocked him, they took the robe 31
off from him, and put his own raiment on him, and led
him away to crucify *him*. And as they came out, they found 32
a man of Cyrene, Simon by name: him they compelled to
bear his cross.

what first came to hand, utterly careless whether it was likely to inflict pain or no.

King of the Jews] Cp. ch. ii. 2, and xxvii. 37.

31, 32. JESUS IS LED TO CRUCIFIXION.

Mark xv. 20, 21; Luke xxiii. 26—32; John xix. 16, 17.

St Luke has several particulars of what happened on the way to Golgotha, omitted in the other Gospels. The great company of people and of women who followed Him; the touching address of Jesus to the women; the last warning of the coming sorrows; the leading of two malefactors with Him.

32. *a man of Cyrene, Simon by name*] (1) "coming out of the country" (Mark and Luke), (2) the father of Alexander and Rufus (Mark).

(1) This has been thought to imply that Simon was returning from work, and hence that it cannot have been the actual day of the Feast. Simon was probably coming into the city for the Paschal sacrifice, the hour for which was close at hand. (2) Rufus is probably the Christian named Rom. xvi. 13, who would be known to St Mark's readers. May not Simon have been one of those "Men of Cyrene" who preached the Word to Greeks when others preached to the Jews only? (Acts xi. 20.) (3) The inference that he was already an adherent of Christ is quite uncertain.

Cyrene] A city in north-eastern Africa, famous for the beauty of its position. A large colony of Jews had settled there, as in other African and Egyptian cities, to avoid the oppression of the Syrian kings.

compelled] See note ch. v. 41, where the same word is used, and the custom referred to of which this is an instance.

33—50. THE CRUCIFIXION AND DEATH OF JESUS.

Mark xv. 22—37; Luke xxiii. 33—46; John xix. 18—30.

St Mark's account differs little from St Matthew's. St Luke names the mockery of the soldiers and the words of the robbers to one another and to Jesus. Three of the sayings on the cross are related by St

33—50. *The Crucifixion and Death of Jesus.*

33 And when they were come unto a place called Golgotha,
34 that is to say, a place of a skull, they gave him vinegar to
drink mingled with gall: and when he had tasted *thereof*, he
35 would not drink. And they crucified him, and parted his

Luke only: "Father, forgive them; for they know not what they do;"—"Verily, I say unto thee, To day shalt thou be with me in paradise;"—"Father, into thy hands I commend my spirit." Among other particulars recorded by St John alone are the attempt to alter the superscription—the commendation of His mother to John—the breaking of the malefactors' legs—the piercing of Jesus—three sayings from the cross: "Woman, behold thy son!" and to the disciple, "Behold thy mother!"—"I thirst"—"It is finished." St Matthew and St Mark alone record the cry of loneliness: "Eli, Eli, lama sabachthani?"

33. *a place called Golgotha*] The site of Golgotha is unknown; it was outside the walls, but "nigh to the city" (John xix. 20), probably near the public road where people passed by (*v.* 39), it contained a garden (John xix. 41). The name, which = "place of a skull," is generally thought to be derived from the shape and appearance of the hillock or mound on which the crosses were reared. This, however, is uncertain. Pictures often mislead by representing the crucifixion as taking place on a lofty hill at a considerable distance from the city.

The English "Calvary" comes from the Vulgate translation of Luke xxiii. 33, "Et postquam venerunt in locum qui vocatur Calvariæ." Calvaria = "a bare skull."

34. *vinegar...mingled with gall*] "Wine mingled with myrrh" (Mark). *Vinegar* = "sour wine" (*vinaigre*), or *posca*, such as was ordinarily drunk by the Roman soldiers. The potion was a stupefying draught given to criminals to deaden the sense of pain. "Some of the wealthy ladies of Jerusalem charged themselves with this office of mercy." (Lightfoot, *ad loc.*) Jesus refuses this alleviation of His sufferings.

35. *they crucified him*] From the fact of the *titulus* or inscription being placed over the Saviour's head, it is inferred that the cross on which He suffered was such as is usually shewn in pictures, the *crux immissa* (†) or Latin cross as distinguished from the *crux commissa* (T) or the *crux decussata* (×) the form of cross on which St Andrew is said to have suffered. The height was from 9 to 12 feet; at a short distance from the ground a projecting rest supported the sufferer's feet, which, as well as the hands, were nailed to the cross.

According to St Mark (xv. 25) the Crucifixion took place at the third hour—nine o'clock. St John (xix. 14) says it was about the sixth hour when Pilate delivered Jesus to be crucified.

This discrepancy has received no entirely satisfactory solution. It has however been suggested that St John, writing at a later period and in a different part of the world, may have followed a different mode of reckoning time.

garments, casting lots: that it might be fulfilled which was
spoken by the prophet, They parted my garments
among them, and upon my vesture did they cast
lots. And sitting down they watched him there; and set 36
up over his head his accusation written, THIS IS JESUS 37
THE KING OF THE JEWS. Then were there two 38
thieves crucified with him, one on the right hand, and
another on the left.

And they that passed by, reviled him, wagging their heads, 39
and saying, *Thou* that destroyest the temple, and buildest *it* 40

parted his garments, casting lots] St John describes the division more accurately; they divided His *himatia*, or outer garments, but cast lots for the seamless *chiton*, or tunic. The latter is said to have been a dress peculiar to Galilæan peasants.

The Greek of the quotation from Ps. xxii. 18 (see below) does not convey the same distinction.

They parted my garments among them, &c.] Ps. xxii. 18. The same psalm is quoted *vv.* 39, 43, and 46. It is not a psalm of David, but was probably "composed by one of the exiles during the Babylonish captivity...who would cling to the thought that he suffered not only as an individual, but as one of the chosen of God. But it has more than an individual reference. It looks forward to Christ." Canon Perowne on Ps. xxii. The leading MSS. omit this quotation, which has probably been inserted from Mark.

36. *they watched him there*] fearing lest a rescue should be attempted by the friends of Jesus.

37. *and set up over his head his accusation written*] It was the Roman custom to place on the cross over the criminal's head, a *titulus*, or placard, stating the crime for which he suffered. St John records Pilate's refusal to alter the inscription, and mentions that the title was written in Hebrew and Greek and Latin.

King of the Jews. See ch. ii. 2.

The inscription is given with slight variations by the four Evangelists. "The King of the Jews" (Mark xv. 26). "This is the King of the Jews" (Luke xxiii. 38). "Jesus of Nazareth, the King of the Jews" (John xix. 19). This variation points to the independence of the different Gospels, and also indicates that a real though not a verbal accuracy should be looked for in the records of the Evangelists.

38. *two thieves*] Rather, **robbers**; in all probability partners in the crime of Barabbas. The mountain robbers, or banditti, were always ready to take part in such desperate risings against the Roman power. In the eyes of the Jews they would be patriots.

Josephus tells of one leader of robbers who burnt the palaces in Jericho (*B. J.* II. 6), and of another who for twenty years had wasted the country with fire and sword.

39. See Ps. xxii. 7.

in three days, save thyself. If thou be the Son of God,
41 come down from the cross. Likewise also the chief priests
42 mocking *him*, with the scribes and elders, said, He saved
others; himself he cannot save. If he be the King of
Israel, let him now come down from the cross, and we will
43 believe him. He trusted in God; let him deliver him
now, if he will have him: for he said, I am the Son of
44 God. The thieves also, which were crucified with him, cast
the same in his teeth.

45 Now from the sixth hour there was darkness over all the
46 land unto the ninth hour. And about the ninth hour Jesus
cried with a loud voice, saying, ELI, ELI, LAMA SABACHTHANI?

40. *Thou that destroyest the temple*] This is the mockery of the Jewish populace, who have caught up the charges brought against Jesus before the Sanhedrin. The taunts of the soldiers are named by St Luke alone: "If thou be the King of the Jews, save thyself" (xxiii. 37).

41. *chief priests...scribes and elders*] members of the Sanhedrin, the "rulers" of Luke xxiii. 35.

42. *He saved others; himself he cannot save*] These words in the original would recall the "hosannas" in the Temple which had enraged the chief priests; see note ch. xxi. 9. They also connect themselves with the name of Jesus ("Saviour").

the King of Israel] A title applied to Jesus only here and in the parallel passage of St Mark's Gospel.

43. *He trusted in God*] See Ps. xxii. 8. The chief priests unconsciously apply to the true Messiah the very words of a Messianic psalm.

44. *The thieves also...cast the same in his teeth*] They would naturally catch at the thought that the deliverer failed to give deliverance. St Luke alone relates that "one of the malefactors which were hanged railed on him...the other answering rebuked him." It is by no means impossible that the penitent robber may have seen and heard Jesus in Galilee.

45. *from the sixth hour...unto the ninth hour*] From 12 to 3 o'clock in the afternoon, the hours of the Paschal sacrifice.

there was darkness over all the land] Not the darkness of an eclipse, for it was the time of the Paschal full moon, but a miraculous darkness symbolic of that solemn hour and veiling the agonies of the Son of Man, when human soul and body alike were enduring the extremity of anguish and suffering for sin.

46. *Eli, Eli, lama sabachthani?*] (Ps. xxii. 1). *Eli* is the Hebrew form. In Mark xv. 34 the Aramaic words are preserved exactly as they were pronounced by Jesus. The repetition, "My God! My God!" gives a deeply pathetic force; cp. ch. xxiii. 37. It is an expression of utter loneliness and desolation, the depth of which it is not for man to fathom. "It is going beyond Scripture to say that a sense of God's

that is to say, My God, my God, why hast thou forsaken me? Some of them that stood there, when they 47
heard *that*, said, This *man* calleth for Elias. And straight- 48
way one of them ran, and took a spunge, and filled *it* with
vinegar, and put *it* on a reed, and gave him to drink. The 49
rest said, Let be, let us see whether Elias will come to save
him.

Jesus, when he had cried again with a loud voice, yielded 50
up the ghost.

wrath extorted that cry. For to the last breath He was the well-beloved of the Father, and the repeated 'My God! My God!' is a witness even then to His confidence in His Father's Love" (Canon Perowne. Ps. xxii. 1).

This was probably the fourth word from the cross; the fifth "I thirst" (John); the sixth "It is finished" (John); the seventh "Father, into thy hands I commend my spirit" (Luke). It is thought by some that after these words the darkness, which had lasted to the ninth hour, rolled away; others think that it lasted till the death of Jesus.

47. *This man calleth for Elias*] This was probably spoken in pure mockery, not in a real belief that Jesus expected the personal re-appearance of Elijah.

48. *took a spunge, and filled it with vinegar*] The soldiers' sour wine (*posca*), the reed, or hyssop stalk (John), and the sponge, were kept in readiness to quench the sufferers' thirst.

49. *Let be*] We must understand this to mean either (1) leave *him*, do not assist him; or (2) leave *it*, do not give the draught to him; or (3) "Let be" in the Greek coalesces with the verb following, and = "let us see." For the construction in the original cp. Luke vi. 42. In Mark the words "Let alone; let us see" are put in the mouth of him who offered the wine to the Saviour. There "let alone" may = "let me alone."

to save him] Here the Sinaitic and Vatican MSS. add, "and another took a spear and pierced his side, and there came out water and blood."

50. *when he had cried again with a loud voice*] Perhaps an inarticulate cry is meant, or perhaps the sixth word from the cross, "It is finished." John xix. 30.

yielded up the ghost] St Luke preserves the exact words, "Father, into thy hands I commend my spirit" (xxiii. 46).

51—56. EVENTS THAT FOLLOWED THE CRUCIFIXION. (1) THE VEIL OF THE TEMPLE RENT; (2) THE EARTHQUAKE; (3) THE SAINTS ARISE; (4) THE CENTURION AT THE CROSS; (5) THE WATCHING OF THE WOMEN.

Of these, (2) and (3) are peculiar to St Matthew.

Mark xv. 38—41; Luke xxiii. 45, 47—49, where the grief of the spectators is an additional fact. St John omits these incidents, but

51—56. *Events that followed the Crucifixion.* (1) *The Veil of the Temple rent;* (2) *the Earthquake;* (3) *the Saints arise;* (4) *the Centurion at the Cross;* (5) *the Watching of the Women.*

51 And behold, the vail of the temple was rent in twain from
the top to the bottom; and the earth did quake, and the
52 rocks rent; and the graves were opened; and many bodies
53 of saints which slept arose, and came out of the graves after
his resurrection, and went into the holy city, and appeared
54 unto many. Now when the centurion, and they that were
with him, watching Jesus, saw the earthquake, and *those things*
that were done, they feared greatly, saying, Truly this was
55 the Son of God. And many women were there beholding
afar off, which followed Jesus from Galilee, ministering unto
56 him: among which was Mary Magdalene, and Mary the

records the breaking of the malefactors' legs and the piercing of Jesus' side.

51. *the vail of the temple was rent in twain from the top to the bottom*] St Luke has "rent in the midst." The veil meant is that which separated the holy of holies from the holy place. The rending of the veil signifies that henceforth there is free access for man to God the Father through Jesus Christ. Cp. "Having therefore, brethren, boldness to enter into the holiest by the blood of Jesus, by a new and living way, which he hath consecrated for us, through the veil, that is to say, his flesh" (Heb. x. 19, 20). The incident would be observed and made known to the Church by the priests, of whom afterwards "a great company were obedient unto the faith" (Acts vi. 7).

54. *the centurion*] in command of the guard of four soldiers who watched the crucifixion.

Truly this was the Son of God] "Certainly this was a righteous man" (Luke).

56. St Mark (xv. 40) specifies the group as "Mary Magdalene, and Mary the mother of James the less (rather, *the little*) and of Joses, and Salome."

Mary Magdalene] Mentioned here for the first time by St Matthew. She was probably named from Magdala (*Mejdel*), on the Lake of Gennesaret; see map, p. 49. She had been a victim of demoniacal possession, but was cured by Jesus (Luke viii. 2), and then joined the company of faithful women who followed Him with the Twelve. Mary Magdalene is not named by St John among those who at an earlier period "stood by the cross of Jesus," but even then we may believe she was watching far off, and early in the morning she was present at the sepulchre.

The great Italian painters have identified Mary Magdalene either

mother of James and Joses, and the mother of Zebedee's children.

57—66. *The Entombment.*

When the even was come, there came a rich man of 57
Arimathea, named Joseph, who also himself was Jesus'
disciple: he went to Pilate, and begged the body of Jesus. 58
Then Pilate commanded the body to be delivered. And 59

with the "woman that was a sinner" who anointed Jesus in the house of Simon the Pharisee (Luke vii. 36—50), or with Mary the sister of Lazarus. But neither identification can be sustained on critical grounds.

Mary the mother of James and Joses] Perhaps the same Mary who was the wife of Cleophas, Clopas, or Alphæus (different forms of one name), mentioned John xix. 25. If so, according to *one* interpretation of the passage in John, the sister of the Blessed Virgin.

the mother of Zebedee's children] Salome. See ch. xx. 20.

57—66. The Entombment.

Mark xv. 42—47; Luke xxiii. 50—56; John xix. 38—42.

Vv. 62—66 are peculiar to St Matthew. St Mark notes the wonder of Pilate that Jesus was already dead, and the evidence of the centurion to the fact. St John mentions the co-operation of Nicodemus—like Joseph, a member of the Sanhedrin, who "consented not to the deed of them;" who brought "a mixture of myrrh and aloes about a hundred pound weight."

57. *Arimathea*] is generally identified with Ramathaim-zophim, on Mount Ephraim, the birth-place of Samuel (1 Sam. i. 1), the site of which is undetermined. Many authorities place it much nearer to Jerusalem than the position indicated in the map, p. 28.

Joseph] From the other two Synoptic Gospels we learn that he was "an honourable (Mark) counsellor (Mark and Luke)," i. e. a member of the Sanhedrin. Like Nicodemus, he was a secret disciple of Jesus, and must undoubtedly have absented himself from the meetings of the Sanhedrin when Jesus was condemned. He "had not consented to the counsel and deed of them" (Luke).

An ancient but groundless legend has connected Joseph of Arimathæa with Glastonbury, where, it is said, he built of osier-twigs the first Christian Church in England.

58. *Pilate commanded the body to be delivered*] after having ascertained from the centurion that Jesus was dead. Usually those who suffered crucifixion lingered for days upon the cross. By Roman law the corpse of a crucified person was not buried except by express permission of the Emperor. A concession was made in favour of the Jews, whose law did not suffer a man to hang all night upon a tree. Deut. xxi. 23. (See Jahn, *Bib. Ant.*, 296.) "The readiness of Pilate to grant Joseph's request is quite in accordance with his anxiety to release Jesus and his

when Joseph had taken the body, he wrapped it in a clean
60 linen cloth, and laid it in his own new tomb, which he had
hewn out in the rock: and he rolled a great stone to the
61 door of the sepulchre, and departed. And there was Mary
Magdalene, and the other Mary, sitting over against the
sepulchre.
62 Now the next day, that followed the *day of the* preparation, the chief priests and Pharisees came together unto
63 Pilate, saying, Sir, we remember that that deceiver said,
while he was yet alive, After three days I will rise *again.*
64 Command therefore that the sepulchre be made sure until
the third day, lest his disciples come by night, and steal him
away, and say unto the people, He is risen from the dead:
65 so the last error shall be worse than the first. Pilate said
unto them, Ye have a watch: go your way, make *it* as sure

displeasure against the Jews. If Joseph had not made this request, the body of Jesus would have been placed in one of the common burying-places appointed by the Council" (Lightfoot, *Hor. Hebr.* ad loc.).

59. *linen cloth*] *Sindon*, or **fine linen.**

60. *laid it in his own new tomb*] "His own" peculiar to St Matthew. St John mentions that the tomb was "in a garden in the place where he was crucified" (xix. 41). It was probably hewn out of the face of the rock near the ground (John xx. 11), and the body of Jesus would lie horizontally in it.

rolled a great stone] assisted by Nicodemus. This stone was technically called *golal.*

61. *the other Mary*] The mother of James the less and Joses (Mark xv. 47).

62. *the next day, that followed the day of the preparation*] It was after sunset on Nisan 14. The preparation (paraskeué) was over, the Sabbath and the Paschal feast had commenced. This explanation of the somewhat unusual phrase accords with the view already taken of the Last Supper and the Passover.

While Christ's enemies were busy this Sabbath day, His friends rested according to the commandment (Luke xxiii. 56).

63. *said...After three days I will rise*] Literally in the Greek, **I rise.** For this present cp. ch. xxiv. 41, xxvi. 2.

It appears from this that the priests and Pharisees understood the true import of Christ's words, "Destroy this temple, and after three days I will raise it up," which they wilfully misinterpreted to the people.

64. *by night*] Omitted in the best MSS.

He is risen] Rather, **He rose.**

error] Better, **deceit.** The Greek word has the same root as *deceiver*, *v.* 63.

65. *Ye have a watch*] The meaning is either (1) that Pilate refuses

as you can. So they went, and made the sepulchre sure, 66
sealing the stone, and setting a watch.

1—8. *The Resurrection.*

In the end of the sabbath, as it began to dawn towards the 28
first *day* of the week, came Mary Magdalene and the other
Mary to see the sepulchre. And behold, there was a great 2
earthquake: for *the* angel of the Lord descended from
heaven, and came and rolled back the stone from the door,
and sat upon it. His countenance was like lightning, and 3
his raiment white as snow: and for fear of him the keepers 4
did shake, and became as dead *men*. And the angel 5
answered and said unto the women, Fear not ye: for I

the request; "Ye have a watch of your own"—(*a*) the Levitical temple guard, or (*b*) a small body of soldiers whom Pilate may have already placed at their disposal—or (2) he grants it curtly and angrily, "Take a watch; begone."

The latter view is generally adopted now. It seems quite clear from ch. xxviii. 14 that the guard was of Roman soldiers.

CH. XXVIII. 1—8. THE RESURRECTION.

Mark xvi. 1—8; Luke xxiv. 1—12; John xx. 1—18.

The discrepancies are slight, and may be accounted for by the agitation of the witnesses of this momentous scene. To the women named in this Gospel St Mark adds Salome; St Luke, Joanna and other women; St John names Mary Magdalene only. St Luke and St John mention the visit of Peter to the sepulchre, St John adding "that other disciple." This Evangelist also records the appearance of Jesus to Mary Magdalene in the garden.

The order of events was probably this: First, Mary Magdalene and the other Mary, having come early to the tomb, were addressed by the Angel and saw the empty sepulchre; they hasten to inform Peter and the other disciples; Peter and John visit the tomb and depart; Mary Magdalene, left alone, beholds her Lord, whom at first she does not recognise; soon afterwards the Lord appears a second time to Mary Magdalene, now in the company of other women.

1. *as it began to dawn*] At the rising of the sun, or properly, "when the sun had risen" (Mark). Both St Mark and St Luke mention that they brought spices and ointments.

2. *there was a great earthquake*] Peculiar to St Matthew.

the angel of the Lord] "Two men stood by them in shining garments" (Luke). "Two angels in white sitting" (John).

5. *Fear not ye*] The pronoun "ye" is emphatic in the original. A contrast with the alarm of the soldiers is implied.

6 know that ye seek Jesus, which was crucified. He is not
here: for he is risen, as he said. Come, see the place where
7 the Lord lay. And go quickly, and tell his disciples that he
is risen from the dead; and behold, he goeth before you
into Galilee; there shall ye see him: lo, I have told you.
8 And they departed quickly from the sepulchre with fear and
great joy; and did run to bring his disciples word.

9, 10. *The Appearance of Jesus to Mary Magdalene and the other Mary.*

9 And as they went to tell his disciples, behold, Jesus met

6. *he is risen*] As in ch. xxvii. 64, **He rose.** So also in next verse.

see the place where the Lord lay] In order that they might be convinced of the fact.

It is hardly possible for us even to conceive the overwhelming joy that the conviction of this truth must have brought to these holy women, whose recollection of the divine words and looks and love-inspiring sweetness of character would be quickened by the painful watching and the passionate sorrow for their seeming loss.

7. *tell his disciples*] "And Peter" (Mark). Peter, more than the rest, would be longing for the Lord's return to win forgiveness.

he goeth before you into Galilee] Lit., "Leadeth you as a shepherd." See ch. xxvi. 32.

9, 10. THE APPEARANCE OF JESUS TO MARY MAGDALENE AND THE OTHER MARY.

Recorded by St Matthew only.

Jesus had already appeared to Mary Magdalene *alone*. We must suppose that she was now joined by the other Mary, and perhaps by Salome, Joanna, and others; and while these were going to announce the great news to the rest of the disciples [Peter and John already knew] the Lord Jesus met them.

The following is a list of the different appearances of Jesus during the forty days:—(1) To Mary Magdalene alone (John xx. 14 foll.; Mark xvi. 9). (2) To Mary Magdalene, the other Mary, and perhaps other women (Matthew xxviii. 9, 10). (3) To Peter (Luke xxiv. 34; 1 Cor. xv. 5). (4) To Cleophas and another on the way to Emmaus (Luke xxiv. 13—35). (5) To the apostles, in the absence of Thomas, at Jerusalem (Mark xvi. 14; Luke xxiv. 36; John xx. 19). (6) To the eleven apostles at Jerusalem (John xx. 26). (7) To seven disciples at the Sea of Tiberias (John xxi. 1—24). (8) To the eleven on the highland of Galilee (Matthew xxviii. 16). (9) To five hundred brethren at once—possibly the same appearance as 8 (1 Cor. xv. 6). (10) To James,

them, saying, *All* hail. And they came and held him by the
feet, and worshipped him. Then said Jesus unto them, Be 10
not afraid: go tell my brethren that they go into Galilee,
and there shall they see me.

11—15. *The Roman Guards are bribed.*

Now when they were going, behold, some of the watch 11
came into the city, and shewed unto the chief priests all the
things that were done. And when they were assembled 12
with the elders, and had taken counsel, they gave large
money unto the soldiers, saying, Say ye, His disciples came 13
by night, and stole him *away* while we slept. And if this 14
come to the governor's ears, we will persuade him, and
secure you. So they took the money, and did as they were 15
taught: and this saying is commonly reported among the
Jews until this day.

the Lord's brother (1 Cor. xv. 7). (11) To the eleven in the neighbourhood of the Holy City (Mark xvi. 19, 20; Luke xxiv. 50; Acts i. 3—12; 1 Cor. xv. 7).

9. *as they went to tell his disciples*] These words are omitted in the best MSS.

All hail] Literally, **Rejoice**; the Greek salutation, both on meeting and on parting.

10. *go tell my brethren that they go*] i. e. tell my brethren (of my Resurrection), in order that they may go.

my brethren] The disciples; "He named them brethren, as being Himself a man and their kinsman according to man's nature" (Euthymius quoted by Ellicott, *Life of our Lord*); comp. Heb. ii. 11, "He is not ashamed to call them brethren." Now that Christ had clearly manifested the power of the Godhead, there was special need of reminding His disciples that He was still man, and that they were brethren.

11—15. THE ROMAN GUARDS ARE BRIBED. **This important testimony is given by St Matthew only.**

12. *large money*] Literally, **many pieces of silver**, a *largesse.*

13. *while we slept*] The penalty for which would be death.

14. *persuade*] By bribes. Euripides says "they say that gifts *persuade* even gods." (*Medea*, 964.) The soldiers might readily believe that Pilate was open to the same inducement which persuaded them.

secure you] "Make you free from anxiety." The only other place where the word occurs in N. T. is 1 Cor. vii. 32, "I would have you without carefulness."

15. *this saying is commonly reported among the Jews until this day*] Hence St Matthew found it especially needful to narrate the true facts.

16, 17. *Jesus appears to the Eleven in Galilee.*

16 Then the eleven disciples went *away* into Galilee, into a
17 mountain where Jesus had appointed them. And when
they saw him, they worshipped him: but some doubted.

18—20. *The Last Charge to the Apostles.*

18 And Jesus came and spake unto them, saying, All power
19 is given unto me in heaven and in earth. Go ye therefore,
and teach all nations, baptizing them in the name of the

16, 17. JESUS APPEARS TO THE ELEVEN IN GALILEE.
Peculiar to St Matthew.

16. *a mountain*] Rather, **the** *mountain.* Perhaps the highland behind Tell Hum or Capernaum (see map), the scene of their earliest intercourse with Christ, and the very spot where the New Law was first proclaimed. There the brethren, possibly five hundred in number [see *vv.* 9, 10 (8) (9)], besides the Eleven, awaited the coming of the Great Shepherd (*v.* 7). As the sacred form appeared on the familiar mountain side they threw themselves on the ground, doing homage to their Lord and God. But some doubted still. Then He drew more near and spake. And as the words sounded in their ears, we may believe they "knew His voice" and dismissed their doubts.

had appointed] Rather, **appointed.**

17. *worshipped him*] See note ch. xx. 20. It is characteristic of St Matthew's Gospel that this word, which indicates the homage and prostration before a king, should occur twelve times, whereas it is found twice only in each of the other Synoptics.

some] Probably not some of the Apostles, but some of the five hundred who had not previously seen the Lord.

doubted] The same word is used of St Peter's doubt, ch. xiv. 31, and in these passages only in N. T.; there too the doubt is followed by adoration, *v.* 33.

18—20. THE LAST CHARGE TO THE APOSTLES.

18. *came*] Rather, **came up to them**, near to them.

power] Rather, **authority.**

is given] Properly, **was given**, cp. ch. xi. 27, and Phil. ii. 8—10. These words, in which the infallible King Himself announces His eternal possession of the Kingdom, St Matthew, who is essentially the historian of the Kingdom, alone records.

19. *therefore*] i.e. because Christ hath all power in heaven and earth. The word however is omitted in the leading MSS.

teach] Properly, **make disciples of.** The same mistranslation occurs Acts xiv. 21, "having taught," see ch. xiii. 52, xxvii. 57, where the same word is used. *Teaching*, *v.* 20, = "instructing." "Make disciples of all nations by baptism and by instruction."

Father, and of the Son, and of the Holy Ghost: teaching 20
them to observe all *things* whatsoever I have commanded
you: and lo, I am with you alway, *even* unto the end of the
world. Amen.

in the name] Rather, **into** *the name*. Jewish proselytes were baptized into the name of the Father; Jesus adds the names of the Son and of the Holy Ghost. In the instances of baptism recorded in the Acts, ii. 38, viii. 16, x. 48, xix. 5, the name of Jesus Christ (or the Lord Jesus) alone occurs in the baptismal formula, but the promise of the Holy Ghost is given (ii. 38), or the gift of the Holy Ghost follows the rite (viii. 17, xix. 6), or precedes it (x. 44, 47).

20. *I am with you alway*] The Lord Jesus had already taught His disciples during the forty days how He could be present with them and yet be unseen by them. They could then the more easily believe this promise.

the end of the world] See note ch. xiii. 39.

Amen] Omitted in the leading MSS. The last words of St Matthew's Gospel fall solemnly on the ear, the sense of the continual presence of Christ is not broken even by an account of the Ascension. No true subject can doubt that the King is enthroned in Heaven.

INDEX TO NOTES.

CAMBRIDGE: PRINTED BY JOHN CLAY, M.A. AT THE UNIVERSITY PRESS.

THE CAMBRIDGE BIBLE FOR SCHOOLS AND COLLEGES

GENERAL EDITORS:

A. F. KIRKPATRICK, D.D., Dean of Ely

R. ST JOHN PARRY, B.D., Fellow of Trinity College

With Introductions, Notes and Maps. Cloth. Extra fcap. 8vo.

An Introduction to the Pentateuch. By the Rev. A. T. CHAPMAN, M.A. 3*s.* 6*d. net.*

The Book of Exodus. In the Revised Version. Edited by the Rev. S. R. DRIVER, D.D. With 11 Illustrations and 4 Maps. 3*s.* 6*d. net.*

The Book of Numbers. In the Revised Version. Edited by the Rev. A. H. McNEILE, D.D. With 2 Maps. 2*s.* 6*d. net.*

The Book of Joshua. Edited by the Rev. G. F. MACLEAR, D.D. With 2 Maps. 2*s. net.*

The Book of Judges. Edited by the Rev. J. J. LIAS, M.A. With Map. 2*s. net.*

The First Book of Samuel. Edited by the Very Rev. A. F. KIRKPATRICK, D.D. With Map. 2*s. net.*

The Second Book of Samuel. Edited by the Very Rev. A. F. KIRKPATRICK, D.D. With 2 Maps. 2*s. net.*

The First Book of the Kings. In the Authorised Version. Edited by the Rev. J. R. LUMBY, D.D. With 3 Maps. 2*s. net.*

The Second Book of the Kings. In the Authorised Version. Edited by the Rev. J. R. LUMBY, D.D. With 3 Maps. 2*s. net.*

The First and Second Books of the Kings. In the Authorised Version. Edited by the Rev. J. R. LUMBY, D.D. In one vol. With 5 Maps. 3*s.* 6*d. net.*

The First Book of the Kings. In the Revised Version. Edited by the Rev. W. E. BARNES, D.D. With Map. 2*s. net.*

The Second Book of the Kings. In the Revised Version. Edited by the Rev. W. E. BARNES, D.D. With 2 Maps. 2*s. net.*

000.6.11

The First and Second Books of the Kings. In the Revised Version. Edited by the Rev. W. E. BARNES, D.D. In one vol. With 2 Maps. 3*s.* 6*d. net.*

The First and Second Books of Chronicles. Edited by the Rev. W. E. BARNES, D.D. With 2 Maps. 2*s.* 6*d. net.*

The Books of Ezra and Nehemiah. Edited by the Very Rev. H. E. RYLE, D.D. With 3 Maps. 3*s. net.*

The Book of Esther. In the Revised Version. Edited by the Rev. A. W. STREANE, D.D. 1*s.* 6*d. net.*

The Book of Job. Edited by the Rev. A. B. DAVIDSON, LL.D., D.D. 3*s. net.*

The Psalms. Edited by the Very Rev. A. F. KIRKPATRICK, D.D.

Book I. 1—41. 2*s. net.*
Books II. and III. 42—89. 2*s. net.*
Books IV. and V. 90—150. 2*s. net.*

The Book of Proverbs. Edited by the Ven. T. T. PEROWNE, B.D. 2*s. net.*

Ecclesiastes; or, the Preacher. Edited by the Very Rev. E. H. PLUMPTRE, D.D. 3*s. net.*

The Song of Solomon. Edited by the Rev. ANDREW HARPER, D.D., Edin. 1*s.* 6*d. net.*

Isaiah. Vol. I. Chapters I—XXXIX. Edited by the Rev. J. SKINNER, D.D. With Map. 2*s.* 6*d. net.*

Isaiah. Vol. II. Chapters XL—LXVI. Edited by the Rev. J. SKINNER, D.D. 2*s.* 6*d. net.*

The Book of Jeremiah together with the Lamentations. Edited by the Rev. A. W. STREANE, D.D. With Map. 3*s. net.*

The Book of Ezekiel. Edited by the Rev. A. B. DAVIDSON, D.D. 3*s. net.*

The Book of Daniel. Edited by the Rev. S. R. DRIVER, D.D. With Illustrations. 2*s.* 6*d. net.*

Hosea. Edited by the Rev. T. K. CHEYNE, M.A., D.D. 1*s.* 6*d. net.*

The Books of Joel and Amos. By the Rev. S. R. DRIVER, D.D. With Illustrations. 2*s.* 6*d. net.*

Obadiah and Jonah. Edited by the Ven. T. T. PEROWNE, B.D. 1*s.* 6*d. net.*

Micah. Edited by the Rev. T. K. CHEYNE, M.A., D.D. 1*s. net.*

Nahum, Habakkuk and Zephaniah. Edited by the Rev. A. B. DAVIDSON, LL.D., D.D. 1*s.* 6*d. net.*

Haggai, Zechariah and Malachi. Edited by the Ven. T. T. PEROWNE, B.D. 2*s. net.*

The New Testament complete

The Gospel according to St Matthew. Edited by the Rev. A. CARR, M.A. With 2 Maps. 2*s. net.*

The Gospel according to St Mark. Edited by the Rev. G. F. MACLEAR, D.D. With 4 Maps. 2*s. net.*

The Gospel according to St Luke. Edited by the Very Rev. F. W. FARRAR, D.D. With 4 Maps. 3*s. net.*

The Gospel according to St John. Edited by the Rev. A. PLUMMER, D.D. With 4 Maps. 3*s. net.*

The Acts of the Apostles. Edited by the Rev. J. RAWSON LUMBY, D.D. With 4 Maps. 3*s. net.*

The Epistle to the Romans. Edited by the Right Rev. H. C. G. MOULE, D.D. With Map. 2*s.* 6*d. net.*

The First Epistle to the Corinthians. Edited by the Rev. J. J. LIAS, M.A. With 2 Maps. 1*s.* 6*d. net.*

The Second Epistle to the Corinthians. Edited by the Rev. A. PLUMMER, D.D. 1*s.* 6*d. net.*

The Epistle to the Galatians. Edited by the Rev. E. H. PEROWNE, D.D. 1*s. net.*

The Epistle to the Ephesians. Edited by the Right Rev. H. C. G. MOULE, D.D. 1*s.* 6*d. net.*

The Epistle to the Philippians. Edited by the Right Rev. H. C. G. MOULE, D.D. 1*s.* 6*d. net.*

The Epistles to the Colossians and Philemon. Edited by the Right Rev. H. C. G. MOULE, D.D. 1*s.* 6*d. net.*

The Epistles to the Thessalonians. Edited by the Rev. G. G. FINDLAY, D.D. With Map. 1*s.* 6*d. net.*

The Epistles to Timothy and Titus. Edited by the Rev. A. E. HUMPHREYS, M.A. With Map. 2*s. net.*

The Epistle to the Hebrews. Edited by the Very Rev. F. W. FARRAR, D.D. 2*s.* 6*d. net.*

The Epistle of St James. Edited by the Very Rev. E. H. PLUMPTRE, D.D. 1*s. net.*

The Epistles of St Peter and St Jude. Edited by the Very Rev. E. H. PLUMPTRE, D.D. 2*s. net.*

The Epistles of St John. Edited by the Rev. A. PLUMMER, D.D. 2*s. net.*

The Revelation of St John the Divine. Edited by the Rev. WILLIAM HENRY SIMCOX, M.A. 2*s. net.*

The Book of Psalms. With Introduction and Notes by the Very Rev. A. F. KIRKPATRICK, D.D. Crown 8vo, cloth, gilt top. 6*s. net.*

The edition of the Psalms prepared by Dr Kirkpatrick for the "Cambridge Bible for Schools" having been completed and published in three volumes, the whole work is now also published in a single volume. The page is larger than in the separate volumes, and, a thinner paper being used, this edition will be found convenient in size, and it is thought that many readers will prefer it to the separate volumes.

The First Book of Maccabees. In the Revised Version. By the Rev. W. FAIRWEATHER, M.A. and J. SUTHERLAND BLACK, LL.D. With Map and Illustrations. 2*s.* 6*d. net.*

The Wisdom of Solomon. In the Revised Version. Edited by the Rev. J. A. F. GREGG, M.A. 2*s.* 6*d. net.*

In preparation (completing the series of the books of the Old and New Testaments)

Genesis. Edited by the Very Rev. H. E. RYLE, D.D., Dean of Westminster.

Leviticus. Edited by the Rev. A. T. CHAPMAN, M.A., Fellow of Emmanuel College.

Deuteronomy. Edited by the Rev. G. ADAM SMITH, D.D., Professor of Old Testament Language, Literature and Theology, United Free Church College, Glasgow.

Ruth. Edited by the Rev. G. A. COOKE, M.A., St John's College, Oxford.

THE REVISED VERSION FOR SCHOOLS

Edited with Introductions, Notes and Maps. Fcap. 8vo. 1s. 6d. net each

The First Book of the Kings. Edited by the Rev. H. C. O. LANCHESTER, M.A.

Isaiah I—XXXIX. Edited by the Rev. C. H. THOMSON, M.A. and the Rev. J. SKINNER, D.D.

St Matthew. Edited by the Rev. A. CARR, M.A.

"The most approved results of recent biblical criticism are embodied in the splendid notes; but independent of its intrinsic value, there are three artistic maps incorporated in the text. An edition as remarkable for its elegance as for its high utility."—*School World*

St Mark. Edited by Sir A. F. HORT, Bart., M.A., and MARY DYSON HORT (Mrs George Chitty).

"Altogether helpful, suggestive, clear, and valuable."—*School World*

"Sir A. F. Hort's little book on St Mark is a model of what such books should be."—*Glasgow Herald*

St Luke. Edited by the Rev. E. WILTON SOUTH, M.A.

St John. Edited by the Rev. A. CARR, M.A.

"A valuable contribution to Biblical study."—*Spectator*

"Mr Carr has succeeded in presenting the best and most approved results of recent theological work on St John in a clear and intelligible form....The introductory matter deserves a special word of praise."—*Guardian*

The Acts of the Apostles. Edited by the Rev. C. WEST-WATSON, M.A.

The First and Second Epistles to the Corinthians. Edited by the Rev. S. C. CARPENTER, M.A.

The Epistle to the Galatians and the Epistle to the Romans. Edited by the Rev. H. W. FULFORD, M.A.

The Epistles to the Ephesians, Philippians, Colos-sians, and to Philemon. Edited by the Rev. W. K. LOWTHER CLARKE, M.A.

The General Epistle of James and the Epistle to the Hebrews. Edited by the Rev. A. CARR, M.A.

The Epistles of Peter, John and Jude. Edited by the Rev. CLAUDE M. BLAGDEN, M.A.

The Revelation of St John the Divine. Edited by the Rt Rev. G. H. S. WALPOLE.

THE CAMBRIDGE GREEK TESTAMENT FOR SCHOOLS AND COLLEGES

General Editor: R. St John Parry, B.D., Fellow of Trinity College

With Introductions, English Notes and Maps
Extra fcap. 8vo. cloth

The Gospel according to St Matthew. Edited by the Rev. Arthur Carr, M.A. 4*s.* 6*d.*

The Gospel according to St Mark. Edited by the Rev. G. F. Maclear, D.D. 4*s.* 6*d.*

The Gospel according to St Luke. Edited by the Very Rev. F. W. Farrar, D.D. 6*s.*

The Gospel according to St John. Edited by the Rev. A. Plummer, D.D. 6*s.*

The Acts of the Apostles. Edited by the Rev. J. R. Lumby, D.D. 6*s.*

The First Epistle to the Corinthians. Edited by the Rev. J. J. Lias, M.A. 3*s.*

The Second Epistle to the Corinthians. Edited by the Rev. A. Plummer, D.D. 3*s.*

The Epistle to the Galatians. Edited by the Rev. A. Lukyn Williams, B.D. 3*s.*

The Epistle to the Philippians. Edited by the Right Rev. H. C. G. Moule, D.D. 2*s.* 6*d.*

The Epistles to the Colossians and Philemon. Edited by the Rev. A. Lukyn Williams, B.D. 3*s.*

The Epistles to the Thessalonians. Edited by the Rev. George G. Findlay, D.D. 3*s.*

The Pastoral Epistles. Edited by the Very Rev. J. H. Bernard, D.D. 3*s.* 6*d.*

The Epistle to the Hebrews. Edited by the Very Rev. F. W. Farrar, D.D. 3*s.* 6*d.*

The Epistles of St John. Edited by the Rev. A. Plummer, D.D. 4*s.*

The General Epistle of St James. Edited by the Rev. Arthur Carr, M.A. 2*s.* 6*d.*

The Revelation of St John the Divine. Edited by the late Rev. William Henry Simcox, M.A. Revised by G. A. Simcox, M.A. 5*s.*

St Mark in Greek for beginners.

The Gospel according to St Mark. The Greek Text. Edited, with Introduction and Notes, for the use of Schools, by Sir A. F. Hort, Bart., M.A., Assistant Master at Harrow School. With 2 Maps. 2*s.* 6*d.* *net.*

Herod was an Idumaen